THE PUBLICATIONS
OF THE
LINCOLN RECORD SOCIETY

PUBLICATIONS OF
THE LINCOLN RECORD SOCIETY
OCCASIONAL SERIES

The Lincoln Record Society has been publishing
editions of historical records since 1910 and it
continues to do so by means of its Main Series and
the Kathleen Major Series of Medieval Records.
Through the Occasional Series the Society will
now additionally issue monographs and similar
publications relating to aspects of the history of the
ancient county and diocese of Lincoln.

CHRISTOPHER JOHNSON *and* STANLEY JONES

Steep, Strait *and* High

The Lincoln Record Society

The Boydell Press

First published 2016

A Lincoln Record Society publication
published by The Boydell Press
an imprint of Boydell & Brewer Ltd
PO Box 9, Woodbridge, Suffolk IP12 3DF, UK
and of Boydell & Brewer Inc.
668 Mt Hope Avenue, Rochester, NY 14620-2731, USA
website: www.boydellandbrewer.com

ISBN 978 1 910653 01 2

A CIP catalogue record for this book is available
from the British Library

Details of other Lincoln Record Society volumes are available
from Boydell & Brewer Ltd

Book designed by Simon Loxley

CONTENTS

ILLUSTRATIONS

COPYRIGHT DETAILS

The editors are greatly indebted to the following for their kind permission to reproduce the various images which appear in this volume, quoted by Figure number:

The Benedictines of Pluscarden Abbey, Elgin: Jacket illustration of the Tophouse, Steep Hill (the Harlequin), by Karl Wood, 1935; The Church Commissioners: *Figs* 6, 37, 63-65, 111; The Diocese of Lincoln: *Figs* 58, 108, 128; The Estate of the late Nicholas Hawley: *Fig* 141; Historic England Archive Service: *Figs* 19, 152-157; Lincoln Cathedral (Dean and Chapter): *Figs* 21, 42, 93; Lincoln Cathedral Library: *Fig* 82; Lincoln Civic Trust: *Figs* 97-98; City of Lincoln Council, Directorate of Development and Environmental Services: *Fig* 18; City of Lincoln Council, Directorate of Resources: *Fig* 30; Lincoln Record Society: *Fig* 143; Lincolnshire County Council, Libraries and Heritage (Lincolnshire Archives): *Figs* 91, 94, 107, 145-46, 148; Lincolnshire County Council, Libraries and Heritage (The Collection: Art and Archaeology in Lincolnshire [Usher Gallery, Lincoln]): *Figs* 104, 138; Lincolnshire County Council, Libraries and Heritage (Lincolnshire Libraries): *Figs* 7, 22, 40, 66, 88-90, 92, 105, 123-27, 136-37, 139, 147 [nos 7 and 66 are from the Banks Collection]; Record and General Photographs Ltd [company no longer in business]: *Fig* 24; Messrs J. and R. Wheeldon: *Fig* 4.

Plans and photographs by Stanley Jones: *Figs* 2, 8-13, 15-17, 20, 23, 26-29, 31-36, 38-41, 43-57, 59-61, 67-71, 73-75, 77-78, 80, 85, 95-96, 100-103, 106, 110, 112-122, 129-132, 140, 144, 150-51.

Photographs by Christopher Johnson: *Figs* 3, 5, 14, 62, 72, 76, 81, 83, 86, 87, 99, 109, 133-34, 142.

Street plans by Dave Watt: *Figs* 1, 52, 84, 135, 143, 149.

Note: The work by T. Hudson Turner (Oxford, Parker), 1851, from which *Fig* 79 is taken, is deemed to be out of copyright; Parker's Bookshop in Oxford ceased to trade in 1993.

The authors and publishers are grateful to all the institutions and individuals listed for permission to reproduce the materials in which they hold copyright. Every effort has been made to trace the copyright holders; apologies are offered for any omission, and the publishers will be pleased to add any necessary acknowledgements in future editions.

ACKNOWLEDGEMENTS

We are greatly indebted to numerous people and organisations for the generous help they have given towards this publication. The archivists, with their Searchroom and Reprographics colleagues at Lincolnshire Archives, have all been of tremendous assistance in the preparatory stage, as have the staff of the Central Library in Free School Lane and the Usher Gallery. This is evidenced by the wealth of documentation, including photographs, pictures and other illustrations which are published here, courtesy of Lincolnshire County Council Libraries and Heritage and other people and organisations. The City of Lincoln Council staff have also been most helpful over many years, providing information on the various buildings covered in this volume. We are most grateful to Arthur Ward and John Herridge (both recently retired) and Graeme Chapman for their advice, and particularly to Mick Jones, formerly the City Archaeologist, with whom we have worked in the Survey of Ancient Houses and its successor organisation the Survey of Lincoln for more than forty years.

Historical advice on various aspects has been given by the Society for Lincolnshire History and Archaeology, Lincoln Civic Trust and the Lincolnshire Family History Society. Information specific to the medieval Jewish community in Lincoln has been offered by Joe Hillaby, the late Robin Mundill, Richard Dale and Marcus Roberts. The *Survey of Lincoln* is very grateful to the Lincoln Civic Trust for their generous grant towards this project.

On the technical side, we need to thank Dave Watt for his assistance with the street plans (*Figs* 1, 52, 84, 135 and 149), based on the OS 1888 Town Plan and copied into a new format by Stanley Jones, and for his adaptation of part of the Padley plan of 1842 (*Fig* 143); also to the staff at the Boydell Press for all their work in preparing our work for publication. We would also like to give particular thanks to the members of the Survey of Lincoln and the Lincoln Record Society, including Prof. David Stocker, Dr Alan Kissane, Ken Hollamby, Dr David Crook, Dr Paul Dryburgh, Dr Nicholas Bennett, the LRS Editor, and Dr Rob Wheeler; without their help and encouragement this volume could not have been published.

Last but not least, Stanley and I are also most thankful to our patient and long-suffering wives, Pat and Rosemary, for their support and understanding, particularly in regard to table tops festooned with our respective paraphernalia, and the time taken up with this work.

C.P.C.J.

MANUSCRIPT SOURCES

The following records are held at Lincolnshire Archives, unless noted below as being kept elsewhere. This is guidance, rather than a comprehensive list of sources.

RECORDS OF THE DEAN AND CHAPTER OF LINCOLN CATHEDRAL (D&C)

A 1.6	*Registrum*
A 1.8	*Liber de Ordinationibus Cantariarum* (abbrev. *Cant*)
A 1.10	Welbourn Cartulary (abbrev. *Welb*)
A 2; A.3	Chapter Act Books
A 4.7	Fabric accounts and rentals 16c
Bj 1	Board and Fabric rentals 15-18c
Bj 2.	Chapter Account Books 14-15c
Bj 5	Draft accounts, rentals (many fragmentary) 13-14c
Bij 2; Bij 3	Chantries, Common Fund and Fabric rentals 14-16c
Bij 3.16-20	Chapter Lease Books 16-17c
Ciij 9.1	Lincoln Common Council Seal Book
Ciij 29 etc.	Parliamentary Surveys, Willson mss
Civ 95	Draft leases 19c
Dij	Charters (mostly those not published in LRS *Registrum Antiquissimum*)
Diij; Div	Miscellaneous Chapter records including Prebendal surveys and rentals
LL	Lincoln Leases: formerly stored as Cj and arranged by Joan Varley
MS 169	The *Burwarmote Book* (abbrev. *BB*): wills and charters of the 14th century, registered with the Mayor and Bailiffs of the City of Lincoln (kept at Lincoln Cathedral Library)
D&C Wills	Probate records 16-19c

Willson Collection (Cathedral Library): albums acquired in the 19th century

VICARS CHORAL OF LINCOLN CATHEDRAL

VC 2/1	Cartulary 13-14c (abbrev. *VC*)
VC 3	Leases, conveyances and miscellaneous papers

RECORDS OF THE CHURCH COMMISSIONERS (FORMERLY ECCLESIASTICAL COMMISSIONERS)

CC; 2 CC: leases (18-19c); Parliamentary Surveys (17c); architects' reports (19c); memoranda (17-19c); rentals (19c)

DIOCESE OF LINCOLN

LCC Wills/Admons; Inventories; Ad Acc: probate records 16-19c

Tithe Awards Plans and books of reference 19c

Visitation (of prebends): Surveys and memoranda 17-19c

PARISH RECORDS

Leases, rentals, account and rate books for several city parishes (see also FL St Mark's, and Lincoln City L1/5/12) 16-19c

RECORDS OF LINCOLN COMMON COUNCIL/CORPORATION

L1/1/1/1 ff	Council Minute Books 16-19c
L1/1/2 ff	Committee Minute Books 19c
L1/3/1	The '*White Book*': custumal, deeds registry; a few wills 15-18c
L1/3/2	Council Lease Book 17c
L1/5/12	St Martin's parish churchwardens' accounts 16-17c
L3	Conveyances and abstracts of title for properties acquired or sold by the Council 18-20c
LC Charters	Conveyances and leases 17-19c
LC Leases	Corporation leases 17-19c
LC Educ	Education files, including school minute books 19-20c
LC Parcels	Clerk's papers 19c
LC Rolls	Chamberlains' Rolls: income from rents 17-19c

ESTATE AND FAMILY COLLECTIONS

Ancaster (abbrev. *Anc*); Andrews (*Andr.*); Brownlow (*BNLW*); Monson (*Mon*); Sibthorp (*Sib*)

SOLICITORS' RECORDS (DEEDS OR CLIENTS' BUNDLES)

Andrew, Race, Midgley and Hill (abbrev. *ARMH*)
Burton Scorer (*BS*)
Danby, Epton and Griffiths (*DEG, 4 DEG*)
Langley, Philips and Coleman (*LPC, 2 LPC*)
Page
Sills and Betteridge (*SB*)
Toynbee, Larken and Evans (*TLE*)
Tweed, Stephen and Jourdain (*TSJ*)
Williams and Glanfield (*WG*)

ARTIFICIAL COLLECTIONS BY LOCAL HISTORIANS OR ANTIQUARIANS

Binnall; Exley (*Ex*); Foster (*FL*); Hill; Lincoln City Library (*LCL*); Lincoln City and County Museum (*LCM*); Miscellaneous Deposits/Donations (*Misc Dep/Don*); Miscellaneous copies of documents (*MCD*)

BUSINESS RECORDS

Padley deposit
Syson deposit

LINCOLNSHIRE COUNTY COUNCIL

Deed packets

LINCOLNSHIRE LIBRARY SERVICE

Mss, printed and photographic material held at Lincoln Central Library:
Unbound Pamphlet series (*LC Lib UP*)
Maps and Plans (*LC Lib Plans*)
Photographic prints and negatives (*LC Lib Photo*)
Banks Collection of drawings and sketches (*LC Lib Banks*)
Ross collection: Annales, Scrapbooks (*LC Lib Ross*)

[See also *Lincs to the Past*, under Website Sources]

RECORDS HELD ELSEWHERE IN THE COUNTRY

THE NATIONAL ARCHIVES, FORMERLY THE PUBLIC RECORDS OFFICE (ABBREV. TNA)

Ref.		Printed form	Abbrev.
C 53	Charter Rolls	*Calendars of Charter Rolls*	*CChR*
C 54	Close Rolls	*Calendars of Close Rolls*	*CClR*
C 60	Fine Rolls	*Calendars of Fine Rolls*	*CFR*
C 62	Liberate Rolls	*Calendars of Liberate Rolls*	*CLR*
C 66	Patent Rolls	*Calendars of Patent Rolls*	*CPR*
C 132	Inquisitions post mortem	*Calendars of Inquisitions post mortem*	*IPM*
C 143	Inquisitions ad quod damnum	*Calendars of Inquisitions ad quod damnum*	*IAQD*
C 145	Inquisitions Miscellaneous	*Calendars of Inquisitions Miscellaneous*	*Inq. Misc.*
C 145	Ancient Deeds	*Calendars of Ancient Deeds*	*AD*
E 9	Jewish Plea Rolls	*Plea Rolls of the Exchequer of the Jews*	*PREJ*
E 101	Jews and Domus Conversorum		
E 159	King's Remembrancer Memoranda Rolls		*KRMR*
E 164	Book of Fees	*The Book of Fees*, otherwise known as the *Testa de Nevill*	*BFees*
E 368	Lord Treasurer's Remembrancer Memoranda Rolls		*LTRMR*
E 371	Originalia Rolls	*Abbreviatio Rotulorum Originalium*	*Abbreviatio*
E 372	Pipe Rolls	Pipe Roll Society series	*PRS*
HO 107/651	1841 Census		
HO 107/2105	1851 Census		
KB 27	Curia Regis Rolls c.1220	*Curia Regis Rolls*	*CRR*
RG 9/2361-2	1861 Census		
RG 10/3373-4	1871 Census		
RG 11/3243-4	1881 Census		
RG 12/2594-5	1891 Census		
RG 13/3062-3	1901 Census		
SC 5	Hundred Rolls		*RH*

BRITISH LIBRARY

Harleian Charters (Newhouse series: transcribed by Canon C.W. Foster)   Harl.
Lansdowne Ms 826, pt.5, transcript 4: transcription from *Originalia* Rolls

SOCIETY OF ANTIQUARIES

Willson Collection (786) *passim* (microfilm held at Lincolnshire Archives)

WESTMINSTER ABBEY MUNIMENTS (ABBREV. WAM)

Jewish *starrs* and bonds

LANCASHIRE RECORD OFFICE, PRESTON

O'Hagan Mss, including deeds for the Blyton and Knight families: photocopies held at
Lincoln Cathedral Library; schedule at Lincolnshire Archives
Townley Mss, including a Wymbyssh family rental: photocopy at Lincolnshire Archives

BODLEIAN LIBRARY, OXFORD

Ms Rawlinson D.687: Christ's Hospital, Lincoln: minutes and accounts 1618–1653
(photocopies at Lincolnshire Archives)

MAJOR WEBSITE SOURCES

Anglo-American Legal Tradition (AALT): image sources from many classes of TNA
records, hosted by the University of Houston
Calendars of Patent Rolls: image source administered by the University of Iowa
Fine Rolls of Henry III Project: Calendar, hosted by King's College, London
Lincs to the Past: catalogue and image source, administered by Lincolnshire County
Council
TNA Discovery Catalogue

Note: All references in the various endnotes to the Fine Rolls were accessed during
2013, and all references to Jewish Plea Rolls, the King's Remembrancer Rolls and Lord
Treasurer's Remembrancer Rolls, from images on the AALT site, were accessed during
2013 and 2014. The authors are indebted to the host universities, and to the staff of the
National Archives and Lincolnshire Libraries and Heritage, for making it possible for
researchers to examine these images and catalogues.

ABBREVIATIONS

AALT	Anglo American Legal Tradition: image source, based at the University of Houston
AASR	Reports and Papers of the Architectural Societies of the County of Lincoln [etc.]
Abbreviatio	The printed digest of the *Originalia* Rolls (TNA E 371)
AD	Calendars of *Ancient Deeds* (TNA C 145 ff)
Anc	Ancaster Estate papers (Lincolnshire Archives)
Andr	Andrews Mss (Lincolnshire Archives)
Arch. Jnl	Architectural Journal
ARMH	Records of Andrew, Race, Midgley and Hill, solicitors, of Lincoln (Lincolnshire Archives)
BB	The *Burwarmote Book* (D&C Ms 169, Lincoln Cathedral Library)
BFees	The *Book of Fees*, otherwise known as the *Testa de Nevill*
BL	The British Library
BNLW	Brownlow Estate papers (Lincolnshire Archives)
BS	Records of Burton, Scorer, solicitors, of Lincoln (Lincolnshire Archives)
Cant	The *Chantries Cartulary* (D&C A 1.8: *Liber de Ordinationibus Cantariarum*, Lincolnshire Archives)
CChR	Calendars of *Charter Rolls* (TNA C 53)
CClR	Calendars of *Close Rolls* (TNA C 54)
CFR	Calendar of *Fine Rolls* (TNA C 60)
CLR	Calendars of *Liberate Rolls* (TNA C 62)
CPR	Calendars of *Patent Rolls* (TNA C 66)
CRR	Curia Regis Rolls (TNA KB 27)
D&C	Dean and Chapter of Lincoln Cathedral
DEG	Records of Danby, Epton and Griffiths, solicitors, of Lincoln (Lincolnshire Archives)
Ex	Exley Papers (Lincolnshire Archives)
FL	Foster Library: Documents, transcripts and printed works collected by Canon C.W. Foster (Lincolnshire Archives)
FoLC	Pamphlets published by the Friends of Lincoln Cathedral
GL	*Georgian Lincoln*, by Sir Francis Hill
Harl	Harleian Mss (BL); Harleian Society publications
IAQD	Calendar of *Inquisitions ad quod damnum* (TNA C 143)
IPM	Calendar of *Inquisitions post-mortem* (TNA C 132 ff)
Inq. Misc.	Calendar of *Inquisitions Miscellaneous* (TNA C 145)
J.Eccl.Hist.	*Journal of the Ecclesiastical History Society*
JMB	*Jews in Medieval Britain*, ed. P. Skinner
KRMR	*King's Remembrancer Memoranda Rolls* (TNA E 159)
LA	Lincolnshire Archives

LAAS	Publications of the Lincolnshire Architectural and Archaeological Society
LAT	Lincoln Archaeological Trust
LCL	Records from Lincoln Central Library, transferred to Lincolnshire Archives
LC Lib	Maps, photographs, unbound pamphlets etc. (Lincoln Central Library)
LCM	Records transferred to Lincolnshire Archives by Lincoln City and County Museum
LHA	*Lincolnshire History and Archaeology*
LLM	*Lincolnshire Life* Magazine
LPC	Records of Langley, Philips and Coleman, solicitors, of Lincoln (Lincolnshire Archives)
LRS	Lincoln Record Society
LRSM	Lincoln, Rutland and Stamford Mercury newspaper
LTRMR	*Lord Treasurer's Remembrancer Memoranda Rolls* (TNA E 368)
MCD	Miscellaneous Copies of Documents: a collection at Lincolnshire Archives
ML	*Medieval Lincoln*, by Sir Francis Hill
Mon	Monson Estate Papers (Lincolnshire Archives)
PREJ	Plea Rolls of the Exchequer of the Jews (TNA E 9)
PRS	Pipe Roll Society (TNA E 372)
RA	*Registrum Antiquissimum*, Lincoln Record Society
RH	The edited transcription of the Hundred Rolls
SAH	*The Survey of Ancient Houses* series
SB	Records of Sills and Betteridge, solicitors, of Lincoln (Lincolnshire Archives)
Sib	Sibthorp Estate papers (Lincolnshire Archives)
SoL	The *Survey of Lincoln* Neighbourhood Booklets series
Thurg	The *Thurgarton Priory Cartulary*, edited by Trevor Foulds
TJHSE	*Transactions of the Jewish Historical Society of England*
TLE	Records of Toynbee, Larken and Evans, solicitors, of Lincoln (Lincolnshire Archives)
TSJ	Records of Tweed, Stephen and Jourdain, solicitors, of Lincoln (Lincolnshire Archives)
TSL	*Tudor and Stuart Lincoln*, by Sir Francis Hill
VC	The Cartulary of the Vicars Choral of Lincoln Cathedral (VC 2/1, Lincolnshire Archives)
VCH	Victoria County History
VL	*Victorian Lincoln*, by Sir Francis Hill
WAM	Records at Westminster Abbey Muniments
Welb	The Welbourn Cartulary (D&C A 1.10, Lincolnshire Archives)
WG	Records of Williams and Glanfield, solicitors, of Lincoln (Lincolnshire Archives)

SELECT BIBLIOGRAPHY

B.L. Abrahams, 'Condition of the Jews of England at the time of their Expulsion in 1290', in *TJHSE*, 2 (1896), 94-96

M. Birch, *Lincoln's Medieval Jewry and uphill Norman Houses* (Heighington, Lincoln, undated [c.2005])

W. de Gray Birch, *The Royal Charters of the City of Lincoln* (1904)

P. Brand, 'The Jewish Community of England in the Records of English Royal Government', in P. Skinner (ed.), *Jews in Medieval Britain: Historical, Literary and Archaeological Perspectives* (Woodbridge: Boydell Press, 2003), 73-83

N. Burgess, *A History of Lincoln Theological College 1874–1974*, typescript notes

K. Cameron, *The Place Names of the City of Lincoln*, English Place Name Society LVIII (1985)

F.W.B and M. Charles, *Conservation of Timber Buildings* (London: Hutchinson, 1986)

Curia Regis Rolls of the Reign of Henry III: 1219–20 (London: HMSO, 1938); 1220 (ditto, 1952)

M.D. Davis, 'The Mediaeval Jews of Lincoln', *Arch. Jnl*, XXXVIII (1881), 178-200

R.B. Dobson, The Jews of York and the Massacre of March 1190, Borthwick Papers 45 (1974)

—, 'The Medieval York Jewry Reconsidered', in Skinner (2003), 145-156

L. Elvin, *Lincoln As It Was 2* (London: Nelson, 1976)

C.W. Foster, *Registrum Antiquissimum I* (Lincoln Record Society 27, 1931)

—, *Registrum Antiquissimum II* (Lincoln Record Society 28, 1933)

T. Foulds, *The Thurgarton Cartulary* (Stamford: Paul Watkins, 1994)

L.M. Friedman, *Robert Grosseteste and the Jews* (Cambridge, Mass: Harvard University Press, 1934)

F. Haes, 'A Report on Aaron's House' [sic], *TJHSE*, 2 (1896–98), 157ff

C. Garton, *Lincoln Grammar School 1792–1850* (unpublished typescript)

P.D. Harvey, *Cuxham* (Oxford: OUP, 1965)

J.W.F. Hill, *Medieval Lincoln* (Cambridge: CUP, 1948)

—, *Tudor and Stuart Lincoln* (Cambridge: CUP, 1956)

—, *Georgian Lincoln* (Cambridge: CUP, 1966)

—, *Victorian Lincoln* (Cambridge: CUP, 1974)

J. Hillaby, 'A Magnate among the Marchers: Hamo of Hereford, his family and clients 1218–1253', *TJHSE*, 31 (1990), 23-82

—, 'Beth Miqdash Me'at: the Synagogues of Medieval England', *J.Eccl.Hist.* 44 (1993), 182-198

—, 'Jewish Colonisation in the Twelfth Century', in Skinner (2003), 1-40

T. Hudson Turner, *Some Account of Domestic Architecture in England from the Conquest to the end of the Thirteenth Century*, vol.1 (Oxford: J.H. Parker, 1851)

R. Huscroft, *Expulsion: England's Jewish Solution* (Stroud: Tempus, 2006)

J. Jacobs, 'Aaron of Lincoln', *TJHSE*, 2 (1896-98), 157-178

T.A. Jackson, J.W.F. Hill, and W.A. Pantin, *The Story of the Cardinal's Hat* (Lincoln: privately published, 1953)

C.P.C. Johnson, 'A Second Jewish *Scola* in Lincoln', *LHA* 13 (1978), 35-36

—, with A.G. Vince, 'The South Bail Gates of Lincoln', *LHA* 27 (1992), 12-16

—, 'The Hospital of the Holy Sepulchre' in A. Walker (ed.), *South-East Lincoln: Canwick Road, South Common, St Catherine's and Bracebridge* (Survey of Lincoln, 2011)

R.H. Jones, *Medieval Houses at Flaxengate, The Archaeology of Lincoln XI-1* (London: CBA, for Lincoln Archaeological Trust, 1980)

S.R. Jones, 'Ancient Domestic Buildings and their Roofs', in the *Programme of the Summer Meeting at Lincoln of the Royal Archaeological Institute* (1974), 49-53

S.R. Jones, *Four Minster Houses* (Friends of Lincoln Cathedral, 1974)

S.R. Jones, K. Major, J. Varley with a contribution by C.P.C. Johnson, *The Survey of Ancient Houses in Lincoln I: Priorygate to Pottergate* (Lincoln Civic Trust, 1984)

S.R. Jones, K. Major and J. Varley, *The Survey of Ancient Houses in Lincoln II: Houses to the South and West of the Minster* (Lincoln Civic Trust, 1987)

—, *The Survey of Ancient Houses in Lincoln III: Houses in Eastgate, Priorygate and James Street* (Lincoln Civic Trust, 1990)

S.R. Jones, K. Major, J. Varley and C.P.C. Johnson, *The Survey of Ancient Houses in Lincoln IV: Houses in the Bail: Steep Hill, Castle Hill, and Bailgate* (Lincoln Civic Trust, 1996)

Lincoln Civic Trust, *Annual Reports*, 1970-1996 *passim*

Lincoln, Rutland and Stamford Mercury, 18-19c: microfilm collection

Lincoln and Lincolnshire Directories: see below

H. Loewe, H.P. Stokes and I. Abrahams (eds), *Starrs and Jewish Charters in the British Museum*, i (Cambridge, 1930); ii Supplemental Notes (London: Spottiswoode, Ballantyne and Co, 1932); iii Indexes (publ. as for vol. ii, 1932)

A.R. Maddison, *Lincolnshire Pedigrees I* (Harleian Society 50, 1902)

K. Major, *Registrum Antiquissimum VIII* (Lincoln Record Society 51, 1958)

—, *Registrum Antiquissimum IX* (Lincoln Record Society 62, 1968)

—, *Registrum Antiquissimum X* (Lincoln Record Society 67, 1973)

D. Mills, *The People of Steep Hill around 1900* (Lincoln: published by the author, 2005)

—, and R.C. Wheeler, *Historic Town Plans of Lincoln* (Lincoln Record Society 92, 2004)

J. Munby, 'J.C. Buckler, Tackley's Inn and Three Medieval Houses in Oxford', *Oxoniensia* 43 (1978), 100-122

R.R. Mundill, 'Anglo Jewry under Edward I', *TJHSE*, 31 (1990), 1-21

—, *England's Jewish Solution: Experiment and Expulsion 1242–1290* (Cambridge: Cambridge University Press, 1998)

—, *The King's Jews: Money, Massacre and Exodus in Medieval England* (London: Continuum, 2010)

K. Naylor, *Richard Smith MD: the Founder of Christ's Hospital, Lincoln* (Lincoln: Governors of the Foundation of Christ's Hospital at Lincoln, 1951)

C. Page, 'Thomas Sawdon, machine maker, and Sawdon's Yard', in A. Walker (ed.), *Brayford Pool: Lincoln's Waterfront through Time* (Survey of Lincoln, 2012), 19-23

W.A. Pantin, 'The Cardinal's Hat, Lincoln', in *The Builder*, 4 September 1953, 343-346

—, 'Medieval Inns', in E.M. Jope (ed.) *Studies in Building History* (London: Odhams Press, 1961), 166-191

—, 'Some Medieval English Town Houses – a Study in Adaptation', in I.LL. Foster and L. Alcock (eds), *Culture and Environment: Essays in honour of Sir Cyril Fox* (London: Routledge and Kegan Paul, 1963)

The Record Commissioners, *Rotuli Hundredorum temp. Hen III & Edw I in Turr' Lond' et in Curia Receptae Scacarii Westm' Asservati*, I (London, 1812)

H.G. Richardson, *English Jewry under Angevin Kings* (London: Methuen, 1960)

J.M. Rigg, *Select Pleas, Starrs and other Records from the Rolls of the Exchequer of the Jews 1220–1284* (Selden Society 15, 1902)

D.L. Roberts, 'The Cardinal's Hat 268 High Street, Lincoln', in the *Programme of the Summer Meeting at Lincoln of the Royal Archaeological Institute* (1974), 84-86

Z.E. Rokeah, 'Money and the Hangman in late 13th century England: Jews, Christians and coinage offences, alleged and real', *TJHSE*, 31 (1990), 83-109; and 32 (1993), 159-218

—, *Medieval English Jews and Royal Officials: Entries of Jewish interest in the English Memoranda Rolls 1266–1293* (Jerusalem: Hebrew University, 2000)

H. Rosenau, 'Note on the Relationship of Jews' Court and the Lincoln Synagogue', *Arch. Jnl*, XCIII (1936), 51-56

C. Roth, *Medieval Lincoln and its Jewry: a Retrospect and a Reconstruction* (London: Jewish Historical Society, 1934)

—, *History of the Jews in England* (Oxford, 1941; 2nd edn, 1942; 3rd edn, 1964)

—, 'The Jews of Medieval Oxford', *Oxford Historical Society*, NS 9 (1951)

R.C. Stacey, 'Royal Taxation and the Social Structure of Medieval Anglo-Jewry: the Tallages of 1239-1242', *Hebrew Union College Annual*, 56 (1985), 175-249

K. Steane, 'Hillside sites in the north-west area', in *Lincoln Archaeology No.1*, ed. M.J. Jones (City of Lincoln Archaeological Unit, 1989), 22-24

D. Stocker, 'Salle et hall, dans les batîments urbains des xiie et xiiie siècles', in *The Medieval House in Normandy and England: proceedings of seminars in Rouen and Norwich 1998 and 1999* (Rouen: La Société libre d'émulation de la Seine-Maritime, 2002)

H.P. Stokes, '*Studies in Anglo-Jewish History*' (Edinburgh: Ballantyne, Hanson and Co., for the Jewish Historical Society, 1913), 33-35

T. Sympson, FRCS, *A Short Account of the Old and of the New County Hospitals* (Lincoln: Williamson, 1878)

E. Venables, 'Walks Through the Streets of Lincoln: a lecture delivered to the YMCA on 11 December 1883' (Lincoln: Akrill and Ruddock, 1884)

Victoria County History of Lincolnshire, 2 (London: Archibald Constable and Co. Ltd, 1906)

R.C. Wheeler, 'Housing Development between Sincil Dyke and Canwick Road', in A. Walker (ed.), *South-East Lincoln: Canwick Road, South Common, St Catherine's and Bracebridge* (Survey of Lincoln, 2011), 18-20

M. Wood, 'Norman Domestic Architecture', *Arch. Jnl*, XCII (1935), 194-198

—, with J.W.F. Hill, 'St Mary's Guildhall and the Lincoln Jews' Houses', *Arch. Jnl*, CIII (1946), 159-162

LINCOLN STREET DIRECTORIES (WITH SOME COUNTY DIRECTORIES)

Chronological list of Directories used in this volume

1828   Particulars and Valuation of the Parishes of Lincoln made in the year 1828, by Edward Betham and Edward James Willson (Lincoln: Drury, 1833) [Quoted as 'Willson and Betham Survey' in the endnotes]

1828/9   Pigot and Co. National Commercial Directory: Northern and Midland Counties

1835   Pigot and Co. National Commercial Directory: ditto.

1842   History, Gazeteer and Directory of Lincolnshire, and the City and Diocese of Lincoln (William White, Sheffield)

1843   The Lincoln Commercial Directory and Private Residence Guide (Lincoln, Victor and Baker)

1849   Post Office Directory of Lincolnshire (London, Kelly and Co.)

1856   History, Gazeteer and Directory of Lincolnshire, and the City and Diocese of Lincoln (William White, Sheffield)

1857   The City of Lincoln Directory (Charles Akrill)

1863   ditto. (Charles Akrill, Steam Press Office)

1867   ditto.

1872   History, Gazeteer and Directory of Lincolnshire, and the City and Diocese of Lincoln, by William White (London: Simpkin, Marshall and Co.)

1877   The City of Lincoln Directory (Charles Akrill, Steam Press Office)

1881   ditto.

1885   ditto. (Akrill, Ruddock and Keyworth)

1888   Directory of the City of Lincoln, with the Surrounding District (Akrill, Ruddock and Keyworth)

1894   ditto. (J.W. Ruddock)

1897   ditto. (J.W. Ruddock)

1899   Lincoln and District Directory (Derby: W.J. Cook and Co.)

1901   Directory of the City of Lincoln with the Villages within a Radius of Ten Miles (J.W. Ruddock)

1903, 1905, 1907, 1909, 1911, 1913: ditto.

INTRODUCTION

This volume not only marks the culmination of 45 years of historical and architectural research on the central and upper City of Lincoln, but also makes continued use of different partnerships and methods to interpret and present the rich topographical history of Lincoln. It builds on the work of a number of local historians of the past 300 years, notably Thomas Sympson, Edward James Willson, the Revd Edmund Venables, Canon Charles Wilmer Foster and Sir Francis Hill.

From 1970 a multi-disciplinary approach was adopted for this work, initially under the auspices of the Lincoln Civic Trust, the result of which was the publication of the four Fascicules of the *Survey of Ancient Houses*, completed between 1984 and 1996. These volumes presented a detailed study of the ancient houses in the Close and Bail of the upper city, combining the rich descriptive architectural detail provided by the drawings, photographs and architectural commentaries of Stanley Jones, and the profuse documentary history of these areas, researched by Kathleen Major, Joan Varley and Christopher Johnson with the invaluable support and assistance of archaeologists such as Mick Jones and Alan Vince, and staff of the Planning Department of the City Council, notably Christopher Bedford, Alan Dobby and Arthur Ward. A fuller list of those who belonged to the *Survey* Working Party may be found in the Appendix, which provides a contents guide to the four Fascicules.

Professor Kathleen Major, who had inherited the mantle of editor for the impressive series of *Registrum Antiquissimum* for the Lincoln Record Society after the death of Canon Foster in 1935, was responsible for volumes iv–x of that series, which were published between the late 1930s and 1973. The final three of these, volumes viii–x, relate to the city of Lincoln, and have been the foundation for the medieval material used in the *Survey* series and also the current volume.

Professor Major was the inspiration and driving force for the *Survey of Ancient Houses* project, and served as Chairman of the working party between 1970 and 1995; she was also a generous donor of both her time and money towards the completion of the original *Survey*. Well into her nineties, she gave her approval to a successor group, the Survey of Lincoln, which has since 1995 continued the detailed research into other areas of Lincoln, and widened the general approach to the subject of urban history with a series of Neighbourhood Booklets, aimed at a general audience.

Joan Varley, former County Archivist, also continued her researches into her nineties, working principally on the records of the Dean and Chapter which contributed in no small fashion to the level of detail found in the four Fascicules. Her work has also proved useful as background for a number of the houses covered in this volume, in particular the Harlequin and Sibthorp House. Mrs Varley and Miss Major together have handed down an invaluable foundation for the research methodology used in this volume, and it is only right that we dedicate it to their memory.

The architectural study of the city was commenced in 1969, when Stanley Jones was first approached by Lincoln Civic Trust to survey some of the buildings in the upper city area. His regular reports to the *Survey* working party formed a valuable adjunct to the survey plans, and formed the basis of the architectural descriptions in the four Fascicules, and in a work entitled *Four Minster Houses*, published by the Friends of Lincoln Cathedral in 1974. During this time he also produced drawings and commentaries for a number of buildings in the central and lower areas of Lincoln, which form a vital component in this volume, which is in essence the fifth and final Fascicule in the *Survey of Ancient Houses* series.

Christopher Johnson, former archivist and latterly Area Service Manager for Lincolnshire Archives, and Secretary of the *Survey* from 1974 until the working party completed its work, has since the 1970s been engaged in a long-term programme of research into the history of these and other areas of the city, in order to provide the requisite documentary source material for the ongoing Survey work. As Chair of the Survey of Lincoln since 2011, he hopes to ensure the continuation of this research and publication effort for the foreseeable future.

The Survey of Lincoln, by participating with the Lincoln Record Society in the preparation of this volume, is not only a partner in the process but also demonstrates, as with *LRS* Volume 92, *Historic Town Plans of Lincoln 1610–1920*, that it is possible to use a variety of formats and take advantage of an ever-increasing range of sources, technology and expertise to further their mutual objectives.

Scope of the Survey work

The geographical coverage of this volume has been largely guided by the availability of historical and architectural evidence. It was decided at an early stage to begin at the point where the original *Survey of Ancient Houses* concluded, i.e. the South Bail Gate, and continue down Steep Hill, through the Strait and into the top section of the High Street.

Steep Hill has rightly earned an international reputation for the quality of its buildings and the unique cultural environment which has developed over the centuries. This was officially recognised in 2011 with the accolade of 'Britain's Best Place', bestowed by the Academy of Urbanism. The present survey documents and illustrates the rich history of a large section of Steep Hill, which includes in its length some of the oldest domestic and commercial architecture to be found anywhere in the country, e.g. the late 12th-century Norman House at 46–47 Steep Hill and the Jew's House of the same era, which forms the dividing line between Steep Hill and the Strait.

The Strait has its own quota of notable architecture, the most prominent example of which is Dernstall House, which was the earliest restoration project undertaken by Lincoln Civic Trust, between 1966 and 1974. Less well known is no.5 in the Strait, which incorporates traces of some original 14th-century timber framing, albeit well disguised by later rebuilding work.

At the top of High Street the outstanding architecture and long history of the Cardinal's Hat and no.262 High Street (Garmston House) are perhaps the most prominent survivals, although there is little of the original fabric left visible inside the latter.

The final section of the survey work in this volume contains a selection of properties which merited particular attention by Stanley Jones during his long connection with the *Survey*: these are the Witch and Wardrobe (no.21 Waterside North), no.195 High Street, Sibthorp House (nos 352–355 High Street) and the Schoolmaster's House (nos 12–14 Broadgate), the last two of which unfortunately no longer exist.

The Appendix brings together a contents list for the original four *Fascicules* of the *Survey of Ancient Houses*. It is to be hoped that there will eventually be a combined index to these to make them more accessible.

Evidence for timber framing

It has been noted repeatedly throughout the course of research into this volume that traces of medieval building methods, particularly timber framing, have been hidden by the accretions of time, under brick, stone and tile used in rebuilding work. One example of this stands out. During demolition work at nos 257–259 High Street in the early 1960s (a very dangerous period for architectural historians in Lincoln, as well no doubt as in other historic towns and cities), Mr Laurence Elvin of the Lincoln City Library Service was on hand to photograph some evidence of timber framing in the late medieval period. Similarly at the next door property, no.260, the later rendering or partial rebuilding of the frontage was sufficiently pronounced, as early as 1649, as to lead the Parliamentary Survey inspector to conclude that this building was of stone construction. Traces of a jettied first-floor, apparently heavily rendered, were evident on an early 20th-century photograph. The Parliamentary surveyors, we think, made similar mistakes in other cases.

Evidence of re-use of timbers, particularly in roof structures, has been noted in certain instances, notably in the north wing of Sibthorp House, 195 High Street and 266–267 High Street. Stanley Jones included a section on medieval and post-medieval roofs in Lincoln in an essay in Part 2 of Fascicule 3 of the Survey: *Houses in Eastgate, Priorygate and James Street*, published in 1990.

Construction in stone

Buildings constructed mainly of stone normally belong to the earliest period of our study, the 12th and 13th centuries. The Norman House (46–47 Steep Hill, with 1 Christ's Hospital Terrace), and the Jew's House, it needs no apology for repeating, are the truly outstanding survivals in this category, and we know from historical research that so many more examples once graced all areas of the current Survey. One superb example of this would have been another property owned by a member of the Jewish community, the double-fronted tenement belonging to Floria at 27–28 Strait, which sported a magnificent entry passage ('*cum pulcro exitu*'). Several other probably similar conformations are identifiable.

The Jewish community

Although this volume is not the most useful format in which to expand on the history of the Jews of medieval Lincoln, nevertheless one cannot help but notice the strong influence this community had on the history of the properties of this area, and of the city in general. The evidence gathered in the course of this research has already enabled us to add considerably to Sir Francis Hill's account of the Jews in medieval Lincoln, not least in identifying some of the houses occupied by particular individuals. Jacob, son of Leo, is the prime example here. Unfortunately immortalised in ballad form as the 'Copin' of the Little St Hugh legend, he is known to have lived in no.13 Steep Hill until his execution in 1255. His widow Marchota (Margot) lived there until c.1280 and is known to have employed a local Christian girl as a maidservant.

Christians and Jews lived in close proximity to each other, noticeably in Brancegate, now Grantham Street, and also in the lower Steep Hill area: Henry Breykaldoun was the occupier of what is now the southern portion of Jews' Court (2 Steep Hill), and John of Hampton lived down a passageway just north of the synagogue. A similar situation prevailed in the area of 261–264 High Street.

Racial tension, when it did surface, was mostly due to external factors (often incited by those with vested interests) or from individuals aggrieved about their personal financial issues. Further exploration of these and other themes connected to the Jews of Lincoln will be the subject of a future project.

Patterns of ownership

The original *Survey of Ancient Houses* was devoted to the uphill area of Lincoln, dominated by Cathedral-owned properties, already noted as being the best-documented group in the whole city. All the 77 or so houses covered in the first three Fascicules were Chapter-owned, except for a few properties under the control of the Vicars Choral, technically a separate corporation. In *Fascicule iv*, however, it is noticeable that the Cathedral owned just over 60% of the properties surveyed, and St Paul's parish accounted for 5.5%. Surprisingly, just under 35% of the houses were freehold, creating several difficulties in tracing early records.

In the area of this Survey, the proportion of Cathedral-owned property (as late as 1870) dropped to 25%; the City of Lincoln owned 20% prior to 1835, and four different parishes accounted for 11% of the total. Freeholds dominated, with 44% of the 92 properties surveyed, posing the same information-gathering problems as encountered above-Hill. Even so, as Chapter and Corporation leaseholds were spread out to some extent in several parts of the Survey area, it was possible to glean boundary evidence for several of these freeholds. More use was made of probate records (wills and inventories), and sources such as the L3 series of Corporation deed bundles, documenting property acquired by slum clearance or road widening schemes. The endnotes show better than this Introduction how a variety of such disparate sources can create a reasonable well-rounded account of most of the properties we have studied.

Digital source material useful to the Survey

More notes about the houses and various sources of information can be found on the Disc accompanying this volume. Please see Disc Menu Page.

Microfiche, though useful in its way and in its time, has now been comprehensively sidelined by digital data, whether in disc form or website-based; students of various branches of urban history now enjoy access to a wide range of primary and secondary material, an advantage your present authors could not have envisaged when the first *Fascicule* was published, just over 30 years ago. The National Archives not only holds at least 32 million records on its *Discovery* database (9 million of which are downloadable), but has also made it possible for a number of very useful digitisation projects to scan and disseminate a vast range of material from the Public Records. Here we list just three:

Calendars of Patent Rolls, administered by the University of Iowa
Fine Rolls of Henry III Project, a consortium approach, including participation by King's College, London and TNA
Anglo-American Legal Tradition (AALT), hosted by the University of Houston, with support from TNA

Dr David Crook and Dr Paul Dryburgh of *LRS* have been associated with some or other of these projects, and Professor Alan Nelson, who undertook research at the Lincolnshire Archives Office in the early 1970s, is also listed among the *AALT* Project Board members. *AALT* holds images of material from Assize records, Pipe Rolls, Jewish Plea Rolls, HM Works records, Memoranda Rolls and many other sources useful for urban history.

Nearer home, the relatively recent database, *Lincs to the Past*, which incorporates the Illustrations Index and the Archives CALM catalogue, is rapidly adding to its contents, giving access information for archive material, printed sources, pictorial collections and archaeological sources. Ever useful also is the *Lincoln Archaeological Research Assessment*, available in CD-Rom format with *The City by the Pool*.

With these additional sources, it is possible to give more consideration to the human element in the historical urban landscape. It is nearly 40 years since there was an explosion of interest in Family History, and even longer since the social and demographic aspects of Population Studies awakened many researchers to the richness of our genealogical records. Some of the personal stories of owners and occupiers, where these are well documented, add considerable value to the building record, giving a wider context to the various accounts to be found in this work. Comprehensive lists (with references) of all known owners and occupiers of the properties in the Survey are included in the data on the disc.

The Survey of Lincoln is greatly indebted to the Officers and Council of the Lincoln Record Society for agreeing to another rewarding publication partnership, which is greatly aided by the fact that several of the Survey members are also involved in various capacities with the Record Society. *The Historical Town Maps* volume, published in 2004, continues to give valuable assistance to urban research in Lincoln, as also will, we hope, this new offering.

Christopher Johnson and Stanley Jones   March 2015

Steep, Strait and High

The Survey

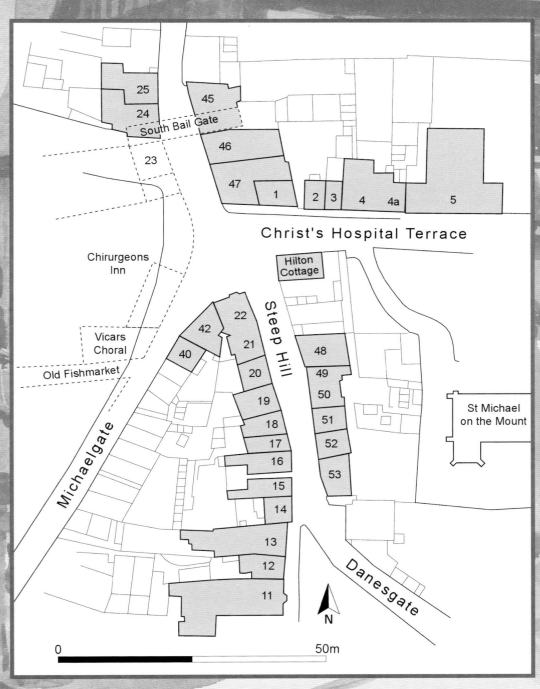

Street plan, no.25 Steep Hill to no.11 Steep Hill

25 and 24 STEEP HILL

This short range of property presents a puzzle, both to the casual observer and the historian, which can only be explained by reference to various events which had an impact on the topography of the area, separated by more than 650 years: the period between the anti-Jewish riot of 1190/91 and the Barons' Revolt of 1217, and the creation of Wordsworth Street in 1881. The area just south of the Roman south gate was of strategic significance, but development was apparently permitted in the twelfth century on the west side, i.e. where nos 24–25 are situated, as it was on the east side of Steep Hill.

It was shown in an article in *Lincolnshire History and Archaeology* in 1992[1] that by around 1200 the south gateway of the old Roman defences had deteriorated, and a new City gate, of limited strategic importance and perhaps more a demonstration of civic pride, was built across the carriageway. The new gate and some new buildings to the west were situated adjoining the south boundary of what is now no.25 Steep Hill, just above where Wordsworth Street adjoins Steep Hill. The gate continued across to join up with the southern part of the present day no.45 Steep Hill, just north of the Norman House.[2]

From a look at the boundaries shown in the 19th-century Padley Plans[3] it seems that nos 25 and 24 Steep Hill (the former Gatehouse) were carved out of a larger original single holding. The boundary between the two properties was not geometrical and may have followed an old pathway. This irregular pattern can be seen today in the curvilinear shape of the rear range of no.25 as seen from Wordsworth Street.

At some point between 1180 and 1184, John son of Augustine released all right in the combined property to William, son of Fulk, his kinsman, but this transaction[4] masks a continuing interest in the site by Benedict the Jew, brother of Aaron, who was in official terms a lessee of William. John owed money to Aaron: a sum of 2.5 marks (£1.66) was still owing after Aaron's death in 1186.[5] William was also in debt to Aaron, and his heirs made a fine of 60 marks and five hawks with the king c.1185, although other debts, including a huge loan on the security of his mill at Washingborough and property elsewhere, took much longer to resolve.

It should perhaps be noted that other neighbouring properties were of relevance to Aaron and his family. He controlled all the property north of the old gate, i.e. 26–34 Steep Hill and 1–4 Castle Hill,[6] and his brother Senior, a Latin derivation from Seigneuret, perhaps equivalent to le Maistre, had land further south of nos 24–25 Steep Hill.[7]

After the 1217 Revolt the Castle authorities acquired by escheat (confiscation) an interest in various properties adjacent to the walls and gates. The Jews, although 'protected' by the king, as his property, were also seen as a ready source of funding, and some of their properties in this area were taken by the Crown, perhaps to facilitate the building of the new gate. Master Mosse Bosse, son of Benedict, was still alive at some stage in 1219 when he responded to official queries about his transactions.[8] Soon after, however, he was murdered by the retinue of Walter de Evermue.[9] The Sheriff of Lincolnshire was mandated by the Justices of the Jews to alert the mayor to this and also to the murder of Sara, wife of Deulecres. Property belonging to Master Mosse, which included land to the west and south of this plot was handed over to Jordan de Esseby, the Constable of the Castle.[10] It is part of this land which was granted c.1221 by Lady Nicholaa de la Haye to Peter the woadseller (*waisdarius/le Weyder*) in return for the sizeable sum of £20 and an annual quit-rent of one pound of wax to be given to her and her heirs. There is an endorsement on this document[11] which states that in the 43rd year of the reign of

Henry III (c.1258/59) it was shown to John de Esseby, then seneschall to the earl, and his servant G. de Brotelby; perhaps this related to a further deed in the series.[12]

Ursell, son of Pucella, a Jew, was known to have been a contemporary occupant of part of this property. The Pipe Roll for 1227[13] records a new imposition of 10s per annum on Peter for 'a messuage which belonged to Ursell the Jew'; he also had to pay for his summons to the Exchequer, as the king had given the property to Lady Nicholaa by his charter.[14] Peter's son John conveyed it c.1244/45[15] to William de Wynchcumbe, canon of Lincoln, who within a few years handed it over to the Cathedral authorities for charitable purposes connected to the Cathedral and St Giles' Hospital.[16] It is interesting to note that the quit-rent of wax was still being paid. This house may be that which was sold to Robert Amys in 1258.[17] The medieval record ends here, and no further owners or occupiers are identifiable until the 18th century, although there may be some connection with lessees and occupiers of the Bail Gate.[18]

25 Steep Hill

Dated to the first third of the 18th century,[19] no.25 was described in the Willson and Betham Survey of Lincoln in 1828 as belonging to the Committee of Isaac Wood. Wood, who had a mental condition, was an inmate of the York Asylum, and his affairs were dealt with by a committee which was representative of the many and various interests of his heirs. Isaac Wood (1773–1849) was the son of another Isaac, Keeper of Lincoln Castle (d.1789) and grandson of Clement Wood who owned several properties in Lincoln, including 8–9 Castle Hill and 2–3 Steep Hill (Jews' Court), as well as no.25 Steep Hill.[20]

As the Wood properties were administered by the Committee and tied up in a very protracted Chancery case which was not finally resolved until 1911, the original deed bundles for these important properties have regrettably disappeared from sight. No.25 Steep Hill may perhaps have been sold off soon after Isaac's death in 1849, as Sarah Horner is listed on the St Mary Magdalene Tithe Award of 1851[21] as owner, with Robert Jackson as the occupier. In 1828 the occupiers had been Elizabeth Sharpe and Ralph Taylor. By 1842 Hannah Taylor, cabinet maker and upholsterer, was listed in the Street Directory and for a while from 1857 Mary Martin, a cooper. Among later occupants were Joseph Mann, grocer and later coal dealer,[22] and Harriet Richardson.[23]

This small tenement has the distinction of having as its northern bound a stone wall of, if not Roman, then certainly one of medieval origin. The same wall in no.26 has a reduced rounded projection in the ground-floor room, a feature thought to have been associated with part of the adjacent South Gate of the Bail. In this tenement the stonework of the wall is exposed to first-floor level, much of its present height relating to post-medieval improvements. A north–south wall in no.25 is three feet thick and fifteen feet in length. In this dimension it is preserved in the basement and the ground-floor shop; above the last level the wall is reduced to twenty-one inches and is held to be of brick construction wholly related to the rebuilding in the later 18th century of nos 24 and 25. When viewed on the 1/500 Ordnance Survey map of the Steep Hill area it may be seen that there is a common alignment of a north–south wall or boundary line extending from no.24 to no.28 inclusive.

It is unlikely that any medieval work has survived above ground-level and one is reluctant to promote the claim that the very substantial wall in no.25 is necessarily of early origin. However, stone buildings are known to have existed on site and the junction of two substantial walls at this point has to be acknowledged as a possible related fragment of something conceivably more extensive.

ARCHITECTURAL
DESCRIPTION

*Fig 2. Plans of cellar,
ground-floor and first-floor of
no.25 Steep Hill*

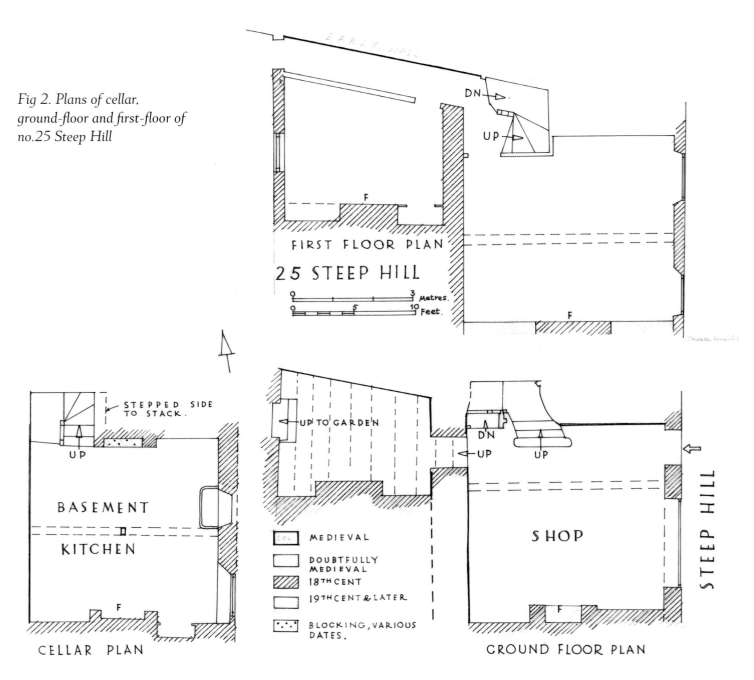

THE PLAN

The house is one of a small group in the upper part of Steep Hill that retains its basement kitchen and, in common with them, was always poorly lit. On the evidence of its external south gable and the general brickwork pattern it displays one may confidently ascribe the present appearance of the building to the mid to late 18th century.[24] The cooking hearths and the smaller domestic hearths in the arrangement are housed in axial chimney stacks; one has to add in some means of storage in the back yard or court for coals etc. The availability of water must have been confined to carrying a supply indoors from a shared well, pump, or water cart. The principal rooms were at first-floor level with the ground-floor, off the street, functioning as a shop or an area for other trades and manufactures. The establishment is two-rooms deep and the uppermost floor level used most likely as family bedrooms. It is possible that servants inhabited the kitchen and the room next to the back yard – or were simply housed elsewhere and employed as outworkers.

Presumably the area immediately to the south of the South Gate had contained a ditch spanned by a bridge of sorts to accommodate wheeled and pedestrian traffic; or, perhaps in lieu of a bridge, there was a road equally defensible from the gatehouse which briefly interrupted the earthwork.

4

The presence of the internal north–south wall in no.25 may be compared to the spinal wall in nos 46 and 47 Steep Hill where it produces a double-range plan. Were this to have been its primary form, the alignment was erected on ground dedicated to the town ditch. It would seem to share this privilege with its eastern counterpart, no.45 Steep Hill.

The South Bail Gatestead, and freehold property to the west: later 24 Steep Hill

This gatestead, described in some detail in the LHA article, was until its demolition in 1776 the property of the Common Council of Lincoln, and we have documentary evidence for the lessees and a few occupiers from 1524 until the end of its existence. Among the lessees were William Hynde, Clerk to the Common Council, who held the lease from 1552[25] and William Darby, pewterer, from 1720[26] to his death in 1732. After Darby took over the leasehold, the gatestead lease became enmeshed in a mortgage, which in 1740, after Darby's death and that of his wife, was assigned to Clement Wood.

In 1774 the lease was surrendered to the Council by Richard Chambers, husband of

Sarah (nee Randes), granddaughter of Clement Wood. A building lease was in 1776 given to Robert Bell, in trust for William Wilson or Willson of the Bail, joiner and carpenter,[27] and a new tenement constructed by him to provide shop accommodation.

In 1807 this lease was transferred[28] to Hadnah Yates, tailor (lessee of the Cardinal's Hat[29]), in trust for Richard East, staymaker. His widow Elizabeth, a grocer, purchased the freehold in 1835, when the newly established Corporation enfranchised the majority of its leaseholds. Her devisees sold it in 1854 to William Greenwood of Boston, and in 1860 the site was acquired by the Governors of the County Hospital.[30]

The tenement on the Steep Hill frontage, now numbered 24, had no recorded occupants between 1860 and 1877, when George Broadway, cook and confectioner, appeared in the Street Directory. A variety of different trades and tenants followed. In 1881, Henry Horner, the owner of the freehold, complained about the taking of some of his land to create Wordsworth Street. He was still owner in 1898, and had added a new tenement on what was left of his property facing the new street. His premises there also included a bakehouse, stable and piggery.[31]

A comparison of the surviving boundary details for nos 25, 24, the gatestead and other property to the south and west has led to the conclusion that the gatestead was in the same position as the current 24 Steep Hill, which places it a little way north of the position identified in the *LHA* account.

As for the freehold which backed on to the west of the gatestead, this was at various times owned by the lessees of the gatestead. Gregory Lowcock, mercer, owner from 1599,[32] passed it on to his son Thomas, who by 1639 had become a Merchant Taylor in London. He sold his interest in the property, at that time called Hinde's House, to Christopher Dales of the Close, tailor, and Anne his wife, in that year.[33]

Christopher died sometime before 1668, and Anne provided for their extended family in a detailed will,[34] leaving various properties to her son John, a cutler, including this freehold, two other parcels of property to the west of the gatestead, and the lease of the gatestead itself, which was in the occupation of George Frewin. John's inheritance found its way into the hands of William Darby, pewterer, in the early 18th century, and in his time it seems to have been absorbed into another holding situated to the west and south.[35]

WORDSWORTH STREET
AND A TENEMENT FORMERLY ON THAT SITE

DOCUMENTARY
HISTORY

There are some sketchy clues from the late 15th century onwards as to early occupation on this site. In 1487 a certain Stephen Skelton is recorded as a boundary detail,[36] then in the period before 1551 John Wyngfield, a goldsmith, had property here. He was succeeded by William Dighton, Alderman of Lincoln, and Christopher his son, both connected with a mansion to the south. Christopher Dighton was also a goldsmith, apprenticed to Robert Agland, one of a number of goldsmiths of that name, in 1520.[37] Agland held property in St Michael's parish, referred to in his will and inventory of 1542.[38]

In 1551[39] the Dightons sold this tenement to Humphrey Suttyll,[40] whose daughter and son in law, William and Elena Dyckson of Howsham, with Thomas their son, conveyed it in 1576[41] to Henry Horner, singing man. Later, in 1640, another conveyance is recorded in the White Book,[42] from John Broughe of London, glover, and Katherine his wife, to Robert Kilne of the Bail, butcher. There is a further gap in the documentation until William Darby, who mortgaged this house with its garden and stable to John Harvey

Fig 4. (above) Print of
anon. watercolour c.1880,
showing (foreground)
nos 24–25 Steep Hill and
the tenement demolished to
form Wordsworth Street
Fig 5. (left)
Contemporary photograph
of no.24 Steep Hill, right,
Wordsworth Street and
Chad Varah House

for £30 in 1730. He assigned this in 1732 to William and Richard Forster, flax dressers. William Forster partitioned the site in 1740, creating a new tenement in a small plot to the rear of the main house for another flax dresser relative, Thomas Forster.[43]

William left the property to his brother John in 1761. At this time one of the occupants was William Singleton, founder of the family business of Singleton Flint, who was also connected with a ropery off Hungate. Thomas sold his plot to John in 1771 for £20, and in the same year John, with Thomas and their wives, conveyed the whole site to Edward Varlow of the Bail, blacksmith.[44]

The property passed through various ownerships until 1791, when it was bought by Thomas Yates, baker. George Lough, a dyer from Branston, came in 1797, and sold it to the Governors of the County Hospital in 1804.[45] The tenement remained standing until at least 1868,[46] presumably used for Hospital purposes, but was demolished at or before the construction of Wordsworth Street in 1881. A view of this building, taken from a high vantage point in the former Hospital building c.1879–80, is shown in a watercolour painting.[47]

Lincoln Corporation, in recognising the need for a link road between Drury Lane and Steep Hill, nevertheless hoped to minimise costs by keeping it a narrow thoroughfare based on the original passageway. Mr Horner, the owner of no.24 Steep Hill, objected to land being taken away from him for the scheme. This was modified to create a carriageway of 25 feet in width, but narrowed at its junction with Steep Hill. Site discussions were held with the Chancellor and other representatives of the Bishop's Hostel, who were to receive £250 in compensation for their portion of the land purchased for the road.[48] Horner eventually had to acquiesce in the loss of some of his land, as by February 1882 some widening had taken place,[49] but he would not have lost out, as he was able to build a house for sale at the west end of his property.[50]

THE CHIRURGEONS' INN
LATER THE SITE OF THE COUNTY HOSPITAL AND SUBSEQUENTLY THE BISHOP'S HOSTEL

DOCUMENTARY
HISTORY

This was an extensive and prestigious property, which was often described in the early deeds as a capital messuage. The name 'Chirurgeons' (Surgeons') Inn', first noted in 1702, aptly described the dual usage of the building at that time, but the owners would have been unaware that it had been owned by a medical man as far back as the late 13th century, and would be the site of Lincoln's first purpose-built hospital of the modern era before the end of the 18th century.

In the medieval period the site originally extended in places from Steep Hill, on the east, to the Fabric Garden, a plot near Gibraltar Stairs on the west, and from the Castle Ditch on the north at least as far as the location of the lane known as the Old Fish Market on the south. This was one of the most extensive holdings anywhere in this area of the city. Several of the buildings on the site appear to have been set back from the main road. The first partition occurred c.1217, and the Vicars Choral of the Cathedral acquired part of the site on the corner of the Old Fish Market in the late 13th century;[51] tenements along the north side of the Old Fish Market are first noted in the 17th century,[52] but were swept away in the 1840s.

We have some excellent evidence of ownership in the early 13th century. The Hundred Rolls[53] relate that it had at one time been owned by Senior, business associate and brother of the famous Aaron of Lincoln, the Jew. After his death, perhaps in 1217, it was escheated to the Crown, but appears to have been inherited by his other brother Benedict.[54] The latter died sometime before March 1250, when there was an Inquisition[55] to establish what had become of the property. It was found that one part of it, worth 14s per annum, was in the hands of Amabel Grimward and her sons, and the other, worth 10s pa, was now owned by Gilbert de Hesel, who was a Royal agent of some kind, based at the Castle. His portion would have descended to his daughter Beatrice and her husband, Master William de Roueston, usually named Le Rus or Ruffy, who was a physician. William and Beatrice also had a lease of the Vicars' property on the corner mentioned above, and owned property across the road in what is now Christ's Hospital Terrace[56] and in Bailgate.[57]

Some names associated with this site may be gleaned from the records of the Board Rentals of the Dean and Chapter relating to rents of assize payable on part of the site, at 10s per annum. The rental for 1461–63[58] gives us the name of John Aleyn, who is otherwise unknown.

During the late 15th century, the capital messuage was in the hands of the Dalyson family. Richard Dalyson's granddaughter Margaret married Thomas Tournay of Gayton, and John, their son, conveyed it in 1487[59] to Robert Dighton and Isabella his wife, William Skelton (Treasurer of the Cathedral), and John Dighton, clerk. The Dighton family, based at Great Sturton, owned land in the county and also had other property interests in Lincoln.[60] Robert Dighton is recorded as paying the rent of assize in 1489,[61] and his assigns in 1529,[62] Christopher Dighton, son of William,[63] continued the family connection, although another goldsmith, John Morley,[64] occupied premises here c.1554 when Dighton sold the mansion to Christopher Wyllesford, a local merchant.[65] He conveyed it in 1585 to Robert Dymoke of Lincoln, Esquire, a member of the Scrivelsby family who were hereditary Champions of England. In 1588 and 1592 Richard and Robert Dymoke respectively paid the rent of assize.[66]

At this time the mansion was occupied by Peter Agland, who may be of the goldsmith family, but by 1597 part of it at least was occupied by George Walker, 'Doctor of Phisick', who died in that year. His probate inventory[67] lists five chambers, including a new sealed (ceiled) chamber, a parlour, little buttery, hall, bowling house, kitchen, dark entry (?), cellar, brewing house, new stable, low study, and a little house adjoining. Hangings, or tapestries, which may be the same as those mentioned in William Dighton's inventory of 1558,[68] were in his own chamber, and four very old ones in the hall. Some squared spars, presumably for building work, were listed in the new stable. He also had a collection of medical books, which were separately appraised by Dr Bonde; their value was unclear, but may have been as high as £9. In his will,[69] he also mentions the two painted tables hanging in his parlour, one being the story of Daniel destroying the dragon;[70] the other was of a gentlewoman. Dr Walker was the first in a series of medical men whose memory was preserved in the name later given to the house, the Chirurgeons. In 1612, Geoffrey Harpur of Lincoln, gent., and Joan his wife, who may have inherited from Robert Dymoke, conveyed the mansion house, with all its houses, buildings, stables, shops, cellars, courts, gardens, orchards etc. to Thomas Enderby of Lincoln, gent., and Robert Becke, draper;[71] Dr Walker was named as a recent tenant. George Dickinson paid the rent of assize in 1615, but died in 1621. His widow Catherine continued to live there, and is recorded as paying the rent of assize in 1633.[72] The freehold was sold in 1622 by Christopher Randes of the Close, Esquire, and Catherine his wife to William Carter, the prosperous glazier whose family acquired a strong portfolio of property in various parts of the city, particularly in Steep Hill.[73] Ralph Mossam, a tailor, was an occupier in 1622, and William Smith, a pinner, was living there in 1629.

Not much is known about the site during the period of the Civil War and the Commonwealth. Some rebuilding work may have been done c.1660, according to a dendrochronological survey conducted by Nottingham University on timbers found on the site;[74] tree ring samples suggest an approximate final date of 1657 for growth. Rents of assize were paid by Catherine Monson in 1661 and just before her death in 1672, but by 1676 James Dickinson, gent., her son by George, above, had taken over.[75] He continued with the payments until 1701, when Thomas Robinson, surgeon, was listed. Although Thomas was listed on the rentals until 1707,[76] he actually died in 1703, having mortgaged the property to William Burnett of the Close for £212.[77] Part of the complex, now divided into two tenements, was occupied by Joseph Rayson, possibly the first landlord of the inn. The premises were appraised for probate,[78] and the contents included a brass clock, ten old pictures valued at 2s 6d, five maps and another picture in the best chamber (£1 8s), and a violin and case (10s).

It was clear that the surgery business was playing second fiddle to the inn. A malting office and kiln had been constructed, and there is also a reference to tenements and a highway on the south side, i.e. The Old Fish Market.[79] Burnett's interests were assigned on his deathbed to the Revd Joseph Lister, who died in 1716; Lister's representatives are listed in the rentals until 1724, when the whole estate was sold to Joseph Banks, junior, of Revesby, grandfather of the famous botanist. In September 1742, it was in the ownership of William Banks, Esq., and, having been renamed the 'Hare and Hounds', then in the tenure of John Browne, it was sold, together with the orchard and a cockpit, to Clement Wood, gentleman.[80]

There were a number of family settlements and mortgages during the ensuing twenty years. This property was settled on Clement's daughter Eleanor and her second husband Thomas Searle of Spilsby, a plumber; sometime during this period the inn had another change of name, to 'The Fighting Cocks'. Searle died before 1775, and Eleanor conveyed the whole of this estate in January 1776 to the Governors of the County Hospital, to be the main site of the new Hospital.[81] The sign of the Fighting Cocks was transferred downhill to another public house which later became the Recruiting Sergeant.[82]

The Hospital was built to replace an old building on Waterside South, the site of which was more recently the premises of Doughty's Cake Mill, which had been taken in 1769, but was unequal to the task it was given. A governing body having been established, John Carr, the York architect who was later to be responsible for the design of the Debtors Prison and Governor's Lodging in the Castle Grounds, was appointed to erect a "substantial red-brick building on the summit of the Steep Hill, just below the Castle".[83] A small tenement, all that was left of the buildings on the Steep Hill frontage from before the foundation of the Hospital, was still present in 1842, as noted on the Padley plan of that year, but was demolished before 1851.

The Hospital buildings were purchased in 1879 for £3,800 by Bishop Wordsworth, and presented to the *Scholae Cancellarii*. Since 1870 the Diocese had been searching for a suitable site for a Hostel or Training College for Ordinands. E.W. Benson preached a notable sermon in that year: "Where are the Schools of the Prophets?", which the Bishop caused to be published in order to move things along. Various venues were trialled, including rooms at the Old Palace, the Central School in Silver Street, and Lindum Holme, below Pottergate Arch.

Goddard, the architect, drew up a scheme to create a Hostel for 30 students and two tutors, and a subscription scheme to include a chapel (proposed by Goddard for the Hospital some years earlier) was launched in May 1880. A "Prophets' Chamber" was to be set aside for visiting Prebendaries, and an annexe for the residence of the Vice-Chancellor and family. A smoking room was to be provided in the Tower. The Hostel was opened in October 1880 but the Chapel, designed by Temple Lushington Moore, was not built until 1905.[84] It is now called Chad Varah House, named after the founder of the Samaritans.

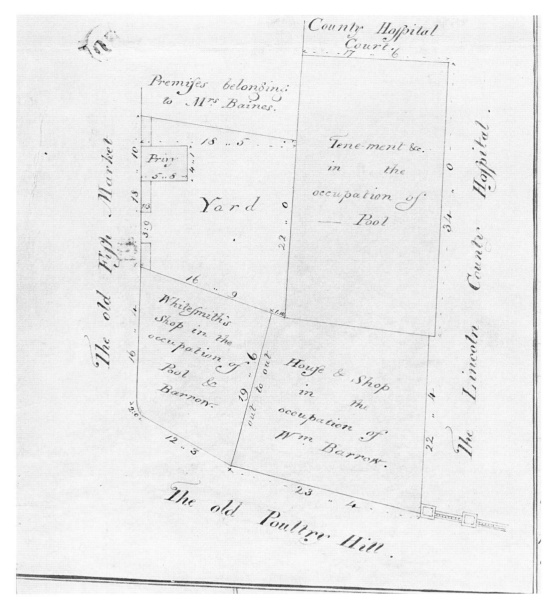

Fig 6. Vicars Choral property: lease plan 1836

TENEMENTS OF THE VICARS CHORAL
ON THE CORNER OF THE OLD FISH MARKET

Although Gilbert de Hesel[85] owned or controlled a large area of land north of the Old Fish Market, a plot at the corner with Steep Hill was apparently outside his remit. At some point around 1270 Ralph, knight of Normanby, granted a rent of 15s per annum from his land at the High Market, situated between land of Gilbert, previously belonging to Beatrice of the High Market, already dead by c.1250,[86] and land of Gilbert Waynpayn, to three representatives of the Vicars Choral. These were Alexander de Winchcombe, the Sacrist, Geoffrey de Folkingham, the Succentor, and Thomas de Banbury, Vicar Choral.[87] This transaction was soon followed by a grant of the land itself.[88]

Richard son of Ralph son of John le Turner granted his land in the same area to Simon in Angulo, son of Nigel, and Alice his wife, for a rent of 4s and one clove pa. This also was snapped up by the Vicars by way of an exchange for property in the Bail.[89] Simon was prominent in the life of the city, and was listed among the 'middling men' as a juror

11

for the inquisition known as the Hundred Rolls (1279/80).[90] This exchange took place between 1272 and 1274. By this time the shop at the corner with Steep Hill was in the occupation of Beatrice, daughter of Gilbert de Hesel, and Master William de Roueston (or le Rus), her husband. They failed to pay their rent of 3s pa for some years,[91] but were forgiven by the Vicars.

By 1294 Beatrice had been widowed, and had adopted the surname Tollecte (or Colet), as her brother John was usually known. She was renovating property once belonging to her father which abutted directly north of the shop owned by the Vicars; but this created a dispute, as a gable she wished to demolish was actually supporting the shop structure. An agreement was reached, for her to repair and maintain the gable, which was of stone.[92] Beatrice died c.1303, having endowed a chantry to the memory of her husband William.[93] No further medieval documentation survives for this site.

There are some leases and supporting records for the period from the late 17th century onwards; the Vicars Choral records for the previous 300 years are very few and far between. A Parliamentary Survey of 1650[94] records a lease which had been given to Robert Kelke in 1634 of a messuage with a barn and lathe in the Old Fish Market, for 40 years, paying 13s per annum. At this time the premises consisted of a shop, hall, kitchen, two chambers, a little stable and a garden. The building was part-timber built, covered with tile rather than thatch. In 1685 William Lillie or Lilly was lessee,[95] probably succeeded by someone called Boole.

Richard Barker held the lease in 1752; a shop or shops on the site were in the occupation of Mrs Lee and others. He was followed by the Revd John Caparn before 1794, who then assigned it to Thomas Yates, baker.[96] A further assignment took place in 1797, the lease transferring to Thomas Watson of Scothern.[97] Watson still held it in 1836, jointly with Thomas Bainbridge.[98] At this time the corner premises was a whitesmith's shop in the occupation of William Pool and William Barrow; the latter occupied a shop just north of the corner, also part of this leasehold. Pool was an inventor, and had patented a design for steam-driven watermill and paddle wheel machinery.[99] He died c.1860 and his widow Catherine moved across the road to 2 Hilton Hill.[100]

The lease was assigned in 1843 to the Hospital Governors, but the site remained the property of the Vicars until their estates were enfranchised at the turn of the century.[101] The shops and other premises were, however, demolished c.1845 when the Old Fish Market was cleared and the site remodelled by the Hospital authorities.[102]

1   CPC Johnson and A. Vince, 'The South Bail Gates of Lincoln', LHA 27 (1992),12-16

2   See further discussion of this below, p.15

3   DR Mills and RC Wheeler, 'Historic Town Plans of Lincoln 1610–1920', LRS 92 (2004),50 (e.g.)

4   RA viii, no.2290

5   Pipe Roll of 3 Ric I, (1191), PRS, NS 2 (1926),21

6   RH, p. 322; LHA op.cit.

7   See below, p.8

8   TNA, E 101/249/13(c); HG Richardson, 'The English Jewry under Angevin Kings' (London: Methuen, 1960),290

9   TNA, Jewish Plea Rolls, E 9/1, m.7; JM Rigg, ed., 'Plea Rolls of the Exchequer of the Jews' PREJ 1, 1218–1272 (Jewish Historical Society, Reprint,1971),31; JWF Hill, ML, 223-4

10 MD Davis , 'The Medieval Jews of Lincoln', in Arch. Jnl. 38 (1880),187-88

11 RA viii, 2297

12 See below

13 TNA E 372/72

14 Unfortunately lost

15 RA viii, 2298

16 ibid., 2299

17 Cant 744

18 See below

19 MLI 94048

20 Willson MSS, Society of Antiquaries, 786/15,82-101;

microfilm copy at Lincolnshire Archives MF 2/124/5. For 8-9 Castle Hill, see also SAH iv (Lincoln,1996),56-61, and for Jews' Court, see below, p.84

21 Tithe Award E 659

22 Directories 1885,1897

23 1901 Census

24 Figs 2,3

25 L1/1/1/2 f.90v

26 LC Charters 21/441

27 LC Leases 414: William Willson was the father of E.J.Willson

28 LC Charters 16/284

29 See below, p.131

30 DEG 4/3-5

31 Exley 12/6

32 L1/3/1 f.194

33 ibid. f. 258

34 LCC Wills 1668 ii, 314

35 See below

36 L1/3/1, f.84v

37 ibid., f.147

38 Sundry Wills 16

39 L1/3/1, f.122

40 Given the Freedom of the City in 1541, L1/1/1/2 f. 2v

41 L1/3/1.,f. 167

42 ibid., f.258v

43 DEG 10/1-6

44 DEG 10/7-12

45 DEG 15-29

46 Padley plan, HTPL,78

47 Print, from a watercolour by an unknown artist, in the possession of Mr and Mrs C. Johnson

48 L1/1/15/3, pp. 30,50,62-3

49 ibid., p. 422

50 Exley 12/6

51 See below

52 DEG 6/1

53 RH, p. 322

54 See above

55 Cal. Inq. Misc., vol. 1, no.57, p. 18

56 See below, p.27

57 SAH iv, 84ff

58 Bj.5.13.13: described in the calendar as a chantries rental

59 L1/3/1 f.84v

60 Notably the Antelope Inn, SAH iv, 71

61 Bj.1.1.2

62 Bj.1.1.3

63 See above

64 He paid 6s for his Freedom of the City in 1561, L1/1/1/2, f.161v

65 L1/3/1, f.123

66 Bj.1.1.6-7

67 Inv 90/284

68 Inv 28/72

69 LCC Wills 1597/98,6

70 From the story of Daniel, Bel and the Snake (or dragon) in the Apocrypha

71 L1/3/1 f.205

72 Bj.1.1.9

73 See below, p.83

74 Survey report submitted to the City of Lincoln Archaeological Unit, 1988

75 Bj.1.2, passim

76 Bj.1.3

77 LCC Wills 1703/186; DEG 2/5

78 LCC Admons 1703/109

79 DEG 2/5

80 DEG 2/7-8

81 DEG 1/5-9, 12-14

82 EJ Willson, Notes on Sympson's Adversaria; D&C Ciij 48/1/4, cf. Willson Coll 786/17; Exley 28

83 Thomas Sympson, A Short Account of the Old and New Lincoln County Hospitals, 1878: Lincolnshire Libraries, L.Linc.362.1

84 Notes abridged from a history of Lincoln Theological College 1874-1974, compiled by Neil Burgess: Lincolnshire Libraries, L.Linc.271

85 See above

86 RA viii, 2271; she may have been Gilbert's mother

87 VC, no.256

88 ibid., no.257

89 ibid., no.180; SAH iv, 132: 69-75 Bailgate

90 Hill ML, 399

91 VC, no.258

92 ibid., no.255

93 See above

94 CC 27/152829 7/7 p. 26

95 VC 3/2/4/1

96 DEG 1/3

97 ibid., 8/1

98 CC 140/298549

99 The patent for this is at LA, ref. LCM 9/8/1

100 See below, p.36

101 VC 3/2/4 passim

102 See above

45–47 STEEP HILL
WITH 1–5 CHRIST'S HOSPITAL TERRACE

Documentary history: medieval development

Prior to the 12th-century civil war between Stephen and Matilda, this site was part of a large area of ground below the wall of the Bail which was kept deliberately open as a potential defensive zone, with a ditch, which may now be represented by the roadway of Christ's Hospital Terrace.

In about 1137 Stephen granted a charter to Bishop Alexander[1] of the land between the church of St Michael and the ditch, up to the City wall, together with land worth 20s from his demesne, to provide a site for the proposed Bishop's Palace. This was confirmed by Pope Innocent II in April 1139,[2] including a clause for maintaining the Palace out of the proceeds from the land. From this it may be noted that the church and churchyard were already in existence. St Michael's was assigned to the Precentor by the Bishop in 1147/48[3] in a notification sent to Adelmus, Dean of Lincoln, and the Chapter.

Stephen's charter was altered before confirmation by Henry II c.1155–58; he removed a grant of the wall made by Stephen, but enlarged the area of land granted, to extend across to the east wall of the city. Pope Eugenius III confirmed his predecessor's grant both to Bishop Alexander in 1147 and to the next Bishop Robert Chesney.[4] Pope Alexander III repeated the procedure in 1163.[5]

It is fairly obvious that no buildings had been constructed anywhere in this zone before 1137, and in view of the impact of civil hostilities in Lincoln, it is also fair to assume that little if any development was put in hand before the accession of Henry II. The Palace development itself does not appear to have commenced until the time of Bishop Hugh of Avalon.[6] The prospect of tax avoidance for properties on this site may have appealed to prospective developers in the early years of Henry II.

It is quite possible that the Bretheren of the Hospital of Lincoln became involved during this period. As a lay corporation charged with supporting the Hospital of St James, later the Holy Sepulchre, the Bretheren had a certain amount of freedom to acquire property and transact financial business on behalf of the Hospital. Although on the same site as the Priory of St Katherine, and under its tutelage from 1163, it maintained a separate existence, as it had been established before the Priory.[7] Founded by Bishop Robert Bloet in the early years of the 12th century, the Hospital built up a wide portfolio of property interests in 18 Lincoln parishes, and also held land in numerous places elsewhere in the county. In several cases there were connections with the Jews.[8]

46–47 Steep Hill and 1 Christ's Hospital Terrace:
the Magna Aula *of Joan of Legbourne*

A business associate of Aaron, Joceus of York is arguably the man responsible for the building of the *Magna Aula* (Great Hall), although his name is only found in a Lincoln connection in the Hundred Rolls as the owner until 'the old war', probably meaning in this context the massacre of the Jews at York in 1190,[9] although the siege of the Castle by the Chancellor, Longchamp c.1193[10] may alternatively be proposed.

The next known owner of the whole site was William de Tilbroc (Tilbrook). He was a magnate, with his origins and substantial estates in the Huntingdonshire/Bedfordshire area. William was an agent for the king, and spent £58 on the king's behalf in 1200 for wine purchased at King's Lynn.[11] Crucially he was also farmer of the Exchequer in Lincoln, and was recorded as being in debit by £32 3s (£32.15) on his account in 1205.[12] This was still owing at his death in 1219.[13] In this role he was also heavily involved in the management of the relationship between the king and the Jews in Lincoln, always a difficult task.

William took as his second wife, c.1207–1210, Eleanor de Baiocis (of Bayeux), widow of Hugh, who held a Barony; she was probably descended from the de Bekering family. Eleanor had royal permission to remarry, for which she had to pay a substantial sum.[14] At some point after 1207 he made over to her as dower some of his Lincolnshire estates, including his capital messuage on Waterside North (opposite the current site of Lincolnshire Archives), land in Wigford held of John the Fleming and the Bretheren of the Hospital, and also his land at the gate of the Bail, with its buildings, rents and all appurtenances, held by him from the said Bretheren.[15] The gate in this context refers to the new South Bail Gate.

In 1217, the aftermath of the Barons' Revolt cost William his property holding on this side of the street, or at least that part which lay between the old and new gates,[16] the site of no.45 Steep Hill. What happened to the *Magna Aula* and its curtilage to the east is less certain: he may have retained this property, which we may speculate was still in Jewish occupation, although there are no records to support this.

Tilbroc was not popular, even with some members of his own family. By a first marriage he had sons named William and Robert, and possibly a daughter Joan, married to Peter of Legbourne (de Lekeburn). Eleanor had two sons by her first marriage, John and Thomas. In the autumn of 1219 Tilbroc was murdered at his house in West Torrington, and suspicion fell on John and Thomas. During a sensational case heard in the Curia Regis,[17] full of the somewhat gory detail of the crime and notable also for two judicial duels, Thomas successfully (if dubiously), pleaded benefit of clergy, but John was committed to the Fleet Prison, his fate unknown. Others outside the family circle were also implicated. It may be that Eleanor's dower holding of the *Magna Aula* was lost as a result of the case. In any event the property as a whole devolved to Joan de Lekeburn and her husband Peter. In 1242 Peter held eight virgates of land, a sixth part of a knight's fee, in Tilbrook, then in Huntingdonshire, corroborating the putative connection with William. He also had land in several parishes in the east of Lincolnshire.[18]

If Peter and Joan spent time away from Lincoln on their other estates, then this gives a further pretext for supposing that the *Magna Aula* was let to tenants. The surviving documentation for the neighbouring properties, i.e. no.45 Steep Hill, and nos 2–3 Christ's Hospital Terrace, despite its quality, does not provide the names of any occupants for the *Aula*, and neither is it included in the foundation of the Ruffy Chantry in c.1302/3 (see below).The evidence we do have for the *Magna Aula* after the time of Joan of Legbourne, derived from boundary information, points to its ownership by the physician, Master William le Rus, who acquired no.45 Steep Hill in the period around 1270[19] and what is now nos 1–3 Christ's Hospital Terrace in 1281 (see below). The charter for the latter transaction places Cecily's house next door to the house where Master William lives; in this context it can only refer to the *Aula*.

In the Chapter Account books of the early 14th century is a series of entries relating to rent arrears, both from properties owned by the Chapter and rents of assize or outrents owed to the Chapter from freehold properties; some of these rent charge payments are from a very early date and relate to some former involvement of the Chapter. There are several such entries relating to a property called the *Magna Aula* in the parish of St Michael, showing a connection to Hagin the Jew and Gilbert de Atherby, who acquired several of Hagin's properties sometime after Hagin's death in 1280. The initial entries are anachronistic, and on the face of it relate well to nos 46–47 Steep Hill, yet there is no other evidence to show a link with either Hagin or Gilbert. The term *Magna Aula*, as David Stocker has pointed out,[20] does occur elsewhere. Other, very convincing, evidence points to no.13 Steep Hill as the location.[21]

This Grade 1 Listed Building, now in three tenancies, is of stone construction dating from the third quarter of the 12th century. Its hillside location at the junction of two streets and fronting an ancient market place allowed the tenement a full-length vaulted cellar and above, at ground-level, shops to exploit passing trade. Its original plan was one of double-range type whereby two conjoined buildings aligned north–south, shared a common spine wall and would have presented, as now, twin gables at both north and south ends of the combined tenement. The gables were rebuilt in brick in the 18th century, a work that accompanied a general reduction in height by roughly a metre throughout the entire building.

The principal access from the west side is by way of a round arched doorway with attached moulded shafts, the whole a more restrained and less exuberant version of the Romanesque entrance to the Jew's House in the Strait; originally both doorways, in common, carried a projection overhead containing the first-floor fireplace and its chimney; a fuller, albeit incomplete, version of this is to be seen in the Strait building (see below). The complete 12th-century first-floor window in the west wall of the Norman House is said to be based on fragments recovered from elsewhere in the building. Its sill level, it may be observed, should be higher to agree with that of the now reduced and fragmentary moulded stringcourse on this front. At the chimney projection the string course followed suit. The same stringcourse returns along the south wall but here too its alignment has been interrupted on this side, most likely a disturbance of the later 18th century.[22] It would be reasonable, given the evidence of the moulded stringcourse, to suppose the south wall may have sported a prestigious first-floor window similar in style and detail to the restored version facing Steep Hill.

The Steep Hill entrance has an opposed east doorway in the spine wall, an opening of plainer and loftier dimensions with a rear arch of joggled voussoirs. Linking both, formerly, was a passage from the street presumably partitioned off from the remainder of the ground-floor by timbered walls, of which no trace now remains. Either side of the passage the ground-floor would have been occupied by shops, and direct access to these, it is assumed, was from the street. Unfortunately there is no surviving structural evidence that might shed light on the form of the original shop openings, such is the extent of alteration and re-facing of the street frontage, unlike that better preserved at the Strait house. At ground-level the spine wall doorway has its door checks on the east face, implying that the eastern half of the tenement was securable against persons using the passage; contrariwise, two flanking coeval lower square headed doorways have their checks facing west, permitting one access back into the western half.[23] Such an arrangement, accessed exclusively from the eastern half of the tenement, would have bordered the passage, with each flanking room probably obliged to be artificially lit when in use.

Proof that all three doorways are of the primary phase of construction is evident in the common masonry courses linking each; moreover, the north jamb of the northern opening may be seen to be integral with the lower part of a large arched recess, described below. The same doorway was later in use to access the cellar, an alteration clearly post-medieval in origin.

What the west front now lacks in detail is more than made up for by the architectural interest of the east face of the spine wall, an observation that applies generally to the eastern half of this double-range tenement. The spine wall has been truncated at its

true
true
true

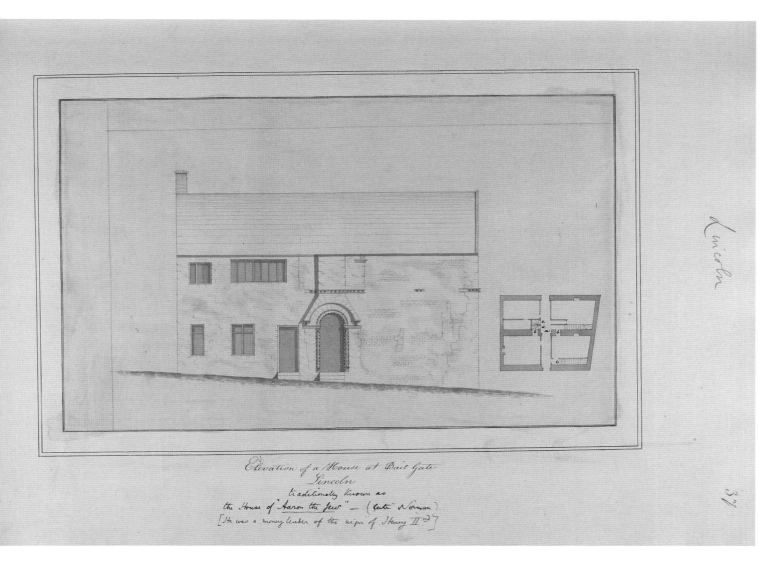

Fig 7. Plan and elevation of nos 46–47 Steep Hill c.1790

northern end, which is unfortunate, as that which is missing is a short length of wall that would have completed a shallow round arched recess of plain appearance, and could have afforded one some idea of a tie-in with the north wall. A perspective drawing has been produced to present the probable arrangements in this, the rear half of the tenement, c.1170.[24]

It is important to note that, as part of the 12th-century establishment, no.1 Christ's Hospital Terrace had at its ground-floor level sufficient evidence, now concealed, of two twinned shops that may be held to have been coeval with the main structure. Both were timber ceiled, with heavy joists carried on stone corbels in the east and west walls. The north wall in its thickness retained two small lockers, now blocked, perhaps for lamps (?), one per shop. From this it would seem that the shops were probably lock-ups and almost certainly lacked access to the main tenement. The ground beyond the north wall of the shops was apparently left unexcavated as intended. It follows from the above evidence that the southern half, or nearly so, of the eastern half of the tenement would have had a plank floor, and this may have carried a gypsum render as a finish.

Alterations to the interior of no.1 Christ's Hospital Terrace in the early 1970s[25] led to the discovery in the spine wall of an original doorway to the first-floor in no.47. This feature was adapted to serve as an additional hearth in a later subdivision of the house, and to this end had its round arch and splayed reveals effectively infilled. After repairs the doorway was again blocked for structural reasons, but not before its details were duly recorded. It is reasonable to suppose that a straight stair flight against the east face of the spine wall, south end, may have provided the principal approach to this doorway; the door checks in this instance were on the west face and the original gudgeons for hanging the door were preserved in the south reveal of the opening.

Whilst one can be certain that the western half of the double range from inception was two-storied, with shops fronting Steep Hill at ground-level, and the possibility of having a two-room arrangement on the first-floor, the interpretation of the eastern half is not at all straightforward. Two major gaps that account for this are, firstly, the total refurbishment of no.1 Christ's Hospital Terrace and the consequent loss of its architectural evidences and the other, just as depleting, the rebuilding and reductions that have affected the rooms to the rear of nos 46–47. Add to this the overall reduction in height of the entire tenement in the later 18th century, with much replacement of masonry by brickwork, and the problem of assigning a function to the eastern half involves much guesswork.

The semi-circular arched recess at the north end of the spine wall may well have had its counterpart in the now rebuilt east wall, and was perhaps repeated in the north wall. Shallow recessed and arched features are known to have embellished the dais ends of major medieval halls of stone construction but these occur mostly on the main axis of the hall and not sited laterally, as in the Lincoln house.[26] Blackened masonry present on the uppermost courses of the present north wall is the result of an earlier and wider flue than that at present being made against its south face. A large hearth at ground-level at this point on the plan suggests the room it served had been a kitchen,[27] and had functioned as such for some considerable time. Could the north end of the eastern extent of the tenement have functioned as an open hall in the 12th century and instead of being warmed by an open hearth, had one confined within a smoke hood? Could one, perhaps, envisage the entire tenement as being two-storied with a line of samson posts in support of a timber upper floor and with other partitions in attendance? Two partition walls that incorporate re-used timber framing elements would seem to demarcate the extent of the post-medieval kitchen area, and not to represent an earlier arrangement.[28]

Heavy stone corbels in the east face of the spine wall pose yet another problem in the interpretation of this half of the medieval tenement. The uppermost corbels in the east face of the spine wall are held to be reset features probably resulting from the general lowering of the walls to accommodate the present roof. However, as supposedly re-located features, they no longer serve any useful purpose and their large size suggests that originally their positions may have been nearer the wall top, where they carried either long timbers against the wall face on which tie beams or rafter couples were fixed, or each corbel, individually, had supported the end of a more substantial and transversely aligned tie beam. In appearance the corbels are of a rough character and therefore inappropriate for a building of such obvious quality. A smaller more refined corbel set immediately above the arched recess is rebated to carry a horizontal timber next to the wall and appears to be in situ; if so this would argue strongly for a storied north end, assuming that the side beam's function was to support ceiling joists.[29] Shown on the same elevation of the spine wall is a further doorway at first-floor level, whose design is similar in style to that of the smaller doorways at ground-level. Thought at first to be of post-medieval origin, there is a case to be made for it belonging to the primary phase, and if so it would imply at least a part-storied eastern half for the tenement.

Within the roof space above both halves of the original tenement, a number of early rafters have been re-used. The attic above the west range retains the bulk of these and they are incorporated in a four-bay roof of clasped-purlin type; there is now no longer attic provision in the east range roof.

A close examination of the roof members should enable one to identify any relocated primary timbers. Renovation work carried out at the Jew's House in the early 1970s[30]

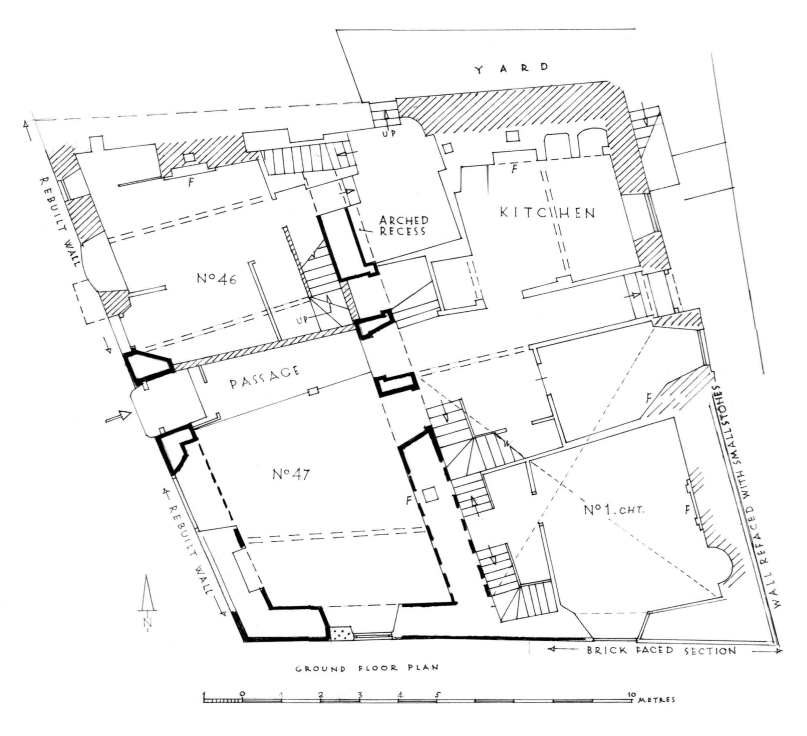

GROUND FLOOR PLAN

Fig 8. Ground-floor plan of 46-47 Steep Hill and 1 Christ's Hospital Terrace

revealed an almost full complement of its former 12th-century roof members re-used in the existing attic roof (see below).

The west range fronting Steep Hill is subdivided between nos 46 and 47 with the east range triply divided to include no.1 Christ's Hospital Terrace in its southern half. To date, no dendrochronology has been attempted on selected timbers in the ceilings or roof spaces of the tenement as a whole. For no.46, whose west wall is a rebuild of the 18th century, there remains on the ground-floor, at the north end, evidence for a chimney and hearth much altered and retaining two sections of its former lintel. Whether this served as a small working hearth in the shop is not known; it would seem to be, in origin, of a date before c.1750; the same chimney with an additional hearth survives intact on the first-floor. This end of the shop has a doorway cut through the spine wall breaching the arched recess, an access point which also incorporated a stair approach to the north end of the long vaulted cellar. Both access cuts were apparently late in origin, coinciding

19

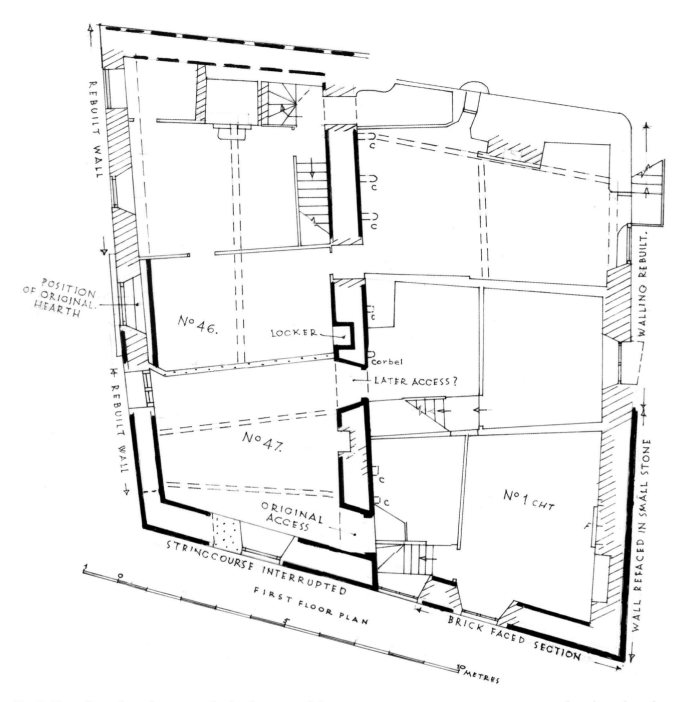

Fig 9. First-floor plan of nos 46–47 Steep Hill and no.1 Christ's Hospital Terrace

with the division of the west range into separate tenancies, and with each making use of allotted space in the basement for additional storage.

The east wall of no.46 at first-floor level has internally a tall mural aumbry with a triangular head, a shape masked today by its door and frame. The west wall of the cellar retains a smaller open version of this type.

Renovation work in 1994 concerned with the consolidation of the cellar's barrel vaulting also exposed lower masonry courses in the west face of the north–south spine wall. In that length of the wall from the line of the cross passage to the south gable, deep rectangular indentations or slots were revealed. An interpretation of these features is that they may have held flat laid horizontal beams, possibly joists of a flooring scheme subsequently superseded by the present barrel vaulting. Before the present cellarage was cleared of its later intervening brick walls, its north end wall retained a high ledge below the crown of the vault. Whether the above slots are indications of preparatory work connected to the building of the vault or a main building phase is uncertain, but it is considered worthy of record, should future investigations turn up further corroborative material. The east face of the spine wall i.e. within no.1 Christ's Hospital Terrace at this point has been greatly obscured by modern brickwork introduced to provide chimney flues. Consequently evidence for a continuation of the above beam slots has been either concealed or destroyed.

As in the Jew's House in the Strait, the Norman House ceilings were floored simply with timber cross beams and carried common joists and planks; another alternative was the employment of plaster in lieu of, or additional to, the planking, as noted above.

Given the considerable spread of the tenement presumably the accommodation of a kitchen to serve the whole establishment should have posed few if any problems. But can one entertain the notion that cooking was carried on in the eastern half of the house, and roughly where the present kitchen is? And if this were so, where does the hall or its equivalent fit in? Limited space for an outside kitchen exists north of the back range, but this would appear to intrude into the curtilage of no.45 Steep Hill.

In the Civil War incursions the earlier juxtaposition of the Norman House with the City Gate clearly presented an obvious and sizeable target for military gunners encamped on Canwick Common to the south of the city. The discovery of a cannon ball lodged in the chimney stack of the nearby Harlequin, c.1900, might persuade one that the Norman House was similarly affected at this time. Unfortunately the replacement of its stone gables by brick in the mid-18th century is unhelpful in this respect. Perhaps of greater significance is the scale of the rebuilding and a refacing that included the east wall and its south angle, both of which would seem to be connected with the provision of new roofs. A view of the newly exposed east wall of no.1 Christ's Hospital Terrace was obtained in the early 1970s by the then Conservation Officer Charles Martin, who realised that a future adjoining development would totally conceal the east face of the wall.[31]

45 Steep Hill

The deeds for no.45 Steep Hill between the 1240s and c.1303 show clearly that the northern boundary of the site was the Bail wall. Peter of Legbourne needed the assent of his wife Joan for the grant to Thorald Copper, given sometime in the 1240s, at a rent of 8s per annum.[32] After Peter died, possibly in the early 1260s, Joan was able to repeat the grant to Thorald, in her own right this time, listing her "large house which is called *Aula*" as the south bound. Measurements were given for the plot: 16 ells in length and 11 ells in breadth.[33] There was an exclusion clause prohibiting assignment to religious or Jews, a fairly standard provision which came into usage during the middle of the century.

Thorald died within a few years, and Warin his son granted the property to Master William de Roueston (le Rus/Ruffy). The 8s pa was to be paid to the chief lord of the fee, with 1d pa to Warin. By this time, probably c.1267–69, Joan had sold off the *Aula*, presumably to William, although there is no direct evidence,[34] and there was a later quitclaim of interest by Walter de Cantebrig and Alice le Calicer, his wife.[35]

The tenement has as its north and south abutments the former Roman and medieval gatehouse – the south gate of the Bail – and the 12th-century building known now as the Norman House respectively. **ARCHITECTURAL DESCRIPTION**

It is of red brick construction, two-storied with attics and has an extensive cellarage. It has a central entrance doorway raised above pavement level that leads into a symmetrical layout of heated end rooms either side of a staircase hall. The street elevation has the principal fenestration and there are grounds for thinking that the house is of a single build erected circa 1780.

Little is known of the building it succeeded then, but, as the ground plan demonstrates, the southern bounds of the property form an obtuse angle with the Norman House[36] (Fig 20). The kitchen was housed in the cellar, the original arrangement, and there is

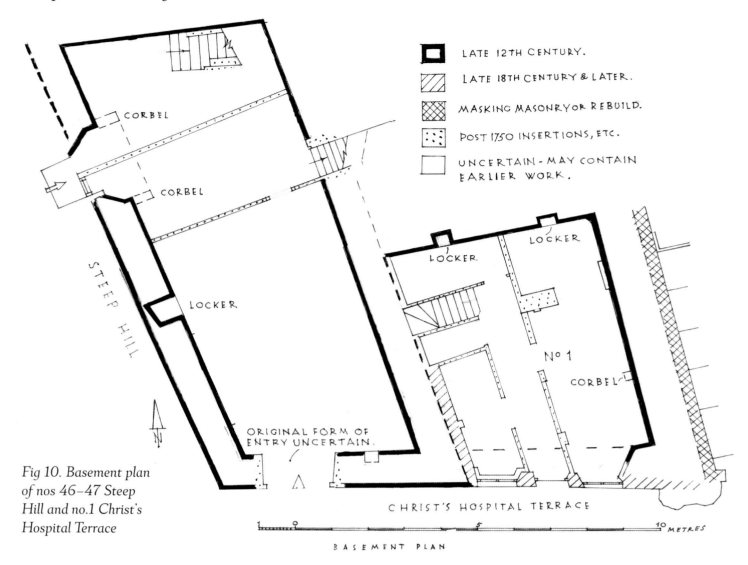

LATE 12TH CENTURY.

LATE 18TH CENTURY & LATER.

MASKING MASONRY OR REBUILD.

POST 1750 INSERTIONS, ETC.

UNCERTAIN - MAY CONTAIN EARLIER WORK.

CORBEL

CORBEL

STEEP HILL

LOCKER

LOCKER

LOCKER

N° 1

CORBEL

ORIGINAL FORM OF ENTRY UNCERTAIN.

CHRIST'S HOSPITAL TERRACE

0   5   10 METRES

BASEMENT PLAN

Fig 10. Basement plan of nos 46–47 Steep Hill and no.1 Christ's Hospital Terrace

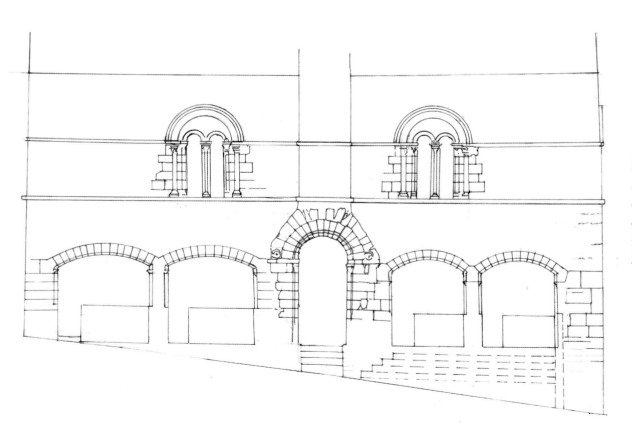

Fig 11. Reconstruction of original west elevation of nos 46–47 Steep Hill

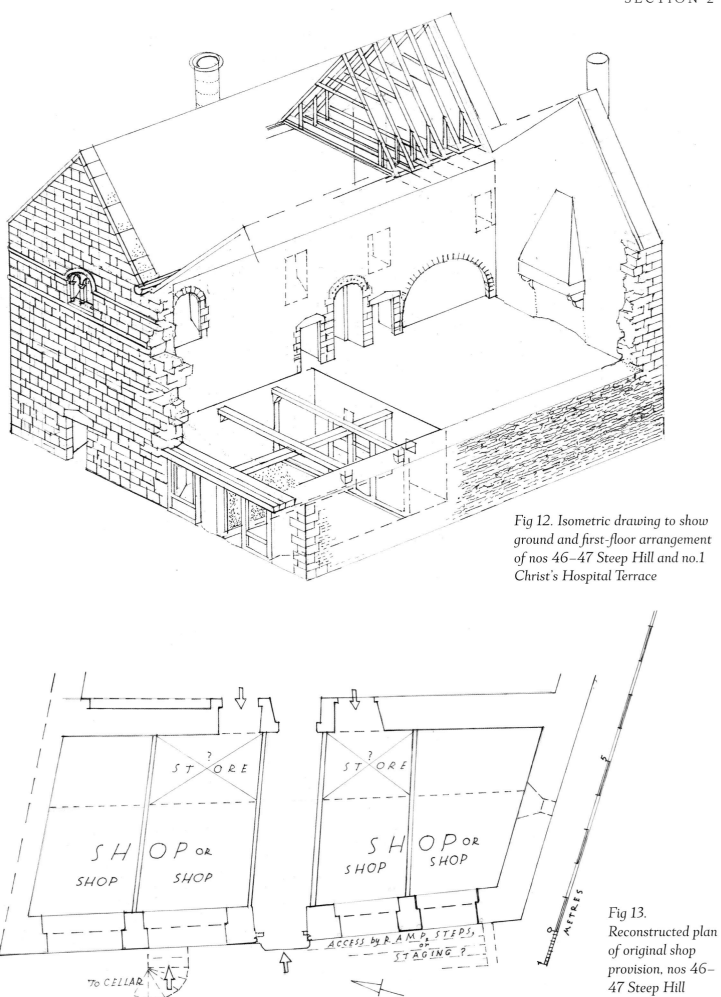

Fig 12. Isometric drawing to show
ground and first-floor arrangement
of nos 46–47 Steep Hill and no.1
Christ's Hospital Terrace

ST?ORE

ST?ORE

S H OP or
SHOP

SHOP

S H OP or
SHOP

SHOP

ACCESS by R AMP, STEPS,
or
STAGING ?

METRES

To CELLAR

Fig 13.
Reconstructed plan
of original shop
provision, nos 46–
47 Steep Hill

23

Fig 14. (top) Contemporary
photograph of the street frontage,
nos 46–47 Steep Hill
Fig 15. (above) Photograph c.1972
showing the vaulted basement,
no.47 Steep Hill
Fig 16. (right) Photograph of the
arched recess in the spine wall,
no.46 Steep Hill

Fig 17. (top) Photograph showing reset corbels in the spine wall, no.46 Steep Hill

Fig 18. (above) Photograph of the exterior of no.1 Christ's Hospital Terrace, prior to rebuilding work (bottom right of p.23 of prototype)

Fig 19. (right) Photograph of doorway and corbel, second floor of no.1 Christ's Hospital Terrace (bottom left of p.23 of prototype)

45 STEEP HILL

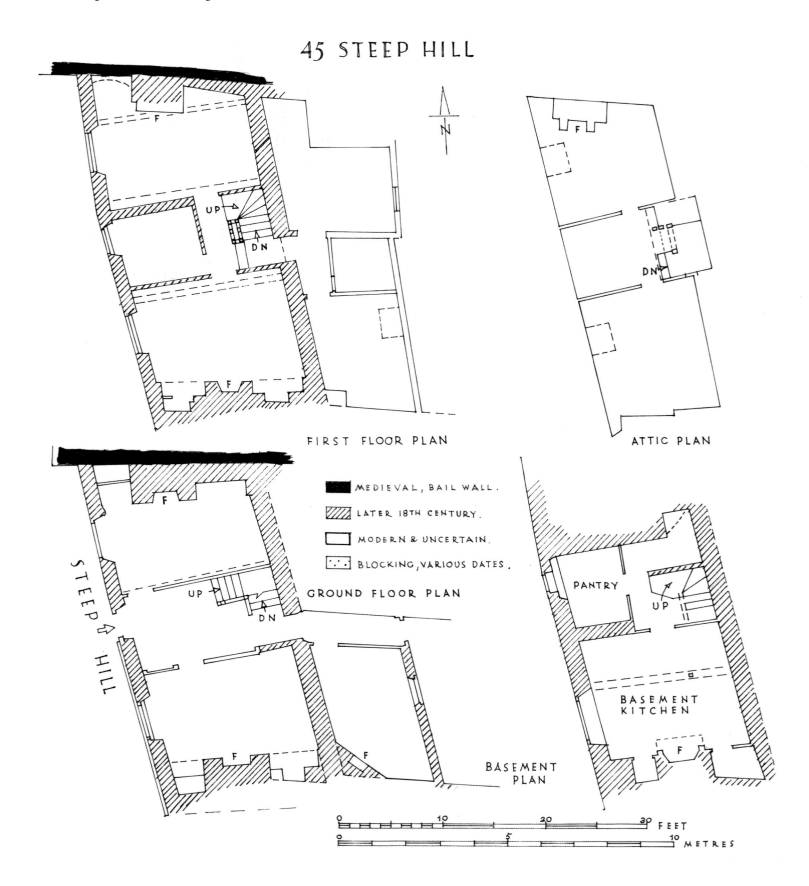

FIRST FLOOR PLAN

ATTIC PLAN

■ MEDIEVAL, BAIL WALL.

▨ LATER 18TH CENTURY.

□ MODERN & UNCERTAIN.

⦙ BLOCKING, VARIOUS DATES.

GROUND FLOOR PLAN

STEEP HILL

PANTRY

BASEMENT KITCHEN

BASEMENT PLAN

0   10   20   30 FEET

0   5   10 METRES

*Fig 20. Plans of ground-floor, first-floor and
basement, no.45 Steep Hill*

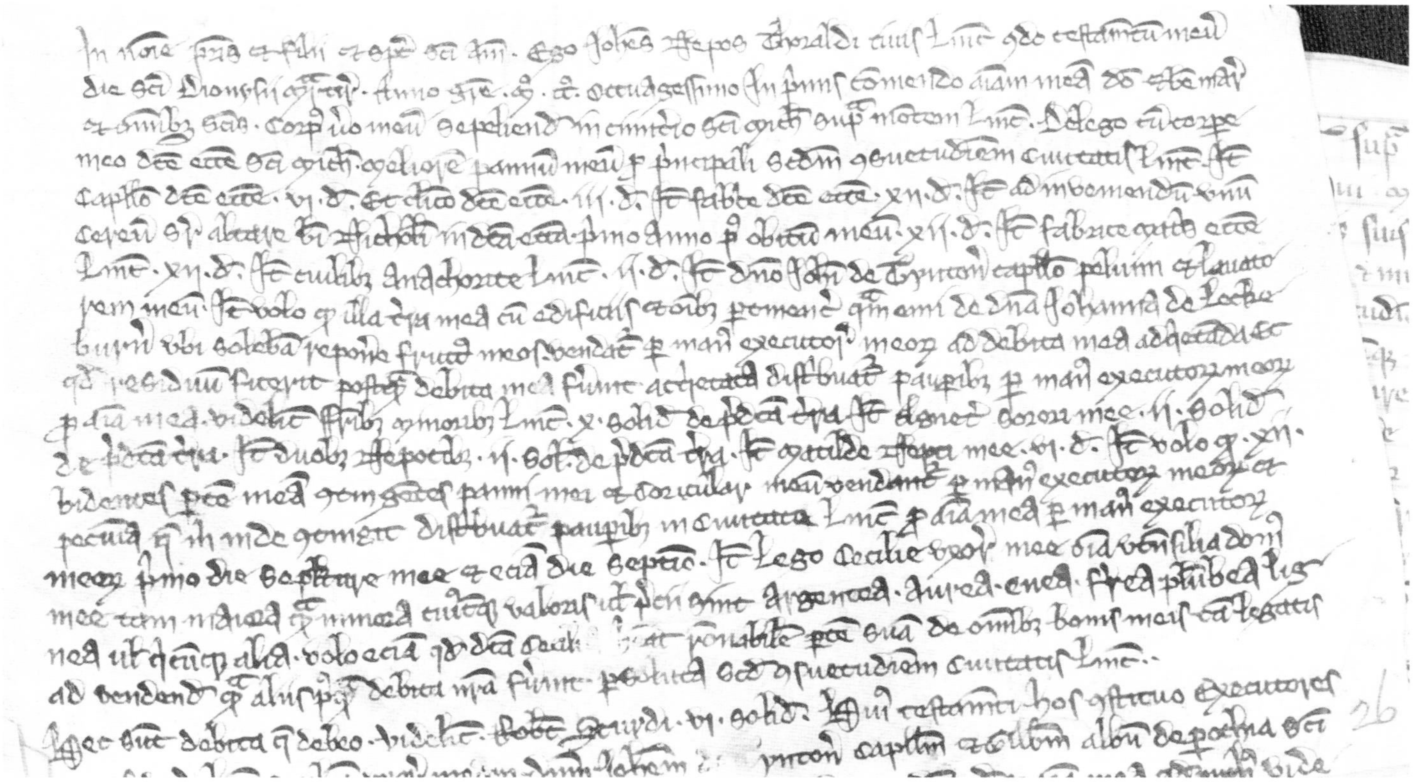

no evidence to show that this function was later transferred elsewhere in the house; at ground-level additions made at the rear served as additional accommodation at the expense of the back yard.

Fig 21. Will of John, nephew of Thorald, 1280

2–3 Christ's Hospital Terrace

A parallel process of dispersal and eventual re-assimilation may be seen in the case of the eastern portion of the property, represented later by East's Court and in more recent times by nos 2–3 Christ's Hospital Terrace. Peter de Lekeburn, with Joan's assent, as above, granted this, situated between land of John the baker by the cemetery gate, i.e. on the east side, and his own house called *Aula* on the west, together with a certain chamber on the north side of the property, near the wall, to Thorald the Fruiterer at a rent of 4s pa. The document is undated but must fall sometime in the late 1220s, based on the script of the original.[37] This grant also was confirmed by Joan in her widowhood, to John nephew of Thorald, who used a building on the site as a storehouse for his fruit.[38]

John died c.1280, leaving one of the few extant 13th-century wills remaining in the Diocesan archives. In this[39] he stipulated that the property should be sold by his executors, John de Tynton, chaplain, Gilbert Albus (White), and Cecily his widow. Among the other provisions of his will was a bequest of 2d to each anchorite in Lincoln. In May 1281 Cecily was given special authority by her co-executors to sell the property to Master William de Roston (sic).[40] The 4s p.a. rent was reserved to the chief lord of the fee. Among the witnesses to this deed, which completed the process of reunification of the properties, were Roger son of Benedict, Mayor of Lincoln, Walter Bek, Constable of the Castle, and Gilbert de Hesel, father in law of Master William.[41]

William le Rus died c.1293, and Beatrice, who was possibly childless, made arrangements for the eventual disposal of their estate. A mortmain licence, enabling her to make grants to religious bodies, was obtained from the king in February 1301 to endow a new chantry at the Cathedral. Called the Ruffy Chantry, it was to be given an annual rent charge of 5 marks (£3.33), allocated from two properties in the Bail,[42] the solar next to the "great hospice called *Aula*" (equivalent to 2–3 Christ's Hospital Terrace), and those shops between the wall of the Bail and the said *Aula* (no.45 Steep Hill).[43] The *Magna Aula* itself was not included: either there was to be a settlement within the family or it would be sold on her death. No further documentation exists for it until the early 17th century.

There is a group of documents, mostly registered in the Burwarmote Book of the city of Lincoln, which add some 14th-century detail to the picture regarding nos 2–3 Christ's Hospital Terrace. William de Waltham, a Vicar Choral who was also chaplain of the Ruffy Chantry, lived in part of this site c.1322; he was related in some degree to Robert de Waltham, who with Alice his wife and Thomas de Lokton and Beatrice his wife sued for possession by writ of right against Odo de Filyngham and Beatrice his wife in 1342. The querents did not appear, so judgment was given in favour of Odo and Beatrice.[44]

Odo, otherwise Odo de Tathwell, and Beatrice both died at the time of the Black Death. Beatrice left the property to Lecia her mother, widow of Robert de Hodelston.[45] Lecia (Leceline) in 1370 left to William, son of Odo, the tenement with its vessels and utensils, together with a rent charge of 12s from the properties connected with the chantry.[46] William died soon after and in his will left the messuage and the rent charge of 12s to executors for sale to the benefit of his soul, those of his parents, Leceline de Hodelston and all other benefactors.[47] This chantry appears from a later legacy given by Thomas Archer to have been based at the church of St Peter at Pleas.[48] No.2 Christ's Hospital Terrace seems from these documents to have gained the name Tathwell House.

4 Christ's Hospital Terrace

The medieval evidence for this site shows that it was unconnected with the *Magna Aula*. Little is known of the occupants prior to 1300, although we know of a John the baker, who lived by the cemetery gate c.1240.[49] This gate may have stretched across the line of the present day roadway, as it is known that the northern boundary of St Michael's churchyard was the Bail Wall. John's house was still mentioned as the boundary in a deed of the mid-1260s, although another deed of the 1240s for a plot to the east (see below) gives the name of Thomas the baker for the west bound. In 1274/75 William Juvene, another baker, occurs;[50] he had other property to the south of the churchyard, on the site of a horse mill, later granted to the Cathedral as part of the endowment of the chantry established by Roger son of Benedict,[51] several times Mayor of Lincoln.

After Juvene, the property was acquired by the Vicars Choral and leased to Stephen de Godwynston, later known as Stephen de Kingston, for 8d per annum. His four daughters (Maud, Elena, Cecily and Alice) released their interest in it in 1322.[52]

4A Christ's Hospital Terrace, later merged with no.4

Between 1240 and 1250 Adam son of Robert son of Astin granted to Nicholas of Spalding, deacon, otherwise known as Burgulun, a plot of land in the cemetery east of the above-mentioned property of Thomas the baker.[53] There was a rent of 3s p.a. which was transferred to the Dean and Chapter soon after, when Nicholas granted this site for the use of the Fabric Fund.[54]

5 Christ's Hospital Terrace and other properties as far as the wall of the Bishop's Palace

There were two or three other holdings which may be distinguished here, between no.4A and the Palace wall. The westernmost property was inhabited by Alan the tailor c.1240–50[55] and c.1275–80 by John the Applemonger, nephew of Thorald the Fruiterer, and his wife Cecily, who was the widow of Master Laurence de Riston, physician, who may have been related to Master William le Rus.

A grant of 1310, which has insufficient contextual information to pinpoint its site, survives in the Foster Library Collection:[56] Thomas Woodruff and Hawise his wife granted a solar with the appurtenances situated north of the churchyard to Roger Totel, clerk, and Margery his wife. Roger had the site to the west, and the east bound was named as William son of Stephen atte Bischophalle.

Lastly, the will of John atte bargate was proved in 1317:[57] he gave his messuage north of the cemetery, which he had by feoffment from Lecia Faukener, to Alice his wife. The bounds for this were John – to the west (the text is deficient at this point) and Robert Harefot on the east.

45 Steep Hill and the South Bail Gate

Although these properties have been the subject of previous accounts,[58] the research for the current volume has led to a new understanding with regard to the site of the South Bail Gate. The point of contact on the east side of the street was not no.46, as previously thought, but the lower portion of no.45. This enables a reinterpretation of the Nattes view, vis à vis the current street frontage. The gap shown in the illustration[59] is the site of the ground-floor room of the eastern gatestead, accounting for a width of approximately 20ft,[60] just under half of the total current frontage of no.45. The whole site was rebuilt after 1792, the doorway and steps being moved slightly southwards to ensure symmetry. A stone boundary post with the City Arms now marks the northern corner of the gatestead, which also happens to be the parish boundary between St Mary Magdalen and St Michael parishes.

In the same Nattes sketch there may faintly be seen in the gap between the standing portion of no.45 and the outline of no.46 a partial view of the rear of nos 2–3 Christ's Hospital Terrace. Realistically the artist could not have seen this from his main viewpoint, and would have had to move into the gap between the houses to take down these details.

The 1618 lease for the eastern gatestead describes a lower room, which Alexander Amcotts, the lessee, later[61] termed a 'Lobbie', one little piece of ground enclosed within a wall. There would also have been a staircase to an upper room, east of the main chamber over the arch belonging to the western leasehold. The upper room (called the Old Hall), and the rest of the archway, was covered with a lead roof. As Amcotts also owned nos 46–47 at this time, there may have been some interconnection with his own premises.

Alexander is known to have devised his leasehold interest to his godson Nicholas Amcotts, and there is no further reference to a City lease until June 1693, when William Carter, plumber, was given a lease,[62] although it is possible that Francis Tooley (died 1677) and Lettice his widow may have been in occupation during the interim period: the name Tooley appears on the Chamberlain's Roll for 1685.[63] Lettice had been married to one of the Thorolds, who were connected to the Amcotts family. The Amcotts/Thorold/Tooley connection seems likely also to have governed the succession in ownership of the main *Magna Aula* holding (see below).

In the mid-18th century the gatestead lease came into the hands of the Wood family. Frances Randes, daughter of Clement Wood, was lessee from 1755,[64] and was succeeded in 1773 by Isaac Wood, Commissioner in Bankruptcy on behalf of George Lewis, her husband. This occurred just a year before the surrender of the lease and the eventual dismantling of the Gate.[65]

POST-MEDIEVAL OCCUPATION

46–47 Steep Hill, with 1–3 Christ's Hospital Terrace

There is an inconvenient and annoying gap of 300 years in the documentation of this fascinating and important group of properties, but the fact that the *Aula* was still a high-status dwelling in the early 17th century indicates that the successive owners had managed to maintain the fabric to a certain extent, and had not allowed it to fall into quite the same level of dilapidation as many other medieval houses in Lincoln.

In 1618, a boundary detail in the Amcotts gatestead lease[66] places Alexander's freehold as south of the archway. This juxtaposition is also mentioned in his will.[67] As mentioned above, there was a Thorold connection, Lettice Thorold, widow, having married Francis Tooley Esq, whose family were prominent in Lincoln. Francis died in 1677, and his probate inventory[68] includes an impressive number of rooms, including six chambers or lodging rooms, and what must have been a fairly extensive suite of coach house and stables, the coach being worth £20 and the two coach horses together at another £20. There was also a saddle nag, at £6 10s (£6.50).

As there were no children the property descended to his sister Martha Foster, but there must have been an agreement for Lettice to remain in occupation, as her own inventory of April 1688 lists many of the same chambers and rooms.[69] Martha had in any case sold on her interest in the property to Thomas Baker, her son by a former marriage. He died c.1705 and his son Francis, of the parish of St Peter in Eastgate, then for £150 conveyed the whole property to George Pinder, a cooper, and Mary his wife.[70] Nos 46 and 47 later in the century became divided into a number of apartments. It is unclear as to exactly when the four tenements known as East's Court were erected, but they probably date from just after the purchase in 1825 of the estate by Richard East, grocer.[71]

4 and 4A Christ's Hospital Terrace

Until 1810 this property was in two distinct holdings.[72] In the 16th century the Vicars Choral leasehold covered the western portion of the site, and the Corporation owned the freehold of the rest. The plots developed separately until the second half of the 18th century, but by 1810 no.4 had been taken under the wing of the growing school known as Christ's Hospital, founded originally in the early years of the 17th century by Dr Richard Smith.[73]

4 CHRIST'S
HOSPITAL TERRACE

The Vicars Choral records for the 16th century have largely disappeared, and few exist for the 17th, so consequently the history of no.4 is difficult to reconstruct. The Parliamentary Survey of 1649, however, did survive, and from it we learn that a lease was granted in 1638 to Francis Camplin of two tenements on this site for 40 years at the rent of 5s 4d per annum. By 1649 it had been assigned to Peter Walter;[74] it is uncertain whether Peter was a relative of the Hugh Walter who was a schoolmaster at Christ's Hospital from 1653. The two dwellings consisted of a kitchen, buttery, cellar, two chambers and two little gardensteads. The building was of stone and "rough vast, with lime and hair and a covering of tile". The tenants were Justinian Walwin (who also held the Corporation leasehold next door at this time, and was associated with other properties), and the Widow Nix and her family; her son Thomas earned 3s in 1642 for allowing the Hospital contractors to use their tenement for the purpose of making plaster.[75] Elizabeth Nix died in 1644: there was a shop within the premises.[76]

In 1685 William Lilly, gent., was the Vicars' lessee.[77] He had been lessee of the Corporation property next door from 1649 to 1652, but had left.[78] After Lilly there was

View of South Roman Gate as seen from the North
Lincoln
Nattes
1789

a period with no surviving documentation, then from 1776 we have a series of leases which with other source material covers the period to 1860.[79]

Henry Stanley, cabinet maker, was tenant in March 1766, and began to rebuild the house, but came to the notice of the Hospital Board because his east gable end was encroaching on their premises, by two feet or more from west to east and 18ft 3ins north to south. The Governors wanted 2s per annum for the encroachment together with a signed agreement with Stanley, which apparently he refused. Legal action was threatened, and no further news was reported in the Minutes.[80]

Katherine Lawrence of the Close, widow, held a lease from the Vicars in 1776[81] which described the property as 'lately rebuilt', in the occupation of Widow Spooner. Daniel Long, stonecutter, lived there for a while before 1785 when Thomasin Winship, widow, took over the tenancy, receiving a new lease in 1790.[82] In 1792 William Haldenby was living there.[83] A Mrs Paddison appears to have purchased the lease by c.1808, and the Hospital Board then bought her out for £580 after a survey by John Hayward.[84] 'Paddison's House', as it became known, was let at £25 pa to William Haldenby from 1809, and insured for £200 with the County Fire Office. It was repaired and repainted in September 1817.[85] William's son George having taken over the occupancy. A new front and steps for the house were agreed by the Board in 1819, and the Master and Governors themselves took on the role of lessee in that year, renewing the lease in 1832, 1846 and 1860.[86]

In 1834 Thomas Foster, the local builder, started to put the building into better order, under the direction of the well-known Lincoln architect William Adams Nicholson, and in 1838, during a massive rebuilding operation at the main school site, there were changes to the eastern section of this building.[87] Edward Betham, in his surveyor's report of 1845, described it as: "a brick and tiled house...in the occupation of Mr Lampray, Unitarian

Fig 22. Nattes' drawing of no.45 Steep Hill and gap to south, c.1790

4 CHRIST'S HOSPITAL
TERRACE.
'GROUND FLOOR' PLAN.

F

DN

UP

*Fig 23. Ground-floor
and basement plans,
no.4 Christ's Hospital
Terrace*

F

F

0   5   10   20   30 FEET

0   5   10

BASEMENT PLAN

N

F

UP

F

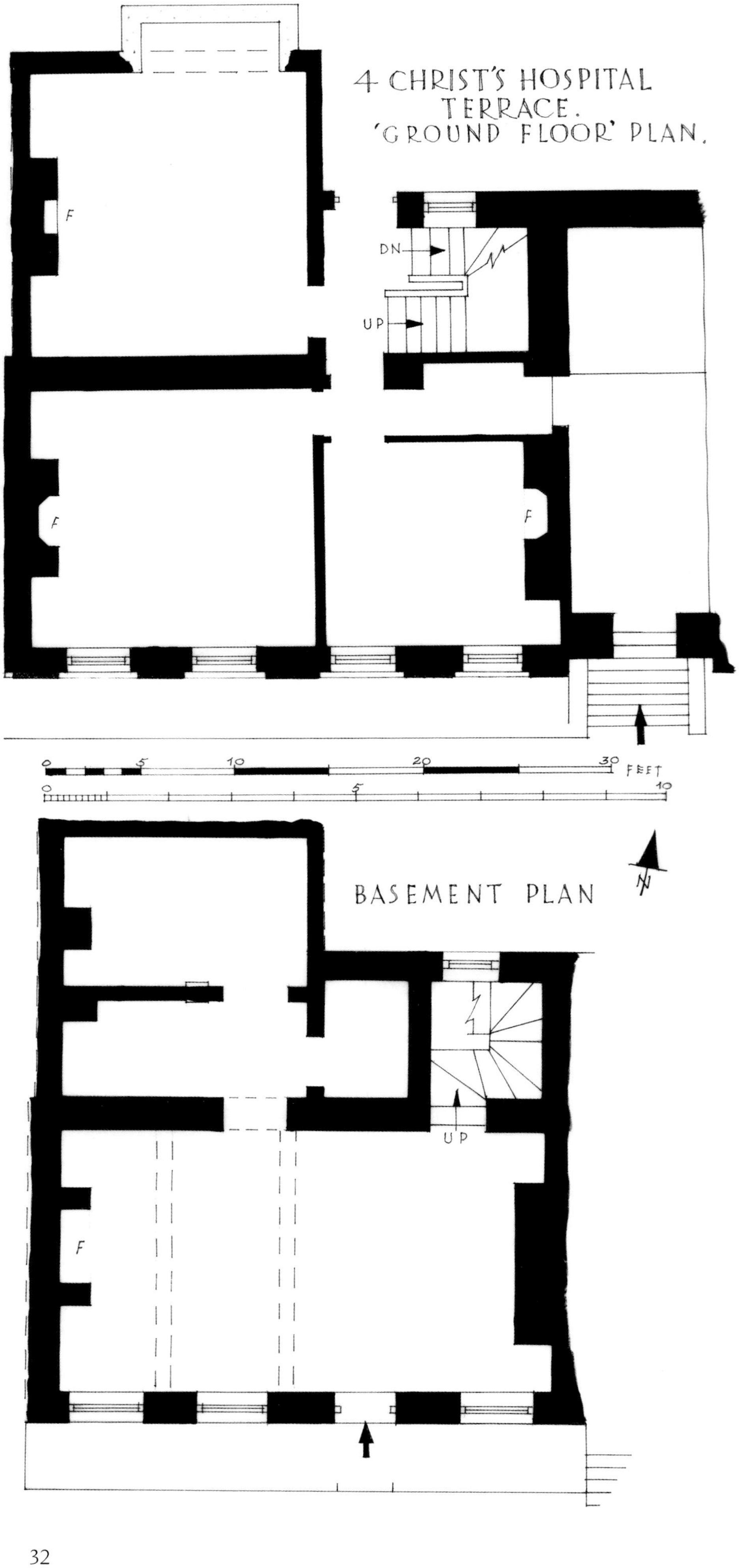

Minister. The house contains in the basement a lower storey, a kitchen and other offices; on the next or ground-floor...lately approached by a flight of stone steps in the centre of the south front, but now through a passage at the east end lately made by lessees[88] over ground belonging to the said Hospital...two parlours (one and a smaller one, late the entrance hall) in front, a larger parlour, passage and staircase behind; two chambers and two attics over them, in front, and one chamber over the back parlour; a small yard with a rain water tank and pump, and, ascended by steps, a small garden extending by a gradual and rather steep ascent, to the wall of the Minster Close next to the garden of the Precentory on the north."[89]

A small residence of distinction, three storeys high, of red brick construction throughout with some stone dressings. The Terrace facade is divided above basement/ground-floor level into four bays each distinguished by a shallow projecting whole height pilaster; each pilaster has a projecting capital and feet. The present principal entrance is contained in a fifth bay at the east end of the facade at first-floor level; an off-centre doorway accesses the basement from the street. The frontage is topped by a modillioned cornice that follows the pilaster projections, and four dormers complete the attic roof space. At the west return of the basement wall this is marked by it being superficially of stone up to ground-floor level. The construction date is thought to have been c.1770. A difference between the window heads of the first-floor windows in which one lacks the double line of brick voussoirs has been singled out as a possible entry site made prior to the present provision at the east end of the facade; this may be part of ground allotted to no.4 by the Hospital Trustees.[90]

ARCHITECTURAL DESCRIPTION

There are early references in the Lincoln City Common Council Minutes to their plot east of the Vicars' leasehold. In 1540 William Sammes was given a twenty-year lease of: "a piece of ground by St Michael's Church, with the tenters there".[91] The rent was 8d per annum, soon raised to 3s 4d. Nicholas Nevell in 1571 and 1584, William Richardson in 1599 and Lancelot Forster in 1603 and 1618 followed in succession.[92] The latter lease, recorded in full in the Lease Book,[93] describes the plot as measuring 31 yards from the Close Wall, north to the churchyard, south, and 8.5 yards wide at each side. The rent was 3s 4d pa, and a fat pig or 2s.[94]

4A CHRIST'S HOSPITAL TERRACE

In 1625, following the purchase from Thomas Forster of the main Hospital site to the east two years earlier, the Master and Governors of the Hospital paid £8 for an assignment of the City lease held by Lancelot Forster.[95] The sitting tenant, Henry Good, continued to occupy the house at a rent of 20s per annum, but fell into arrears c.1630. Apparently he had sublet his basement to "a poor body" for 5s, which was paid to the Hospital Nurse, but did not pay his proper rent.[96] The Civil War disturbed regular record keeping, but we do hear that Samuel Good was tenant in 1642. Daniel Good was there in 1647 and was replaced by Justinian Walwin, instrument maker, who stayed until 1649, and William Lilly, 1649–52.[97]

John Wanless was tenant c.1653–57, and after him came Guy Dickinson, paying £3 pa; he stayed until his death in 1686 and contributed half the cost of repairs and a new ceiling to the house in 1663. He also made a silver seal for the use of the Hospital.[98] After a Mr and Mrs Smith, 1694–97, John Powell, who we know was a schoolmaster, took over; after his death in 1722 his widow continued as Matron until 1756.

Samuel Graves was tenant 1757–59, then followed the lengthy incumbency of William Putterill, 1760–96, during which time the Hospital agreed a 998-year lease with the Corporation.[99] William had his rent halved in 1787 as a class of girls was now being taught at the house. On his death his widow carried on as Matron and girls' teacher until her resignation in 1806. Her daughter Mrs Caparn took over the role and the house until

1809. William Wilkinson then took over the girls' school rent-free and Mrs Caparn was allowed to occupy the old garden, also rent-free: she died in 1814. The house was now fully absorbed into the main Hospital structure.[100]

The garden was let separate from the house. Originally mostly orchard, it was let to the Subdean from 1675 at a rent of 20s per annum.[101] Successive Subdeans continued to hold it until 1754. Thomas and Richard Barker successively held it from 1755–66, after which it reverted to the holding of the Master. Mrs Caparn used it as a cow yard in 1809.[102]

5 Christ's Hospital Terrace: Christ's Hospital, later Church House and Institute

In the late 16th and early 17th centuries this extensive property was a freehold in the ownership of the Forster family. Lancelot Forster was also tenant of the Corporation property to the west of this site. In 1623 Thomas Forster sold the freehold of this site to the Master and Governors of Christ's Hospital in Lincoln[103] which had been founded in 1602 and from 1614 until 1623 was established at St Mary's Guildhall.[104]

The Guildhall proving unsuitable, it was decided to move the school into the city. The master and Governors paid 2s annual ground rent to the parish of St Michael from 1623,[105] but continued to pay rent to the Corporation for St Mary's Guildhall until 1634,[106] as they were able to derive rents of £14 per annum from subletting. Over a period of several years many repairs were needed at the new site, to the walls, well and churchyard gates in particular.[107]

In 1684 a passageway leading to the 'house of office' in the Hospital garden was ordered to be fenced off, not so much to ensure privacy as to prevent the boys from entering the garden.[108] Little more is recorded about the buildings on the site until 1758, when it was decided to cap the well and draw water via a pump set up against the Hospital wall. Two years later there was a further improvement in water supply with the installation of a ground cistern of 60 hogsheads capacity and an improved pump.[109]

The Hospital apothecary, Mr Brown, was in 1777 authorised to inoculate (for prevention of smallpox) such of the Hospital boys who wished to be treated, and if he considered them proper subjects.[110] We are not told the results of this.

With the gradual growth of the school, there were developments in its infrastructure. A dairy on the site being too small, the Governors sanctioned a replacement facility in 1805. The buildings as a whole were insured for a total of £650 in 1809. A new schoolroom was constructed in the garden in 1817 and the existing room converted to a dining room. There were to be new gates and a door, and a ventilator fitted to the schoolroom. In 1828 the principal staircase ceiling in the Hospital House was to be properly washed and cleaned and the walls painted in French Grey, and the Boardroom was fitted out with matching furniture and décor.[111]

Gas lighting made an appearance in the schoolroom and dining room in October 1829, and a 'batswing' burner gas light in front of the House. New paving was provided for the yard. Witton Dalton later commented that the school started out with 12 boys in the 17th century and had grown to 56 boys in c.1835. A thorough review was made of the estates, with a view to revising rents, and of the school facilities, in 1837. The dormitories were found to be most unsatisfactory both in repair and cleanliness: improvements were put in hand. W.A. Nicholson was asked to draw up a plan for an increase in capacity to 100 boys, later revised upwards to 120.[112] The School continued until closure in 1883, and Canon E.T. Leeke later established his Church House and Institute here.[113]

1   *RA i*, 54-55
2   *ibid.*, no.249, pp. 190-193
3   *ibid.*, no.302, pp. 262-3
4   *ibid.*, nos 251 and 250, pp. 193-6
5   *ibid.*, no.254, pp. 202-4
6   *ibid.*, pp. 267-76
7   *VCH Lincolnshire, vol ii*,189; Hill, *ML*,345; Chris Johnson, 'The Hospital of the Holy Sepulchre', in *South-East Lincoln, Canwick Road, South Common, St Catherine's and Bracebridge*, ed. Andrew Walker (Survey of Lincoln, 2011),9-10
8   e.g. *RA viii*, no.2314: land in Mickelgate, held by Abraham, son of Aaron, of the Hospital, for which see below, p.141
9   *RH*,322a; *LHA op. cit*,16
10 Hill, *op.cit.*,90
11 Pipe Roll 2 John, *PRS* NS vol 12,87-91
12 Pipe Roll 7 John, *PRS* NS vol 19,213
13 Pipe Roll 3 Hen III, *PRS* NS vol 42,121
14 Pipe Roll 10 Ric I, *PRS* NS vol 9,62; there are similar entries in several Pipe Rolls
15 *RA x, no.2943*: whether the Bretheren of the Hospital were involved here in Joceus' time is unknown. See also Pipe Roll 12 John, *PRS* NS vol 26, 8
16 *RH*, 322a
17 *CRR* (1219-20),381-3; (1220),27,167-8,307,329; Fine Rolls of the Reign of Henry III,15 February and 11 March 1220, available on the Fine Rolls Projects website (http://www.finerollshenry3.org.uk), and within *Calendar of the Fine Rolls of Henry III 1216–1234*, ed. P. Dryburgh and B. Hartland, technical ed. A. Ciula and J.M. Vieira, 2 vols. (Woodbridge, 2007), nos 97 and 116
18 *BFees i*, 888, 895, 1002, 1053-55, 1058-59, 1078
19 See below
20 D. Stocker, *pers.comm.*
21 See below, p.63
22 *Fig 7*
23 *Fig 8*
24 *Fig 12*
25 *Fig 9*
26 *Fig 16*
27 *Fig 8*
28 *ibid.*
29 *Fig 16*
30 *Fig 74*
31 *Fig 18*
32 *Cant 729*; Dij. 76/2/18
33 *Cant 730*; Dij. 76/2/31
34 *Cant 733*; Dij. 76/2/27
35 *Cant 734*; Dij. 76/2/24
36 *Fig 20*
37 Dij. 76/2/30; *Cant 731*
38 *Cant 732*; Dij 76/2/29
39 *Cant 737*; Dij 76/2/26: a contemporary copy rather than an original or probate
40 *Cant 736*; Dij. 76/2/23
41 *Cant 735*; Dij. 76/2/25
42 *SAH iv*, 84, 89: nos 12a and 15 Bailgate
43 *Cant 739*; Dij. 76/2/34
44 *BB*, f.157v, no.512
45 *ibid.*, f.191v, no.624
46 *ibid.*, f.271, no.961
47 *ibid.*, f.272v,no.968
48 *IAQD* 3 Hen V, no.21
49 *Cant* 731
50 *RA* viii, no.2296
51 *Cant* 602-605
52 *VC*, nos 261-2
53 *RA* viii, no.2292
54 *ibid.*, no.2293
55 *ibid.*, no.2292
56 *FL Deeds* 3219
57 *BB*, f.83, no.46
58 *LHA op.cit.*,1992; *SAH iv*, 1996,21-24
59 *SAH op.cit.*, 22, *fig*.19; although undated, it must have been drawn c.1790
60 Dimensions given in 1618 lease: L1/3/2 f.65v
61 LCC Wills 1636,103
62 L1/1/1/6, p. 486; Ciij 9.1/97
63 LC Rolls 1/150, North Ward
64 LC Charters 38/868
65 *ibid.*,38/869
66 L1/3/2 f.65v
67 LCC Wills 1636,103
68 Inv 219A/31
69 Inv 188/69
70 L3/2530/13-14
71 L3/2530/35-36; Willson and Betham Survey 1828
72 For convenience, no.4A is used to identify the Corporation holding, although part of it actually fell later within the curtilage of the Hospital building proper, which for this purpose is given no.5
73 See Kate Naylor, *Richard Smith M.D.: The founder of Christ's Hospital School* (Lincoln, 1951); Hill, *TSL*,135
74 CC 27/152829 3/7, p. 14
75 Christ's Hospital Accounts, Bodleian Library, Oxford, MS Rawlinson D 687: transcript from photostat copy at Lincolnshire Archives, *MCD* 794/2,f.57
76 LCC Wills 1643&4,198
77 VC 3/2/4/1
78 *MCD loc.cit.*, f.62v; *LCL* 5078
79 CC 140/298536,38,40,42,47 and 51; 3*LCL* 3/1/6
80 *LCL* 5081
81 CC 140/298536
82 CC 140/298538
83 L3/2530/33
84 *LCL* 5082
85 *ibid.*
86 CC 140/298542,47,51; *LCL* 5084
87 *LCL* 5083
88 Lessees of the Corporation
89 *VC* 3/2/4/58: Lampray had been tenant since 1842 – cf. rentals in *LCL* 5083
90 *Fig 23*
91 L1/1/1/1, f.277
92 L1/1/1/3, f.58, 143v; L1/1/1/4 f.2, 25
93 L1/3/2, f.61
94 The pig, costing 2s anyway, was usually sent in as the quitrent
95 *MCD* 794/2, f.35v
96 *ibid.* f.47v
97 *ibid.* ff.56v,58,61v,63v
98 *LCL* 5078 *passim*
99 LC Charters 41/946
100 *LCL* 5082 *passim*
101 *LCL* 5079, p. 8
102 *LCL* 5082
103 *MCD* 794/2, f.29
104 David Stocker, *St Mary's Guildhall, Lincoln: the survey and excavation of a medieval building complex*, CBA for City of Lincoln Archaeological Unit, 1991, 8-9
105 *MCD* 794/2 f.31ff
106 *ibid.*, f.52
107 *ibid.*, f.47v, 49, 51
108 *LCL* 5079 p. 81
109 *LCL* 5081 12 Sept 1758, 16 Oct 1760
110 *ibid.* 7 Oct 1777
111 *LCL* 5082 *passim*
112 *LCL* 5083 *passim*
113 *WG* 6/2A/1-3 *passim*; LC Educ 5/1

HILTON COTTAGE AND THE HARDING HOUSES
(INCORPORATING MANNOCK'S HOUSE)

No medieval documents have been positively identified for this range of properties built into the hillside between Steep Hill and St Michael's Churchyard. The goldsmith John Morley was the first person we know to have had property in this location, in the period before a lease was given in 1565[1] to William Mannock, a shoemaker and jerkin maker who had been given the freedom of the City c.1550 by a former mayor.[2] We know very little about him apart from this, but his name somehow remained interlinked with the properties until 1835.

An official Ministry inspection report of 1957[3] suggested that two houses, nos 49–50 Steep Hill, restored in 1962, were essentially of 15th- to early 16th-century origin, with arched brace timber framing in the main structure. No.48, on the site of the original Mannock's House, was thought to be 18th-century,[4] and no.51 (Harding's House) originally of 16th-century construction remodelled in the 18th century: it was thought that the upper floor may have been timber-framed.[5] There was also some 19th-century infilling behind this row, on land belonging to the parish, to form a group of cottages called Hilton Hill. The parish also owned a house on the corner by the Mayor's Chair which was probably of 17th-century build.[6]

William Mannock held this range of property until 1586, and Anthony Osgarby was here from 1587 until the early 17th century.[7] Mark Fenne, apothecary, was lessee in 1627,[8] but died a few years later. In his lease he was to arrange for "honest artificers of good and sufficient trade" to occupy the tenements below the main house, the tenements being converted two into one to create larger units. Perhaps this is an early example of a trading estate?

Anthony Topham, Dean of Lincoln, was lessee in 1638 and Robert Marshall in 1652.[9] Timothy Heardson was recorded in 1685 and 1711,[10] then his son Timothy took over; as a ship's surgeon in the Royal Navy he had to arrange for rents to be paid via his wife Ann, and his will[11] was entered on Navy printed forms. Ann died in 1761[12] after having arranged the assignment of the lease to Eleanor Searle, daughter of Clement Wood. William Wetherall of the Bail, devisee in trust under Clement's will, was lessee in 1792.[13]

In 1824 William Wilkinson, schoolmaster, bought the lease, then in 1835 acquired the freehold from the Corporation during the mass enfranchisement of leaseholds at the time of local government reform.[14] John Wilkinson sold the properties to Christ's Hospital in 1841 for a total of £730, although he had to redeem certain mortgages out of that sum.[15] By 1846 rents from the properties were being paid into the Christ's Hospital accounts, but the individual tenants were not listed regularly until 1854, when Wilkinson's houses, and his other property in Hilton Hill, were joined in the record book by Elizabeth East's houses, including nos 46–47 Steep Hill.[16]

Fig 24. Photograph of the Harding Houses, from the south-west

42–40 MICHAELGATE

It seems probable, on the basis of boundary information for the Harlequin site (see below), that these tenements were owned in the mid-14th century by Thomas de Carleton, but nothing else is known about them except for the architectural evidence. Carleton had two messuages and 10s 8d in rents, and with his wife Cecilia seven messuages, all in Lincoln.[17]

There is a remarkable lack of documentary evidence for the early modern period before 1828; earlier deeds have either not survived or are lurking in some solicitor's basement. Leases for neighbouring properties fail to provide boundary information until 1835.[18] This dearth of information is surprising, given that the owner as recorded in the Survey of 1828[19] was none other than E.J. Willson, the occupiers of nos 42 and 40 being given as Joseph Kidd and George Shipton respectively. Willson's historical collections have nothing to add.

DOCUMENTARY
HISTORY

Fig 25. Pre-restoration photograph of no.40 Michaelgate, showing the south gable

These tenements changed occupiers at frequent intervals during the 19th century, and the historian's task is not made easier by the changes in street numbering prior to 1880. At some point before 1901 William Robert Lilly, an insurance inspector, mortgaged the five properties here to Emma Howsin of Southport for £500. Lilly was an enterprising gentleman who had the interesting but wholly impracticable task of installing a funicular railway up Steep Hill. He also bought up some of the poor tenements at the foot of the hill as part of his plan, which was turned down by the Corporation in 1909.[20]

Demolition Orders were prepared for all the properties except no.42 in February 1932, but Canon N.S. Harding stepped in to preserve no.40 by purchasing the range up from no.36 in January 1933 for £100.[21]

ARCHITECTURAL
DESCRIPTION

The site plan showing the junction of Michaelgate and Steep Hill draws attention to the restricted space to the rear of properties at this point. The opportunities afforded by the proximity to a market place and a well-used thoroughfare clearly outweighed the lack of ground overall in favour of the benefits accruing from trade. It is unfortunate that this thesis with an emphasis on shops cannot be supported by physical evidence in the

structure of either of the tenements under discussion. No.42, abutting the Harlequin, although of brick construction outwardly, preserves framework and an early roof truss of medieval origin in the wall next to the former inn. The truss[22] is of crown-post and collar-purlin type and is similar to, but predates, on stylistic grounds, the trusses above nos 29–30 Steep Hill.

Unfortunately the roof space of no.42 was converted to attics when the house was rebuilt in brick c.1700, and the truss is now the sole visible relic; the tie beams of the early roof may yet remain in situ, serving to support the attic flooring. It was further noted that at least the timber wall-plates from the medieval house appear to be undisturbed. The wall-plate fronting Michaelgate has mullion mortices for a four-light window, along with evidence of former studding at first-floor level; a long splayed scarf joint to the east of the same window position makes it likely that the wall-plate formed a junction with the frame of the Harlequin. At ground-level in no.42 the stair is squeezed in against the west side of the chimney stack in the larger of the two-room plan, and is lit from the street front – a location dictated by the small size of the tenement. It is assumed that in the primary phase the tenement may have been two-storied but not necessarily jettied towards Michaelgate.

No.40 adjoining the south end of no.42 has exposed timber framing on all elevations; originally it extended by at least a further bay to the south. It can be shown that, as a framed structure, it was reared against the south end of no.42 and thereby took advantage of what was then an existing wall, thus obviating the need to provide infilling for the new work. Such 'borrowings' of party walls have a long history and were common in both urban and rural contexts. Although one is dealing with merely a single bay of framing 15ft.×15ft. its interest is nevertheless of considerable significance. It started as an open hall of probable early 16th-century origin, close studded, and with an entrance from the street whose location is now uncertain.[23] The removed south bay is held to have been two-storied from inception.

Fig 26. Post-restoration photograph of no.40 Michaelgate, from a slide

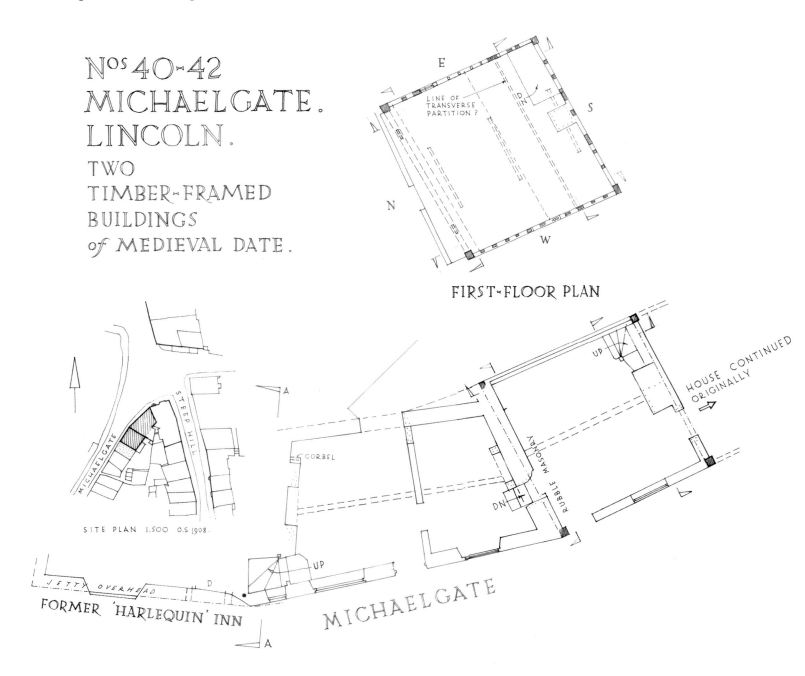

NOS 40~42 MICHAELGATE. LINCOLN.

TWO TIMBER~FRAMED BUILDINGS *of* MEDIEVAL DATE.

FIRST~FLOOR PLAN

SITE PLAN 1.500 O.S 1908.

FORMER 'HARLEQUIN' INN

MICHAELGATE

JETTY OVERHEAD

HOUSE CONTINUED ORIGINALLY

Fig 27. Nos 40–42 Michaelgate: plans

The hall fronting the street in length is only one of two known ground-level examples to have survived, present day, in Lincoln. There is reasonable evidence for an early window of five lights high in the east wall, and notches in the opposed wall-plates may have carried the head beam of a partition of sorts, possibly a dais canopy over the family bench. The bay retains its original roof of clasped-purlin type and the purlins have up-swinging wind-braces from the end trusses. It would seem that both no.40 and no.42 formed a single entity after c.1700, based on a central doorway in the common party wall; that this may have occurred after the demolition of the contiguous and in-line buildings to the south and therefore a more recent amalgamation is to be considered. Improvements to the hall include the insertion of an upper floor, stair and chimney, which are all of post-medieval origin. What is now the southernmost roof truss, but which originally would have been internal, appears to have been open in its lower half, permitting access between the former conjoined bays; the upper half has large inverted braces from the side posts to the spanning bressummer. Given the restrictions of the site perhaps cooking was carried out in the hall itself.

40

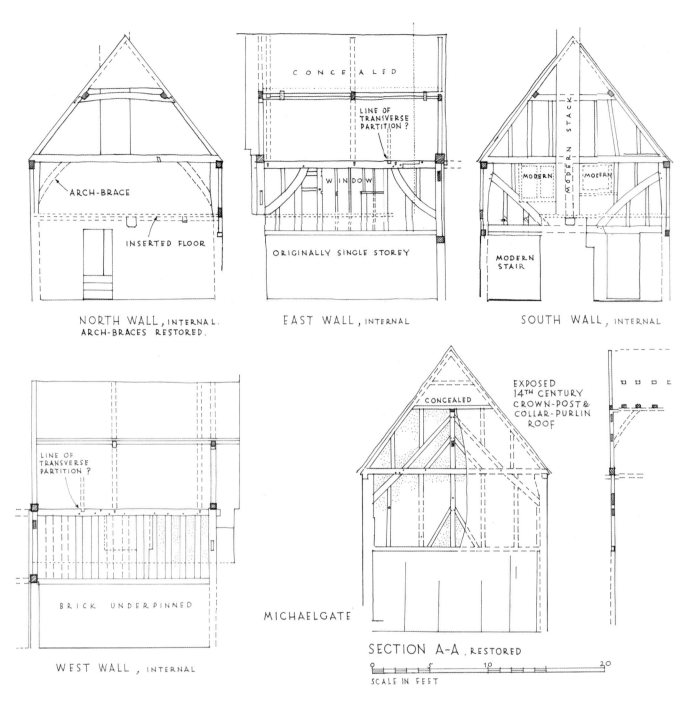

NORTH WALL, INTERNAL.
ARCH-BRACES RESTORED.

ARCH-BRACE

INSERTED FLOOR

EAST WALL, INTERNAL

CONCEALED

LINE OF
TRANSVERSE
PARTITION ?

WINDOW

ORIGINALLY SINGLE STOREY

SOUTH WALL, INTERNAL

MODERN STACK

MODERN

MODERN

MODERN
STAIR

WEST WALL, INTERNAL

LINE OF
TRANSVERSE
PARTITION ?

BRICK UNDERPINNED

MICHAELGATE

SECTION A-A, RESTORED

CONCEALED

EXPOSED
14TH CENTURY
CROWN-POST &
COLLAR-PURLIN
ROOF

0   5   10   20
SCALE IN FEET

Fig 28. (above)
Nos 40–42 Michaelgate:
sections
Fig 29. Photograph of
immured truss, no.42
Michaelgate, from a slide

41

19–22 STEEP HILL, KNOWN AS THE HARLEQUIN
TOGETHER WITH 17–18 STEEP HILL

Jacob son of Leo, was one of the most prominent Jews in Lincoln during the first half of the 13th century, and owned several houses in Steep Hill[24] and the surrounding area. After his alleged implication in the death of the boy Hugh in 1255, and his subsequent execution, all his property became forfeit to the Crown. In January 1257 the king, as a sign of favour to Hagin, son of Master Moses, soon to be appointed Arch-Presbyter of the English Jewry, made a grant to him of Jacob's properties, which included a house in the parish of St Michael, situated between the land of Robert le Turnur south and the High Market (*altum mercatum*) north.[25] This description can realistically apply only to the complex of buildings later known as the Harlequin and the houses now nos 17–18 to the south of it, as noted below.

As has been established regarding the Lincoln properties of Hagin, noted elsewhere in this volume,[26] they came after his death in 1280 into the hands of Queen Eleanor, and thence, via Stephen de Cheynduit and Stephen his son, to John of St Ives and Gilbert de Atherby (of Atterby).[27] John relinquished his interest to Gilbert in 1299.

The property south of the High Market remained in Gilbert's family for two further generations, descending through his son John, who also owned land near to Jews Court, to a grandson William, heir to John. In July 1349 William granted to Robert Hare, bowyer, a messuage with the appurtenances, situated between the land of the cathedral on the south (i.e. nos 15–16 Steep Hill) and the king's way on the north, abutting the king's way east and land of Thomas de Carleton west.[28] Hare possessed other property in St Michael's and St Andrew on the Hill at the time of his death in 1362, some unidentified as to location. It is possible that the Harlequin site was among those tenements in St Michael's which were noted in his will,[29] and entrusted to Peter de Belasise and John de Blythe to establish a chantry in the church of St Michael.[30]

Nos 17–18 Steep Hill, which have no separate identifiable source material of direct relevance, must have formed part of the Harlequin curtilage, according to the bounds of the 1349 grant noted above. There is, however, one earlier boundary reference to land belonging to William son of Fulk, situated north of Hugh Paynel's holding, in the early 13th century.[31]

The Harlequin was once stated to be England's oldest public house, but the documents do not corroborate this. The name 'Harlequin' or 'Harlequin and Colombine' are first noted only from c.1791, continuing until 1931, when the licence was withdrawn, according to Mr Exley's notes on the building.[32]

The building, consisting of four tenements in common ownership from the 16th century, was in the hands of the Common Council from at least 1551, when William Atkynson was given a 21-year lease at the rent of 16s per annum.[33] He was succeeded in 1562 by Alexander Walker, a tailor, and in turn by Henry Horner, singingman, in 1563: he held the lease until 1599.[34] William Proctor, next lessee[35] was followed by Robert Morcroft in 1613.[36] Morcroft renewed in 1629, Edward Freshney being the recorded occupier.[37] Robert Morcroft, an Alderman, was a leading figure in the business life of the city at this time; an entrepreneur of some stature, he was behind a petition to the king for aid for the Fossdyke, and he helped the Cordwainers Guild to apply for a new charter c.1606.[38] He was mayor in 1607 and 1617, and a great supporter of the local textile industries.

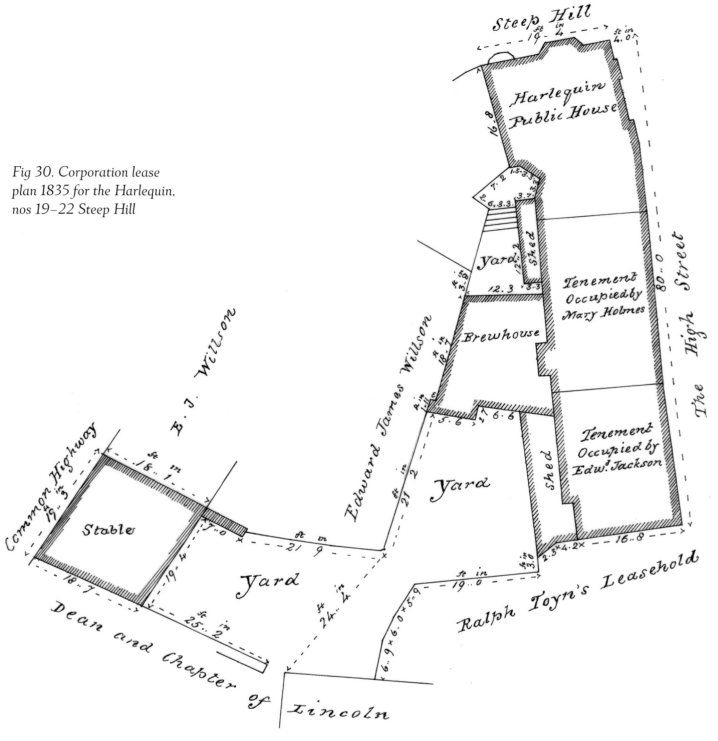

Fig 30. Corporation lease plan 1835 for the Harlequin, nos 19–22 Steep Hill

There is a gap in the lease history of the site until 1681 when Richard Hesslewood or Haslewood, painter, took it over from Edward Kelham, gent.[39] Haslewood held several properties in the area of Steep Hill and the Strait; his last recorded lease was in 1708.[40] In 1739, when Ald. William Raynor was lessee in trust for Ald. George Brown, the property was said to be divided into two tenements, in the occupation of William Smith, Jonathan Wood, Edward Beeston and Mary Darby.[41] It was assigned in 1740 to Clement Wood. By the time of the next renewal in 1771 there had been further subdivisions into several tenements.[42] John Brown, gent., was now lessee, in trust under the marriage settlement of Eleanor Mellor, daughter of Wood, and Thomas Searle, her second husband. John Clark, Richard Billiatt, William Cook and William Rogerson were the tenants. These four, with John Carline, were still in residence at the following renewal in 1804, granted to John Caparn in trust under John Brown's will.[43]

Messrs F. & C. Winn, brewers, took on the lease in July 1835, just before enfranchisement:

William Brown, Mary Holmes and Edward Jackson were tenants.[44] The Winns purchased the freehold for £231 in September 1835. After the break-up of the Winn estate the Harlequin came into the hands of W. H. Brooke, senior, another brewer. He died in 1862, leaving behind a complicated family trust and assorted mortgages, which persisted until 1931. The description in a schedule of 1862 included yards, a brewhouse and a smith's shop, formerly a stable.[45] In 1931 the property was conveyed to the brewing firm of Hall Cutlack and Harlock, but it did not survive as a public house: instead it was sold to Canon Norman Sydney Harding on 9 March 1932 for £550.[46] The jacket illustration for this volume is from a superb 1935 watercolour of the Harlequin by Karl Wood, which is now at the Usher Gallery.

ARCHITECTURAL DESCRIPTION

SUMMARY This large and attractive medieval timber-framed building at the junction of Steep Hill and Michaelgate is remarkable in many respects, the most notable being that it contains a first-floor open hall complete with its dais canopy for the high table, and was heated by an open hearth, as evidenced by its smoke-blackened roof. Later modifications include the insertion of chimneys and a ceiling in the hall itself, to which must be added the subsequent removal of partition walls and materials in a manner which reflects change of use over the lifetime of the tenement. The Harlequin is now, and for many years has been, a renowned antiquarian bookshop, the consequence of which, for the historic buildings surveyor, has meant, understandably, an inability to either reach or see parts of the structure obscured by book stacks. Overall such gaps have not detracted greatly from the analysis of the building as a whole. The building at its north end had served as a public house from at least the early 19th century and ceased trading in 1931.[47] The following account marks the first investigation and assessment of this well-known landmark in Steep Hill, a survey that has revealed a combination of features that single it out as a monument worthy of a higher grading and one deserving of the closest attention for its future well-being by the owners, the local authority.

DESCRIPTION The original form of the tenement in the medieval period comprised a northern cross wing of two bays and two stories aligned roughly east–west, and having off its south side a long range flanking Steep Hill, in part of two and three stories in height. Roof divisions showed the long range to be of four bays originally, terminating in a hipped roof at its south end. The two southernmost bays represent the three-storied section of the structure; the remaining two bays have smoke-blackened roof members and originally formed a small open hall, heated by means of a brazier or hearth on the floor. It is held that a generous application of gypsum plaster to the floor planking under and around the hearth position may have been a means of proofing and preventing the timber frame from accidentally igniting.

The fall of ground north to south on Steep Hill was skilfully exploited by the constructors in adopting the higher level from which to access the tenement, and to adhere to this level throughout for the main hall floor and rooms beyond. Masons were obliged, therefore, to build a high wall at the south end of the tenement, rising no higher than the main floor in order to carry the timber-framed superstructure. At the north end, and carrying the sill beam of the cross wing, a lesser wall was constructed whose other clear function was to divert water and other effluents from the sloping medieval market away from the long side of the wing. As intended, the lower storey or basement was divided into at least three shops as a means of exploiting the potential of passing trade on the Hill; in all probability these were lock-up shops having no access to the floor overhead. The shop area below the cross wing has a stone west wall marking the division with no.42 Michaelgate; it is uncertain whether this wall, now mostly obscured, had once extended further to the south.

The main floor is jettied out continuously on its east side to Steep Hill; the cross wing is also jettied out at first-floor level on both its north and east sides on exposed joists; the dragon-beam arrangement for this dual projection is visible within the bookshop. Large inverted braces distinguish the upper frame of the north side to the wing and it is held that similar bracing was once common to the east wall of the same chamber.[48] Smaller versions of such braces are employed at the south end of the hall range, east side. Here the timber-framed structure rises to three stories, i.e. from pavement level, to incorporate a chamber and superimposed solar, both abutting the south side of the dais.[49] Access from the former market place was at the west end of the cross wing and remains so today, less its original door head. It is envisaged that this, the principal approach to the hall and its ancillary rooms, was partitioned off within the end bay of the wing. In all probability the wing room so truncated may have functioned as a parlour if further undivided, though strictly speaking its location at the socially 'lower' end of the hall could point to some other role conceivably connected to the market place and the transaction of related business.

Entry into the hall proper may have encountered either a screen or a portal serving to discourage draughts.[50] The hall itself was a lofty affair, cross lit from opposed windows, and sporting a crown-post roof with a central truss whose component parts, though somewhat irregular in profile, are structurally robust.[51] At the north end of the former hall the insertion of a chimney stack after c.1600, serving the ground- and first-floor rooms plus the chamber in the cross wing, accounts for the destruction of the framed wall dividing hall from wing. As noted earlier, the preservation of the dais canopy in its entirety at the south end of the hall is quite remarkable given the robust interventions the tenement has experienced in modern times.

The canopy was so contrived that its overhead fixing to the south end hall truss formed a deep dais that protected the family at meat from the sooty particles emanating from the open hearth or brazier.[52] The high ceiling introduced into the hall, together with the chimney stack, made novel use of the spandrels of the open truss and that of the dais truss in which to lodge its side joists; however, the ceiling was not intended to carry an attic floor and consequently the roof space was left untouched, along with its large areas of smoke-blackened surfaces from the primary phase. The greater part of the west wall of the hall range is now of modern brickwork, but retains sections of its principal posts at bay intervals; this, a major intervention, has effectively stabilised the structure on that side.

Between the dais and the south end of the tenement are two-rooms, one above the other, the upper serving as a small but lofty solar exposed in part to the dais canopy's ribs and its planked cove. The lower room in turn may have provided the diners with a buttery and have had more general uses, and the solar, though awkwardly set up, was a reasonably securable point in the house given its distance from the north end entrance. It can be seen that the layout of rooms in the Harlequin does not depart radically from the customary disposition in which a central ground-floor hall is flanked by storied ends each usually allotted socially distinct functions.[53] Where the difference lies is in the elevated position that the Harlequin hall occupies and, whilst attention has been drawn to the main access being off the market place, it is unlikely that this was the only access point serving the establishment. Reference to the site plan and the emphasis on the small yards available to both the Harlequin and no.42 Michaelgate indicates, for the former, a short stair flight as a means of gaining the large brewhouse in the yard from the cross wing passage at its south end; this particular approach may well date from when the tenement was licensed to sell ale in the later 18th century.[54]

For the house in its medieval phase and as an unusually sited urban dwelling, one's curiosity extends to how this lofty household functioned. Where, for example, was the kitchen on this restricted site? Would cooking have been permitted in the hall? Could

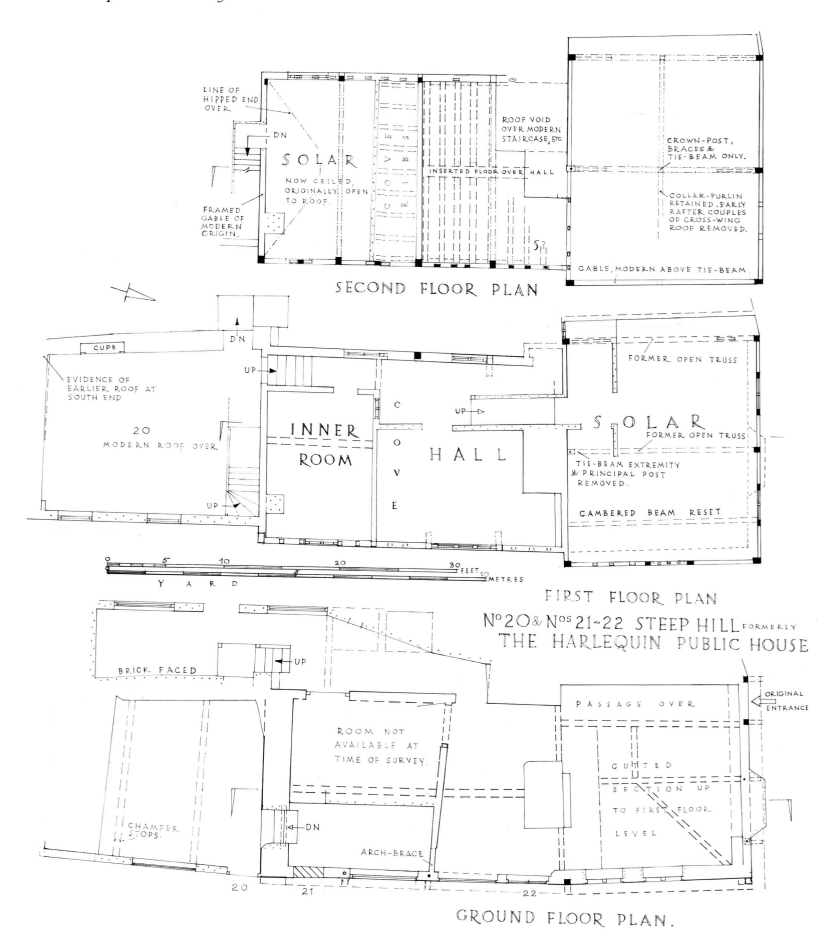

LINE OF
HIPPED END
OVER

DN

S O L A R

NOW CEILED,
ORIGINALLY OPEN
TO ROOF.

FRAMED
GABLE OF
MODERN
ORIGIN.

ROOF VOID
OVER MODERN
STAIRCASE, ETC

INSERTED FLOOR OVER HALL

CROWN-POST,
BRACES &
TIE-BEAM ONLY.

COLLAR-PURLIN
RETAINED. EARLY
RAFTER COUPLES
OF CROSS-WING
ROOF REMOVED.

S?

GABLE, MODERN ABOVE TIE-BEAM.

SECOND FLOOR PLAN

CUPB

EVIDENCE OF
EARLIER ROOF AT
SOUTH END

D'N

UP

20

MODERN ROOF OVER

INNER
ROOM

UP

C
O
V
E

HALL

UP

FORMER OPEN TRUSS

S O L A R

FORMER OPEN TRUSS

TIE-BEAM EXTREMITY
& PRINCIPAL POST
REMOVED.

CAMBERED BEAM RESET

0   5   10   20   30 FEET
                              METRES
Y A R D

FIRST FLOOR PLAN

Nº 20 & Nºs 21-22 STEEP HILL FORMERLY
THE HARLEQUIN PUBLIC HOUSE

BRICK FACED

UP

PASSAGE OVER

ORIGINAL
ENTRANCE

ROOM NOT
AVAILABLE AT
TIME OF SURVEY.

G U T T E D

S E C T I O N U P

T O F I R S T F L O O R

CHAMFER
STOPS.

DN

L E V E L

ARCH-BRACE

20   21   22

GROUND FLOOR PLAN.

Fig 31. Plans of ground-floor, first-floor and second floor, the Harlequin

the rooms to the rear of the dais have functioned wholly in a service capacity? Such questions related to cooking in urban medieval housing are rarely resolved satisfactorily. There was one certain hearth, that in the hall, and the storage of wood for this could conveniently be made in the back yard. One assumes there to have been a well or source of water close at hand; at a later date a large brewhouse was built in the yard against the west wall of the main range and it is likely that this tapped a source on site. Those persons renting, and shown as such on the lease plan of 1835, would presumably also have had access to the back yard, and their individual sheds.

Reference above to the insertion of a chimney and ceiling into the hall relates to the manner in which a great part of the medieval housing stock in the later 16th and early 17th centuries saw a wholesale improvement and transformation. For the Harlequin the obvious change externally would have been the presence of a chimney on its skyline, replacing an outmoded louvre. Possibly by c.1700 the timber-frame may have been concealed beneath a plaster rendering at all levels and with glazed window frames of mullion and transom type installed. Modern repairs account for the loss of the cross wing roof above tie beam level and its east gable facing the Steep. Reference to the long section of the hall range illustrates the now-encased medieval hipped end to the roof at its south end, the present vertical gable there being a product of the early 20th century.[55]

Fig 32. Longitudinal section of part of the Harlequin, nos 21–22 Steep Hill

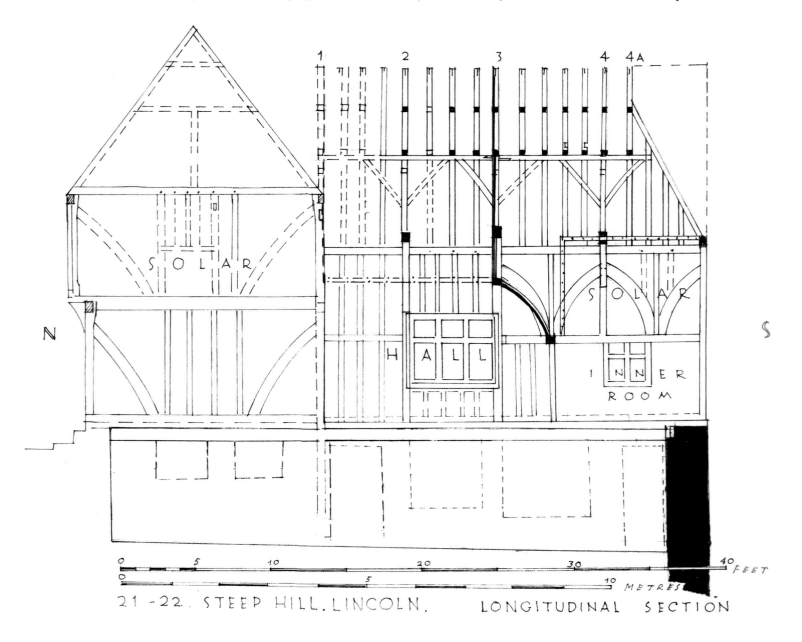

21-22. STEEP HILL. LINCOLN.   LONGITUDINAL SECTION

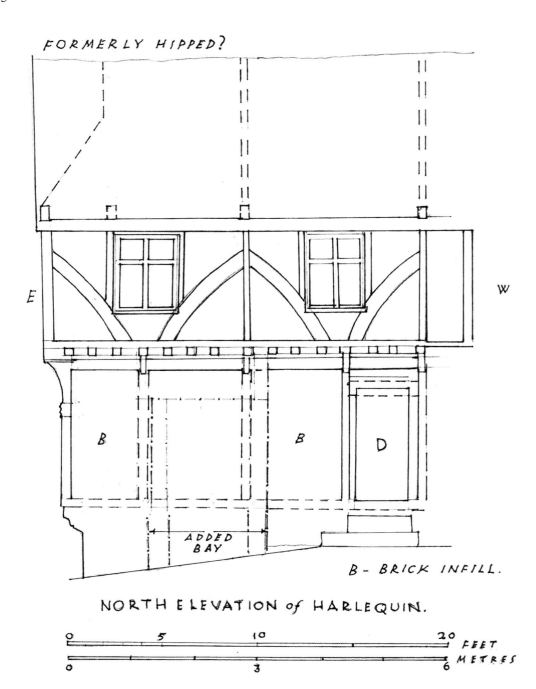

FORMERLY HIPPED?

E

W

B

B

D

ADDED
BAY

B - BRICK INFILL.

NORTH ELEVATION of HARLEQUIN.

Fig 33. North elevation
of the Harlequin,
no.22 Steep Hill

0   5   10   20 FEET

0   3   6 METRES

No.20 Steep Hill

This property now forms an extension to the Harlequin bookshop, and is accessed both from the latter and the street. It is two-storied, one room deep, and formerly two to three bays in length, being roofed parallel to the street. In the modern period its ground-floor area has been reduced. Its north wall is formed by the south end of the Harlequin and much of its external historic interest was lost in a total rebuild or re-facing in brick of the elevation to Steep Hill; in tandem with this, c.1900, went a wholesale re-roofing and the loss of earlier trusses. Within the roof space at the west end of the south wall are the embedded remains of one such truss comprising a tie beam and rafter the latter apparently incorporating a curved brace (?) at its base; its original form, however, is difficult to determine. In the ground-floor shop a ceiling beam chamfered and stopped a short distance in from the front wall would seem to imply either that it was lodged in a more substantial wall, i.e. one of stone, or that it marked the line of a deposed timber-framed wall, implying that the upper storey may have been jettied to the street. On the soffit of the same beam a mortice, some few feet in from the back or west wall, probably

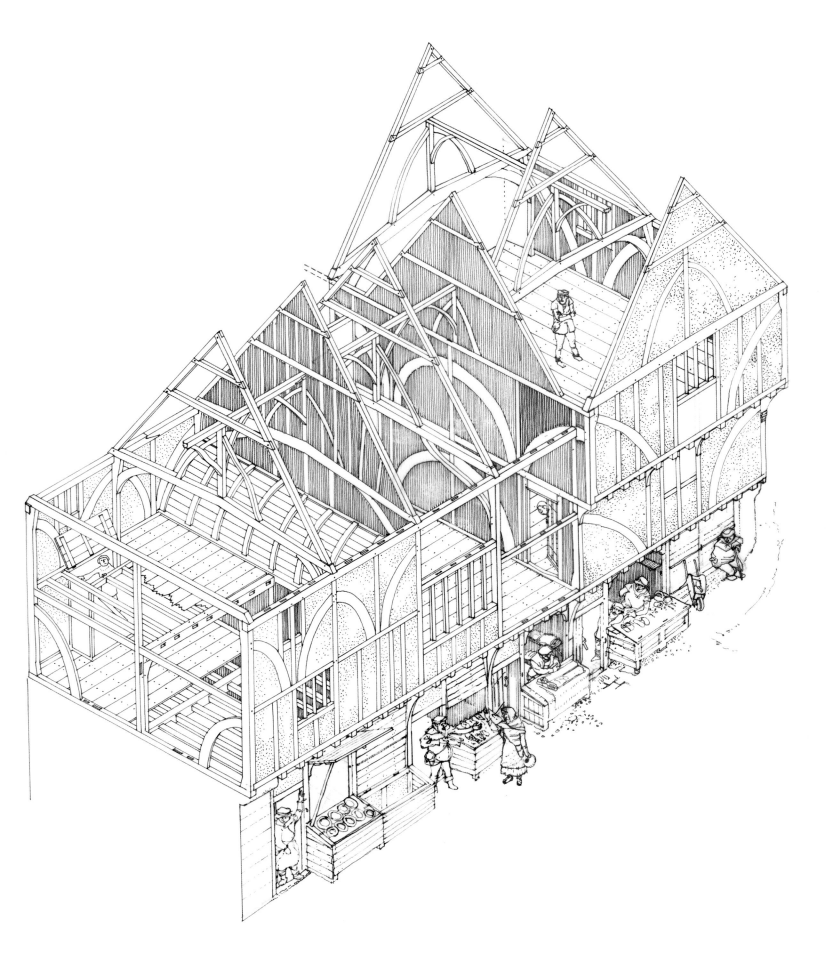

Fig 34. Isometric drawing of the entire Harlequin site, nos 19–22 Steep Hill

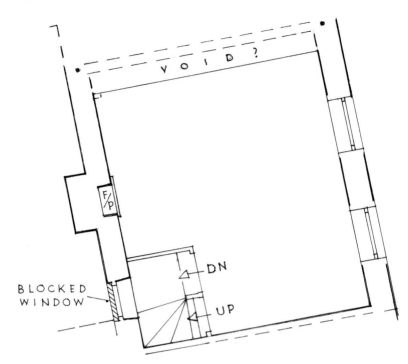

FIRST FLOOR PLAN

Fig 35. Plans of no.19 Steep Hill, part of the Harlequin

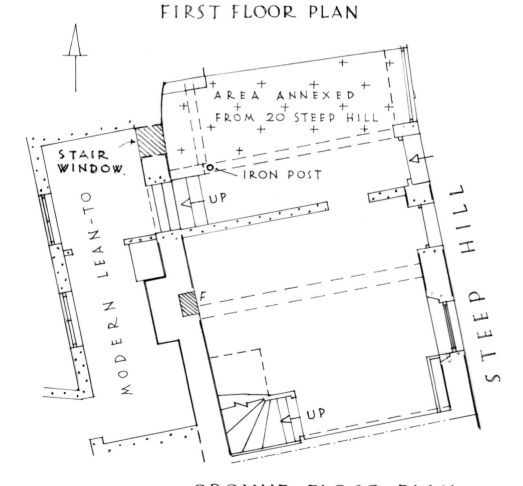

GROUND FLOOR PLAN.

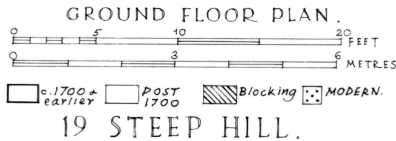

19 STEEP HILL.

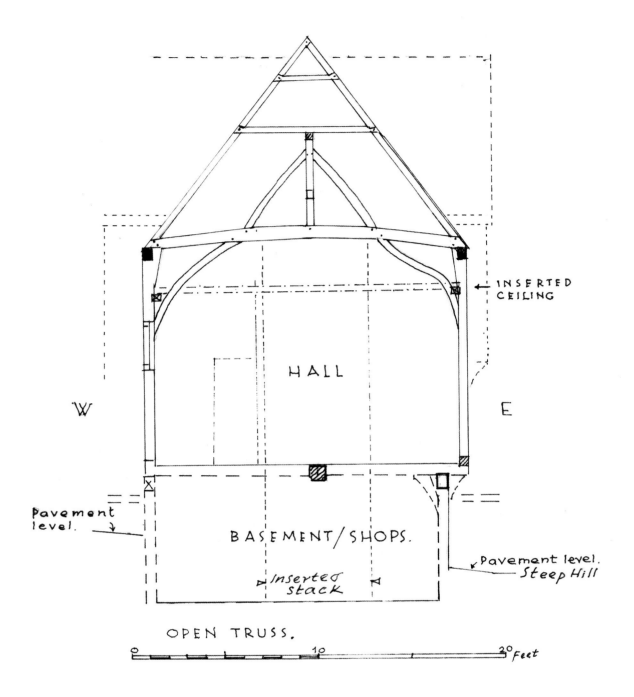

INSERTED
CEILING

HALL

W

E

Pavement
level.

BASEMENT/SHOPS.

Inserted
stack

Pavement level.
Steep Hill

OPEN TRUSS.

0   10   20 Feet

Fig 36. (above) Section from south side, no.19 Steep Hill
Fig 37. (left) Former Harlequin quoits ground, behind nos 15–16 Steep Hill

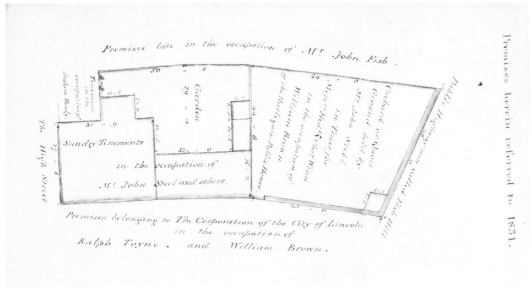

Fig 38. (*left*) *Photograph of the Harlequin from the south-east*
Fig 39. (*below*) *Photograph of first-floor hall and cove, the Harlequin*
Fig 40. (*above*) *Photograph of roof space, the Harlequin, showing reverse side of cove*

secured a vertical post. Openings made in the north and west walls of the shop possibly relate to when the south bay of no.21 and nos 19 and 20 were sub-let in 1835 to Mary Holmes and Edward Jackson respectively, or from an earlier stage.[56]

At first-floor level, a blocked opening in the west wall of no.20 has served as a former window, in this instance lighting a corner stair connecting to the shop; another blocking in the same wall appears to be that of a suppressed hearth. The west wall, rendered internally, is of stone construction and faced externally in part in brick. It is envisaged that the tenement would always have had rear access to the yard. The heating of the tenement was provided by a chimney in the west wall serving both floors.[57] There is no cellar. The only dating criteria available resides in the form of the chamfer stop on the ceiling beam and the embedded relic of the deposed roof: for the former a post-medieval origin and for the latter possibly an earlier and uncertain origin. The fact that the house makes use of the Harlequin's stone south wall could be seen as a borrowing available at any point in time after the latter's inception. A timber-framed structure as an initial phase for no.20 is a possibility, and one where use of the convenient north end wall would have left little or no evidence of attachment once removed.

No.19 Steep Hill

From a superficial viewing of its brick exterior it may be claimed as a structure of one or more builds, with the usual proviso that only an internal inspection might help to establish its true age and development. The fact that its south gable is rendered, and not made up in brick, ought perhaps to alert one to the possibility that the core of the house may retain some elements of timber-framed construction. A further pointer in this direction is that the brick frontage is of two periods, its lower half being the earlier, implying that for an unknown period in the transition from timber (?) to brick it may have retained

Fig 41. Photograph of the hipped south end of the main roof structure, the Harlequin

a framed upper storey. Currently, and on the evidence of its street front, what one is presented with is a two-storied brick-built house, post-1700, whose roof space provided attics. Reference to the plan,[58] however, shows the structure to have substantial walling that could well belong to an earlier build. Equally interesting is the manner by which the ground-floor area has been increased northwards into and at the expense of no.20; at this level the north wall of the enlarged shop is unrelated to divisions overhead, and one might infer from this that the former cross wall divisions in both tenements were of stud construction, and consequently their removal more easily effected.

Both nos 19 and 20 on plan have similar features and appear, perhaps mistakenly, to have originated as a unitary build, regardless of present external differences. Emphasising this pairing is the west wall with its lateral chimney stacks and corner staircases, and a near common north–south alignment. A small window in the same wall lit both the stair and its continuation to the attics, a similar arrangement implicit in no.20. What is less evident is confirmation that both tenements were ever timber-framed entities, in whole or part, prior to 1600.

17–18 Steep Hill

This tenement has been associated with, but in practical terms separated from, the Harlequin since the 16th century, since it was regarded even then as a separate leasehold. It was described in its leases as a cottage or tenement, but by the mid-19th century had been divided into two units.

The first lessee who is identifiable was William Richardson, given a 21-year lease at a rent of 5s per annum and a quitrent of 50 wardens, in 1597; this was renewed in 1609.[59] Alderman Roland Lillie is noted in 1617; his quitrent was 100 wardens.[60] Edward Kelham, lessee here from 1626,[61] also held the Harlequin for a while. James Thornhill lived here c.1685,[62] and after him in 1719 a baker named William Boole, possibly an ancestor of the famous George Boole.[63] William also owned a freehold house nearby called the Mayor's Chair House, probably just round the corner in Danesgate, but alternatively on the site of the present Steep Hill House. He had been left this in the will of his father, also named William.[64] Anne Sturtevant was given a lease in 1748, although as not being free of the City she had to have a proxy lessee, John Garmston.[65] From 1780 to 1820 Sarah Trotter, spinster, through her proxies, held the tenancy.[66]

From its external features the building is superficially of early to mid-18th-century origin, two-storied with a tiled roof, and of brick construction. What seems to be an uneven division of the building is reflected in the shop area on the ground-floor, although it is not clear whether this was indeed the original arrangement or a later encroachment. Some evidence for timer-framing, noticeably in the street frontage of no.18, came to light during recent rebuilding work, albeit too late for detailed investigation in this account.

1   L1/1/1/3, f.4v
2   L1/1/1/2, f.179v
3   MLI 94063
4   MLI 94062
5   MLI 94064
6   *Ex* 12/6 includes a
    photograph of this before
    its removal in the 1920s to
    provide a parish meeting
    room
7   L1/1/1/3, f.162v
8   L1/3/2, f.100v
9   Ciij 9.1/78
10 LC Rolls 1/150; Ciij 9.1/326
11 LCC Wills 1758/76
12 LCC Wills 1761/87
13 LC Leases 516
14 L3/2530/7-8
15 *ibid.*,11-12
16 *LCL* 5083
17 *BB*, f.204 no.694; *Cal.IPM*
    13 Edward III,91, no.45; 17

    Edward III,109, no.16
18 Lease plan for the Harlequin,
    LC Leases 748
19 By Willson and Betham
20 Hill, *VL*, 227n; deeds in
    the custody of Lincoln City
    Council; L3/721,722
21 Harding's deeds, Lincoln City
    Council
22 *Figs* 27, 29
23 *Fig 27*
24 See below, p.56
25 *CChR* 1226-1257,460; *RA viii*,
    nos 2279-2281
26 See below, pp.63, 141
27 *Cant* 274-278
28 *BB*, f.204, nos 694-5
29 *ibid.* f.236, no.825; f.250v,
    no.884
30 *Rot. Chartarum et Inq Ad Quod
    Damnum*, 37 Edw III, Record
    Commissioners 1803, p. 333

    no.5, and 45 Edw III p. 340
    no.11
31 *RA viii*, no.2278
32 *Ex.* 12/6
33 L1/1/1/2 f.87v
34 *ibid.*, f.166v, 184; L1/1/1/3
    f.71v
35 L1/1/1/4 f.2
36 L1/3/2 f.13v
37 L1/1/1/4 f.274
38 Hill, *TSL*,130
39 L1/1/1/6 p. 343
40 *ibid.* p. 642
41 LC Leases 201
42 LC Leases 395
43 LC Leases 594
44 LC Leases 748
45 Harding's deeds, Lincoln City
    Council; Exley 12/6
46 Harding's deeds
47 Notes by Joan Varley in the
    Survey of Lincoln files

48 *Fig 25*
49 *ibid.*
50 *Fig 27*
51 *Fig 41*
52 *Fig 34*
53 *Fig 31*
54 *Fig 30*
55 *Fig 41*
56 *Fig 35*
57 *Fig 31*
58 *Fig 35*
59 L1/1/1/3 f.238; L1/1/1/4
    f.68
60 L1/3/2 f.47
61 Ciij 9.1/127
62 LC Rolls 1/150
63 LC Leases 86
64 LCC Wills 1714/24
65 LC Leases 248
66 LC Leases 431 and 630

14–16 STEEP HILL

From an examination of the 19th-century street plans and boundary details, the properties now represented by nos 14–16 Steep Hill appear to have been part of the same unit for a considerable age, even though no.14 is the only one of the three which has retained any real trace of its medieval architectural features. Fortunately the historical records are sufficiently informative, despite the difficulties of interpretation, as to enable a reconstruction of the tenemental history of the group from the late 12th to the early 14th century. The involvement of the Jews, particularly Jacob son of Leo, in the history of this part of the city adds a new facet to one of the most tragic and well-known stories of medieval Lincoln.

The starting point is the grant of a tenancy c.1190–95 by Gerard, priest of Newport, to Robert Turnur, minister or servant in the Cathedral, of all his land situated next to Robert's house to the south, at a rent of 18d per annum.[1] Turnur within a few years granted this and his own tenement to the Dean and Chapter,[2] and Gerard supported this with a grant or quitclaim from himself.[3]

The Chapter also acquired in the early 13th-century land from Newhouse Priory which had been the property of Hugh Paynel; this became merged with the other holdings.[4] They also re-granted to Alan, son of Robert Turnur, the property which his father had given them.[5] Richard, son in law of Robert Turnur, often called Richard le Fitheler, was also a tenant of part of the Chapter property here in the early 13th century.

Alan's son, another Robert le Turnur, granted a part of his holding c.1250–55 to Jacob son of Leo, an influential Jew.[6] To leave no doubt as to the importance of this transaction (a *starr*, relating to what is now no.14), the plot was precisely measured: from east to west 11 royal ells and a handsbreadth, approximately 42 feet/12.8 m, and from north to south 5⅞ royal ells, about 23 ft 6 ins/7.2 m, extending from Jacob's own house (no.13) on the south to Robert's land on the north, and from the street on the east to Robert's land on the west. Jacob's rent was to be 12d per annum.

The witness list entered on this document is almost unprecedented in Lincoln; this was one of the only documents we have which record both Christian and Jewish names side by side, six from each group. Christians: Master Laurence de Riston, physician and probably a relative of Master William le Rus, also on the list; Gilbert de Hesel, whose links with the castle, the Jews and Master William have already been discussed;[7] William le Denesman; John, nephew of Thorald; Warner the clerk to the Christian Chirographers (scribes who worked with their Jewish counterparts to administer Jewish land and financial transactions). On the Jewish side there were: Isaac son of Benedict, Garsie *Episcopus*, son of Judah, Peytevin le Grant, son of Manser, proprietor of one of Lincoln's synagogues, Hagin son of Master Moses, Benedict his brother, and Samuel son of Abraham, a Jewish Chirographer. To make this charter even more noteworthy, it has a Hebrew attestation at the foot.

Jacob's tenure, however, was to be cut dramatically short within a few years by his execution in 1255. He is now identified as the 'Copin' of the Little St Hugh story, and his end has been immortalised in ballad and in the pages of Hill's '*Medieval Lincoln*', as noted below.

After this, nothing is heard of no.14 for several years. As it was still technically part of the Turnur fee, it was not forfeited to the king on Jacob's execution, as were his other properties to the south, and his widow Marchote or Margot was allowed to continue

Fig 42. No.14 Steep Hill: starr of c.1250–55, with Hebrew subscript

living in no.13. Alice le Turnur, widow of Robert, died between 1263 and 1272, and nos 14–16 were transferred to her daughters Ivetta and Sarra. They sold their interest in the properties to the Chapter before 1272[8] and it was leased en bloc to Robert de Riston, the apothecary. The lease included the 12d pa rent from no.14 and also a rent of 3d pa from land held by John, nephew of Thorald in what is now Christ's Hospital Terrace. Robert was to pay one mark per annum for his lease.[9]

In 1277/78 Robert granted nos 15–16 to Isaac, son of Samuel, a Jew known to all as Hak the Chanter; Samuel could have been the man of that name, who was Jacob's brother in law.[10] Hak fell foul of the authorities in 1279, at the time of the coin-clipping pogrom, and his property was given to Osbert Long, who received several grants of former Jewish property both from the king, and also, later, from his brother John. Osbert transferred the property to Jacob, son of Hak,[11] which raises interesting questions about the inter-relationships between Christians and Jews at this time.

The cellar and solar at no.14 were excepted from the grant to Jacob, and were leased by Robert de Riston, here described as a spicer (alternative name for an apothecary) to Philip the carpenter at a rent of 3s 4d per annum, with an out-rent of 9d pa to John Stoule. This was a short-term arrangement, presumably to facilitate repairs or alterations. Only a year later Robert assigned the rental to William Findeluve, goldsmith, who received quitclaims from both Philip and John Stoule, indicating that he was now full owner of the site.[12]

In 1296/97 William sold it to Simon de Holm and on to William Wolman of Burreth, whose successor Roger le Wolleman granted it to Thomas de Haverholm, tailor to the Friars Preacher, and Agnes his wife, widow of Alexander Vigilis (the verger or wait at the Cathedral).[13] Alexander and Agnes had in 1291 received a lease of nos 15–16 from the Chapter and are known to have been lessees of other Chapter property in the parish of St George.[14] By 1312 Thomas had died,[15] and Agnes in 1320 granted the cellar and solar to Master Richard de Stretton for the augmentation of the Thornton and Gare Chantry.[16]

The 14th-century Chapter Accounts hold several references to nos 14–16, particularly no.14, as it was a chantry endowment. Cecilia Hare was the tenant from or before 1332.[17] There was a disastrous fire which occasioned a complete rebuild of no.14 c.1335; this cost £15 4s 11¾d (£15.25), and Cecilia received a rent abatement of 4s 10d (24p).[18] She may have been the mother of Robert Hare, bowyer, whose name supplants hers in the accounts before 1359;[19] he had already acquired the Harlequin in 1349. Although he died in 1362[20] his name still appeared on the rent rebate lists until at least 1400.[21] He was one of the bowyers after whom Bower Hill was so named.

15–16 Steep Hill

This tenement was allocated to the Common Fund of the Dean and Chapter at the Reformation. The first available and identifiable lease for this property is that of September 1566, given to George Woodruff, a 'poynder' or joiner, for 31 years at a rent of 8s per annum. It had an orchard or garden to the rear, which extended to the "Fyshe Markett", and the south bounds were the Dean and Chapter property at no.14 at the Steep Hill frontage and property belonging to St Paul's Parsonage (no.13) further westward. The north boundary was the property of the Mayor, Sheriffs and Commonalty of the City (nos 17–18 and the Harlequin); no separate mention was made of nos 40–42 Michaelgate.[22] After George's death his widow Ann renewed the lease in 1593, for a term of 40 years.[23]

John Lyon, a musician, was given a lease in 1602;[24] he died in 1616 and his probate inventory is memorable not only for having several bedsteads in the three main chambers and the parlour, but particularly for the long list of musical instruments described in the section 'In Implements'. He had two 'boundaries', a viola da gamba, a bass violin, a 'bandom', a tenor violin, three treble violins, a sithern (cittern), a 'gittare', two tenor clarinets and four treble cornets. Which musical group met there: perhaps the parish church orchestra or even a group associated with the Cathedral? He also had a pair of virginals in the Great Chamber.[25]

John Davy, a butcher, succeeded Sara Lyon, widow of John, and took a lease, also for 40 years, in 1627. By the time of the Parliamentary Survey of 1649 this had been assigned to William Wetherall, the tenement and orchard then being in the occupation of Edward Ripley. The property consisted of a hall, shop, kitchen, four chambers and a gardenstead.[26]

In 1668 begins a series of original leases. Richard Haslewood, painter, was given the same term, but for some reason his rent was increased from the original 8s per annum to 10s; very few Chapter leaseholds were revalued in this way, so it may be thought that some rebuilding work or other improvement had been made. Thomas Holmes had been occupying the property.[27] Haslewood died c.1708 and his widow Ellis stayed on, marrying c.1717 Thomas Thorp, an innholder from the Bail. Thorp received a lease in 1717.[28]

Daniel Wickham, a vintner from the Close, became lessee in 1731, followed by Elizabeth Rance, widow, in 1745. An occupant named Robert Fox is noted there throughout the period 1728–56.[29] One owner of no.13, the main south bound, during the first half of the 18th century was Thomas Sympson, well known to local historians as the antiquary and author of the 'Adversaria'.

Luke Trotter and Alice his wife were lessees of nos 15–16 in 1759.[30] After his death in 1773 Alice took over the lease, but she died at some point between 1777 and 1784, at which time both of their wills were proved.[31] The reason for the delay in probate is unknown, but there may have been family complications. Luke left the lease to Alice, with the proceeds of assignment of the lease after her death going to their son George and granddaughter Sarah. Alice, making her will in 1777, left her pots and crockery in trust for the sole use of Sarah, and also her ring and wearing apparel. In the event, Hannah

Trotter, widow and daughter in law, took the lease in 1787.[32] She remarried, taking the surname Hales, but was again widowed before 1801, when she renewed her lease:[33] it was renewed again in 1815.[34] By 1831 three additional lodgers were being housed here, and the rear part of the holding, nearest the Old Fish Market (Michaelgate) had been taken over unofficially by the landlord of the Harlequin for use as a quoits ground.[35]

John Steel took over in 1831, and the rent was reduced to 8s 10d pa because of the assignment of the quoits ground, for which the lessees of the Harlequin now had to pay 1s 2d pa to the Chapter. A note endorsed on the lease records 'Expired July '69'. In 1851 the Chapter rental book mentions the rent adjustment.[36]

Robert Peel, clock and watchmaker, was among the late 19th-century occupants of no.16, noted in the street directories from 1872 to 1891. Alois Sattele, also a watchmaker, had lived there in 1863.

This is a pair of semi-detached tenements having between them a central through passage leading to a common back yard. Each dwelling had a back kitchen in a short rear wing. The date of their erection probably lies in the mid-19th century. In 1831 the overall shape of the property on the lease plan differs considerably from that of the present building and is captioned: 'Sundry Tenements in the occupation of Mr John Steel and others'. From notes in pencil on the dorse of a lease of 9 September 1815 the house was occupied as follows: in front Wm Coulson 1 low room, front and 2 chambers; in middle John Stoker 1 low room and 1 chamber; at west end John Steel (present owner), 2 low rooms; in front 1 chamber Sarah Maltby; south side in front Chas. Woodhall, 1 low room and 1 chamber.[37]

This combination of low room and a chamber focuses on the small tenement currently carrying the street number 14 and included on the 1831 plan, its caption noting the name of the occupier as Joshua Kealey. What is striking on the lease plan is the impression that Kealey's tenement is an intrusion into what otherwise would be a regular rectangular plot. Could it be that, far from being intrusive, this small house is the sole relic of a continuous range fronting Steep Hill, of which the greater part, i.e. nos 15–16, had survived to the early 19th century, and whose pencilled basic details are preserved? The Kealey tenement then formed part of the south bounds, the remainder being premises in the occupation of Mr John Fish and which may be confidently identified as no.13 Steep Hill. In an earlier lease of 1825, John Fish's land is cited as a northern bound to what, today, is no.12 Steep Hill.

From the Parliamentary Survey in 1649,[38] nos 15–16 are represented as follows: 'William Wetheral, assignment of all that tenement in St Michael's parish in tenure of Edward Ripley, a hall, shop, kitchen, 4 chambers and gardenstead, Henry Tutty south, city lands north, old fish market west, high street east. In the margin, 8s'.

14 Steep Hill

The first lease recorded in the post-Reformation period was given to William Gillowe, glover, who was already in occupation, in September 1601, for 40 years at the modest rent of 2s per annum; this may have been because the tenement was decayed and dilapidated, but apparently habitable.[39] It was still in poor condition when Ann Cullis, the new lessee, was contracted to rebuild her tenement at her own costs, with "timber, tile and other stuff" within a year.[40] In the Parliamentary Survey of 1649 Henry Tutty was lessee, probably by assignment, and William Denton was the occupant of the one low room and one chamber mentioned as being the accommodation, which may not have changed much from the medieval cellar and solar referred to earlier.[41] Amy Tutty, widow of Henry, renewed the lease in 1668, 1681 and 1697.[42] This tenement on a number of occasions was leased with property in St Swithin's parish.[43]

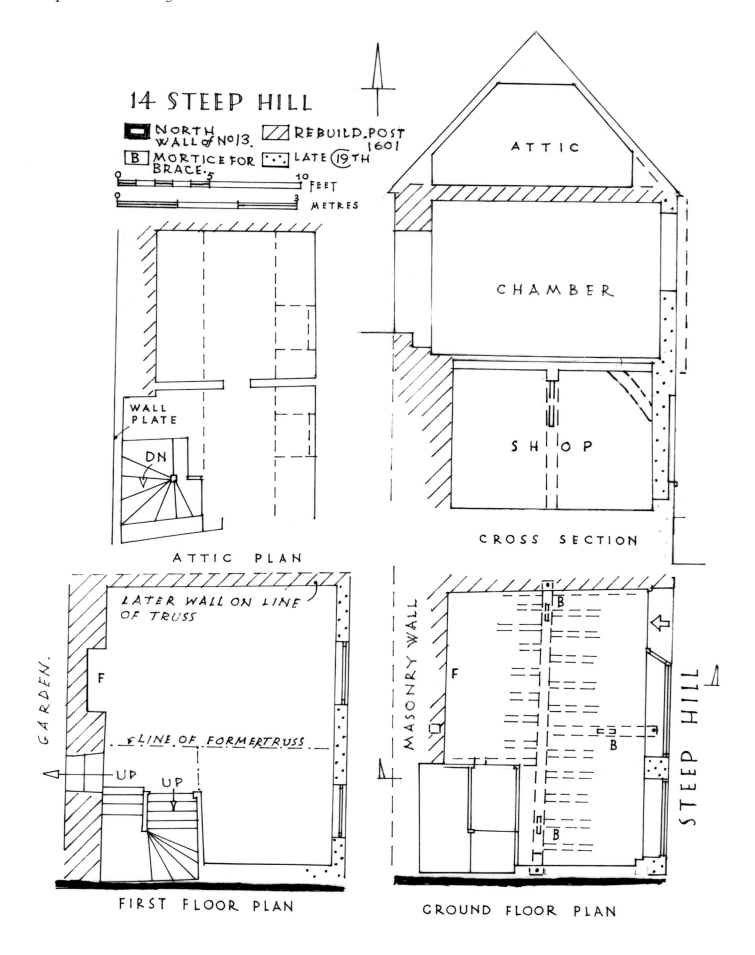

14 STEEP HILL

▭ NORTH WALL of Nº13.
▨ REBUILD. POST 1601
B MORTICE FOR BRACE.
⋯ LATE 19TH

FEET
METRES

ATTIC PLAN

WALL PLATE

DN

LATER WALL ON LINE OF TRUSS

GARDEN.

F

LINE OF FORMER TRUSS

UP   UP

FIRST FLOOR PLAN

CROSS SECTION

ATTIC

CHAMBER

SHOP

GROUND FLOOR PLAN

MASONRY WALL

STEEP HILL

F

B

B

B

Fig 43. Plan and cross section, no.14 Steep Hill

Fig 44. Photograph of street elevation, no.14 Steep Hill

Joseph Durance, mason, was given a lease in 1849, and renewed in 1856 and 1863.[44] Three years before he entered, the Chapter asked Edward Betham, the surveyor, for a report on the fabric, which shows it to be a regular architectural puzzle, with walls built of three different types of material. Some building work was undertaken from 1849. A William Nicholson was occupier in 1849, but it cannot be confirmed if he was the architect.

This small building has firm evidence of a timber-framed structure that was two-storied, aligned as now, north–south, with its upper storey jettied towards the street. The present facade in brick would seem to be work of c.1900 that has effectively removed the jettied overhang. What survives internally consists of an open joisted ceiling within the shop area and the remains of principal posts on the upper floor. An axial main beam in the shop and into which the ceiling joists are tenoned was formerly supported by brackets

ARCHITECTURAL
DESCRIPTION

61

from the north and south end walls. In the south wall a bressummer has similar evidence for bracing from the east and west walls. At the rear (west) of the building, the ground/garden is at first-floor level.

A chimney which may be fully integral to the same west wall is of indeterminate age; its location in the back wall recalls similarly sited hearths in tenements elsewhere on this side of the street. Some advantage appears to have taken of the north party wall to no.13, a stone structure serving as a substantial revetment and marking the considerable difference in ground-levels from north to south. In this instance it appears that the frame of no.14 took advantage of the wall for stability and may have lodged timbers in it for further support (?). The description of the tenement in the lease book would appear to suggest that originally it occupied much the same ground as today.[45] If the identification is correct its condition structurally in 1601 is described then as "late decayed and fallen down", the leaseholder William Gillow, glover, lately dwelling there.[46] A covenant in 1632 attached to the lease to Anne Cullis directed her at her own proper costs to "re-edify and build upon the said messuage, tenement, or toftstead lately decayed, in good sort with all manner of tymber, tyle and other stuffs within one year next after the date of these presents and to keep so much tyled as hath heretofore been tiled".

By 1649 the description of the tenement in the parliamentary survey entry as "consisting of one lowe roome and one chamber, the building of rough stone, the covering of tile with a small toft or backside", suggests a somewhat rugged product of the earlier covenant. It is also at variance with the standing building, although the importation of second-hand timber-framed components and their employment at this period would not have been unusual nor beyond the capabilities of the average carpenter. A clear indication of how the bounds were arranged is shown on the lease plan of 1831 for nos 15–16 Steep Hill, and its accompanying description throws light on the shared south bounds to this plot; it will be seen that the north and south boundary walls run back to Michaelgate, formerly Fish Hill or the Old Fishmarket, and contain what is described as an orchard or quoit ground, then leased separately to the lessee of the Harlequin public house and held in trust.

11–13 STEEP HILL

DOCUMENTARY
HISTORY

In the discussion on no.14 above, there was a reference to Jacob's personal residence situated to the south of it.[47] This is without doubt the site of the present day no.13 Steep Hill. After Jacob's arrest and execution for the alleged murder of the boy Hugh (he was the 'Copin' mentioned in the contemporary accounts and subsequent ballads perpetuating the barbarous anti-Jewish myth), the Sheriff of Lincolnshire was ordered to take into custody the houses of those Jews who had been hung or had fled; their estates were to be appraised and the chirographers' chests examined to seize all their assets. This process was not yet complete by August 1256, when the Sheriff was ordered to sell the properties so seized and to enquire concerning their chattles (meaning particularly the debts owing to them).[48] Jacob's widow Marchote (Margot) was allowed to stay on in no.13, and was still alive c.1281, when her house was mentioned as the south bound of no.14.[49] She had a Christian maidservant named Emma, as did several of the wealthier Jews. This was contrary to statute, as Christians were not allowed to live with or serve Jews, but was generally ignored; there was, however, a concerted attempt to enforce the measures in 1278, and this unfortunately resulted in excommunication for Emma and a number of others.[50]

The king had decided in January 1257 to grant all of Jacob's houses, lands and rents to Hagin 'of Lincoln', son of Master Moses, who in that year was appointed Arch-Presbyter of all the Jews in England. This was more of an administrative than a religious role: the grant bound him to the king and distanced him somewhat from the local Jews, and he had a difficult balancing act to perform. Among the properties were three houses situated between the land of Henna (Hannah), Jewess, on the south and land of Robert le Turnur on the north, of which one was in the parish of St Cuthbert, another, in which Jacob dwelt, in the parish of St Michael on the Mount and of the fee of Newhouse Priory, and the third house, also in St Michael's, of the fee of Robert le Turnur. Jacob's own residence has been identified as no.13, so therefore he also owned no.12, and it is also established[51] that he had acquired no.14. It is reasonable then to suppose that Henna's property was no.11. The Charter Roll entry also establishes the medieval parish boundary between St Cuthbert and St Michael as being between nos 12 and 13.[52]

Hagin retained control of the three properties until 1275; his fall from grace (he was frequently in prison during this period and had a tower in the Tower of London named after him) was signalled by his being given a licence to sell them to Sir Stephen de Cheynduit, a favourite of Queen Eleanor with extensive estates in Oxfordshire and other Midland counties.[53] Stephen was also heavily in debt.[54] He was obliged in turn to sell the houses to the queen in July 1278, although she granted them back to him in 1286, but initially without power to sell.[55] In 1294/95 instead he leased a part of no.13, a plot measuring 5½ ells by 4½ ells (approx. 21ft × 17ft/6.4m × 5.2m) to Alexander Vigilis (the wait/verger) and Agnes his wife for the nominal rent of a clove of gillyflower, a common arrangement which no doubt masked the true terms and payment.[56] This appears to relate only to the street frontage. This document is a curious survival among the Chapter archives, because at no time did the house actually belong to them in later years, whereas we know that nos 14 and 12, with which it was closely linked, did so.

There is, however, one very good reason for the presence of this document in the archives. No.13 was among those properties formerly belonging to Hagin which were eventually sold by Stephen, son of Sir Stephen de Cheynduit, in 1299 to Gilbert de Atherby (of Atterby) and John of St Ives.[57] Soon afterwards John relinquished his rights to Gilbert.[58] This house was retained by Gilbert until his death, thought to have occurred between 1316 and 1320, but was probably leased as early as 1312 to dom. John de Drax, rector of Collingham. Some of Gilbert's properties[59] descended to his son John.

The succession from Hagin through to Gilbert and particularly the reference to John de Drax exactly mirrors the enigmatic entries in the Chapter Accounts to arrears payable from the *magna aula* of Hagin from 1304/05 onwards.[60] In these accounts the name of Hagin, although anachronistic, merely shows a previous connection with the annual payment of 12d per annum to the Chapter; this sum is identical with those payable to the Chapter from no.14[61] and part of nos 15–16.[62] The name J. Drax occurs in the Arrears lists only once, in 1312/13,[63] which, as noted above, could correspond with his occupation of the house, and is followed by a gap of several years, denoting the payment of rent. Gilbert's name recurs in the list owing 3s in 1317/18.[64] He may have died during this period. In 1333/34 John de Atherby is recorded as owing 12d.[65]

12 Steep Hill was the third of Hagin's properties to devolve to the Cheynduit estate,[66] but there are no extant deeds for the final transfer to the Chapter, which may have taken place in the time of John de Atherby or even later.

No.11, also a freehold, was, as mentioned above, in the mid-13th century the property of Henna the Jewess. She may be the lady of the same name who was the widow of Judas mentioned in the Jewish Plea Rolls of 1272.[67] The bonds detailing debts due to her were the subject of another entry in 1278.[68] What became of her property in 1290 at the Expulsion has not yet been discovered, unless it had previously been transferred to one of the other known Jews whose property in St Cuthbert's parish is listed in the *Abbreviatio*.[69]

13 Steep Hill

Apart from an interesting run of 18th- and 19th-century deeds, the majority of references gathered for this account have come from stray deeds, wills, inventories and boundary references. In the 16th century and the early part of the 17th, this freehold was owned by the parish, or strictly speaking the parsonage of St Paul, the rents being paid to the incumbent; how far back this arrangement went in time is unknown, and there are no relevant parish records extant. Robert Nixon is mentioned as a tenant in 1589/90,[70] and in 1601 Oliver Huddlestone, tailor.[71] Oliver left to his wife Cecily one room for her to dwell in, i.e. the kitchen, and also a little house adjacent; the kitchen abutted Oliver's leasehold, and there was a courtyard to the west of it. The will was proved in 1604,[72] and Oliver left a very scanty inventory, with assets worth not much more than £5.[73]

In 1728 Thomas Sympson, gent., purchased the house from George Houghton and Thomas Fitchett. He was a scrivener, and also at some point lessee of the Cardinal's Hat, but more importantly for us was a noted antiquary and local historian, the author of 'Adversaria'. He lived at no.13 until his death in 1752, having in 1732 placed the property in a family trust. Ann, his widow, continued to live there, but ownership passed to their son, the Revd Thomas Sympson (d.1786), and after his death to Mary Sympson of the Bail, milliner. By the late 1760s the Sympsons were no longer in residence, the house being let: Dr Malcolm Fleming was the occupant in 1763, Matthew Hickson and others in 1771, followed by George Miller (1784), Elizabeth Miller, widow (1791) and Penelope Miller (1801).[74]

Mary Sympson sold up in 1812, the Steep Hill house being conveyed to John Fish, glass warehouse man, who owned property in several parts of the city. The plot was partitioned and some parts sold to a developer named Ashton. John Fish set up a lodging house, and in 1854 sold no.13 to Thomas Stephenson, after whose death it was acquired by Edward Coulson, clerk in the Probate Office.[75] For a long period from 1895 onwards, A.E. Syson, furniture dealer and French polisher, conducted his business from here.[76]

ARCHITECTURAL DESCRIPTION

No.13 provided useful detail when undergoing repairs at the time of the survey, with particular reference to altered floor levels within the street range; there were also indications of former intercommunication by way of common floor levels with no.12 to the south. The building, now two-storied throughout, is stone walled in its greater length and has a rendered frontage to Steep Hill which, internally, has pointers to a timber-framed predecessor in its upper storey. The shop on the ground-floor front is now a generously high-ceiled room, a height obtained at the expense of a reduced cellar and the blocking of a fireplace in the west wall chimney stack. The stack originally served both the shop area and the back room in the range to the west, and may itself be an insertion. Related to this is a now concealed hearth (FP 1) in the shop face of the stack, and which has above it, embedded in the wall face, a long mortised timber, the relic of a superseded flooring scheme and is *ex situ*. A much smaller hearth was formed subsequently to serve the front room at its present level.

On the west face of the stack, the hearth has made use of a wave-moulded length of timber to serve as a lintel.[77] Linking both front and back parts of the tenement is a passage from the street an alignment on the north side next to the high stone wall that forms the boundary with no.14. A baulk of ground forming the passage floor adjoining the shop curtails the cellar area, and may represent an ancient arrangement. There is a considerable difference in levels between the passage and the adjoining shop floor, the latter being much lower – as witness the cross section. One therefore has to visualize the passage level as that of a missing ground-floor in the shop area, in order to reinstate the former original heights of cellar, shop and chamber.[78] Unfortunately the chamber fronting the street is difficult to interpret as to whether an east facing gable was intended

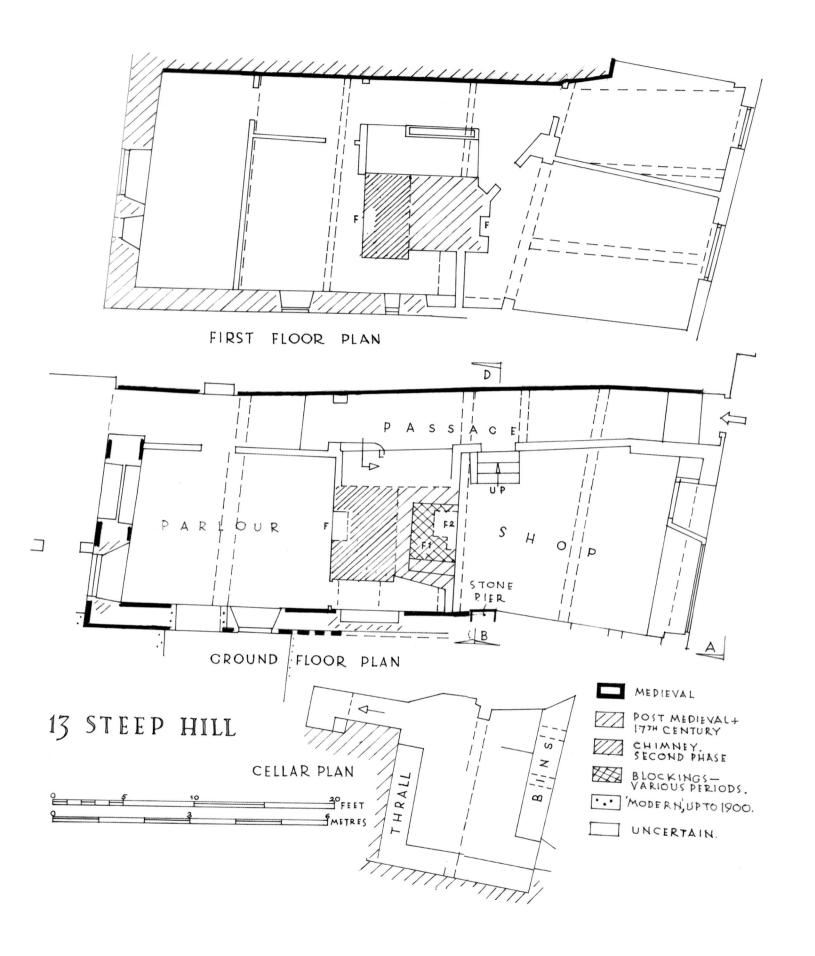

FIRST FLOOR PLAN

D

PASSAGE

UP

PARLOUR   F

F2

F1

SHOP

STONE
PIER

B

A

GROUND FLOOR PLAN

13 STEEP HILL

CELLAR PLAN

THRALL

BINS

0   5   10   20 FEET

0   3   6 METRES

▮ MEDIEVAL

▨ POST MEDIEVAL +
17TH CENTURY

▨ CHIMNEY,
SECOND PHASE

▨ BLOCKINGS—
VARIOUS PERIODS.

⋅⋅⋅ 'MODERN', UP TO 1900.

▭ UNCERTAIN.

*Fig 45. Ground-floor, first-floor and cellar plans,
no.13 Steep Hill*

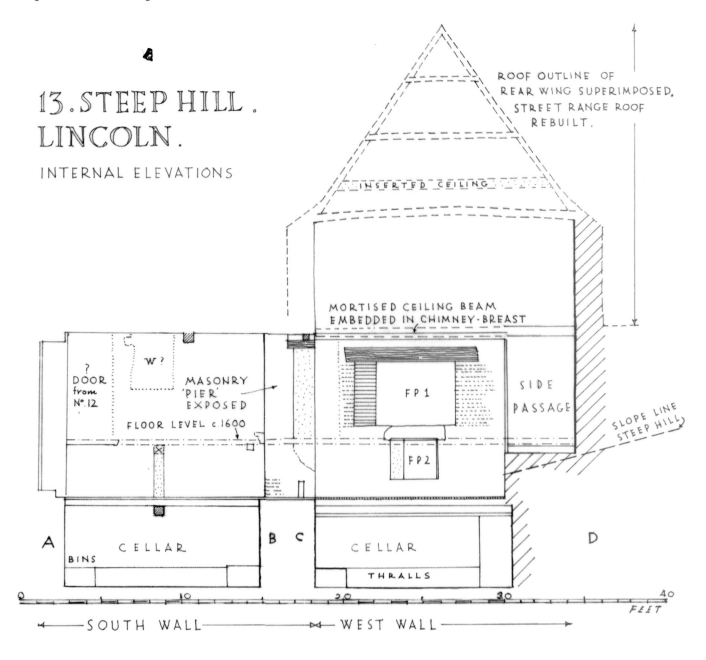

13. STEEP HILL.
LINCOLN.
INTERNAL ELEVATIONS

ROOF OUTLINE OF REAR WING SUPERIMPOSED. STREET RANGE ROOF REBUILT.

INSERTED CEILING

MORTISED CEILING BEAM EMBEDDED IN CHIMNEY-BREAST

W ?

? DOOR from N°.12

MASONRY 'PIER' EXPOSED

FLOOR LEVEL c.1600

FP 1

FP 2

SIDE PASSAGE

SLOPE LINE STEEP HILL

A CELLAR

BINS

B C CELLAR

THRALLS

D

0 10 20 30 40 FEET

← SOUTH WALL → ← WEST WALL →

Fig 46. (above) Sectional drawings, no.13 Steep Hill
Fig 47. Photographs of former fireplaces in shop wall, no.13 Steep Hill

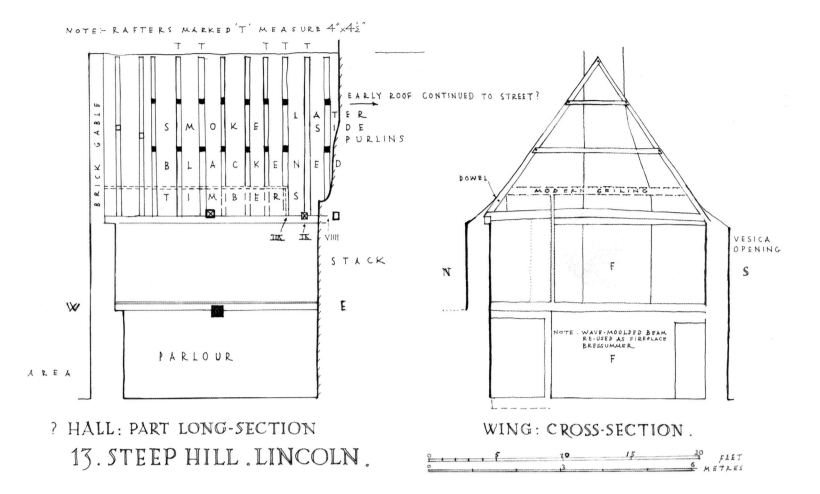

? HALL: PART LONG-SECTION
13. STEEP HILL. LINCOLN.

WING: CROSS-SECTION.

and then abandoned in favour of one aligned, as now, north–south, such is the mix of timbers that confronts the investigator.

The roof of the rear wing to no.13 is of a simple A form, and one first encountered in the 13th-century roof of Deloraine Court, James Street,[79] where each rafter couple has two well-separated collar beams and no lengthwise stiffening for support.[80] The existing purlins in the Steep Hill roof are later insertions related to a disruption of the rafters when the large chimney stack was built at the junction of the street range and the wing. A window, now blocked, has an ovolo moulded frame and mullions of 17th-century character and, because it lit a small lobby next to the south side of the stack originally, it could indicate, roughly, the period of alteration for this end of the house. Coeval with the stack insertion is the upper floor in the wing. The wing roof timbers are soot encrusted, suggesting their having been exposed to the open hearth of a single-storied hall. To date it has not been possible to examine the junction between wall top and rafter ends in order to confirm that the roof is in situ and not transposed from elsewhere; interestingly, the wing roof has avoided being used for attic accommodation. The hall, if such was the role of the wing originally, occupies the full width of the plot in a similar manner to that of the hall and street range that one may still observe at no.29 Steep Hill.[81]

12 Steep Hill

Thanks to the allocation of this tenement to the Cathedral Fabric Fund, a relatively long list of lessees can be identified. There are Fabric rentals which are sporadic but reliable, going back in date to just before the Reformation, and a series of leases dating from 1590 to 1839. The name of John Hyppes appears in rentals of 1521 and 1536,[82] but there is a slight problem as the rent differs from that levied in later years, normally 4s pa. From 1572 to 1589 there is a much firmer identification, from a volume of Fabric rentals.[83]

Fig 48. Internal elevations, no.13 Steep Hill

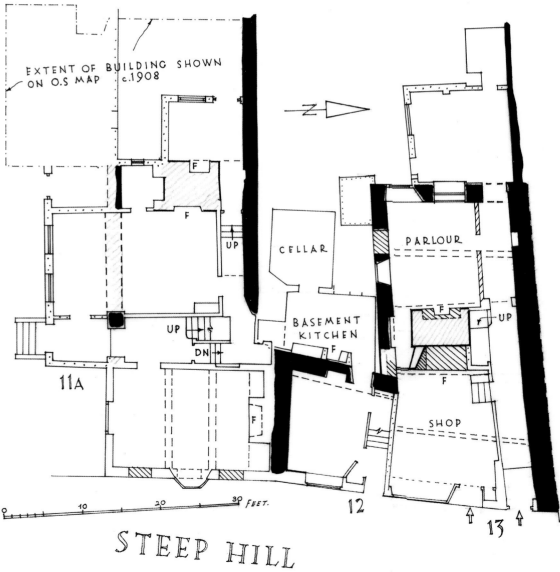

Fig 49. (left) Ground plan for no.12 Steep Hill, showing relationship with nos 11 and 13

Fig 50. (above) Exterior photograph of nos 11–13 Steep Hill, from a slide

In 1590 John Beteson or Beeston took a 40-year lease at 4s per annum.[84] Here we may learn that the western boundary was not the present-day Michaelgate but another holding, that of John Towneley Esq. Lancelot Forster was lessee and occupier from 1601 or 1602.[85] Dr Jeffrey Fieldhouse received a lease in 1633,[86] and also held for a while the two neighbouring freehold properties, nos 11 and 13 Steep Hill. From the late 17th century, however, no.12 was generally held by the owners of no.11.

The Revd George Yarbrough of Scampton took a lease in 1670. He was the husband of Mary (nee Fieldhouse), and he appears to have bought the former Towneley land to the west. Yarbrough obtained the leasehold by assignment after the Doctor's death in 1661 and Madam Trout, daughter of Dr Featley the Precentor, was living here just before 1670.[87] At this time the house contained a hall, a parlour, a little buttery next to the hall and another between the hall and parlour. There were three chambers over and also a garrett; the rent was now 5s per annum, a rare increase in the customary level of rental which is not explained.[88]

George assigned the lease to William Morrice c.1677,[89] having recently also sold to him the freehold of no.11 (see below). Morrice was the father of Abraham Morrice, mercer and well-known Quaker, who took over the Chapter leasehold on William's death in 1683[90] albeit unofficially, as Quakers were still denied certain civil rights at this time. Abraham's mother Susanna continued to live there until her death in 1692, and Abraham managed to secure a lease in 1698 after relaxation of some of the restrictions.[91] He died in 1705. Samuel Everatt, a family trustee, acted as lessee and in 1718 arranged an assignment of the lease to Stephen Long of Lincoln, gent., who was also connected to the Morrice family.[92]

Occupiers from 1828 onwards are known from the Willson and Betham Survey, census returns and street directories. Among them were Jonas Lazarus, clothes broker, c.1828–51, Abraham Moses, clothier, 1856–67 and Nathaniel Middleton, a labourer in 1881 but later a toy dealer, c.1881–99. John Everett and his wife were cabinet makers and furniture dealers here from 1901 to 1907, succeeded by A.E. Syson.

ARCHITECTURAL DESCRIPTION

Reference to the inclusive plan that covers nos 11, 12, and 13 makes it reasonably certain that, on structural grounds, no.12 originally marched with no.13.[93] This would explain the thin dividing wall between the two houses and the close conformity in former first-floor levels between each tenement.

The house itself is one room deep with a later kitchen at the rear, an extension made possible by part excavation into the hillside. Superficially the brickwork of the street elevation suggests a date in the late 17th to early 18th century,[94] but the thick walls to the remainder of the tenement must belong to an earlier phase when, conceivably, the frontage was of timber framing and one shared, presumably, with no.13.

Lease Book evidence citing details for no.12 Steep Hill notes in 1589/90 that the tenement forming its northern bounds was on 'lands of St Paul's church wherein Robert Nixon did of late dwell'.[95]

11 and 11A Steep Hill

This is an impressive freehold site on the hillside, with a larger than average plot size, possibly because of the steepness of the terrain in places, and it accommodated several tenements at one time. During the mid-16th century the owner was Ambrose Sutton of Burton, Esq., and then it passed to Agnes Duffield and Grace Maidenwell, who may have been his daughters. They sold it in 1576 to Alderman Thomas Winterbourne.[96] Cottages and tenements on the site were in the occupation of Henry Riche, Matthew Wiggeslay, Isabella Slater and Henry Knowles.

Around 1633 this property was acquired by Dr Jeffrey Fieldhouse, who, as noted above also held nos 12 and 13 at this time; Winterbourne's former holding was quoted as the south boundary in a lease of no.12.[97] Fieldhouse died in 1661 and, as with no.12, George Yarbrough took over, noted in a 1670 lease.[98] In 1675 it was conveyed to the Quaker William Morrice; the deed has since been lost, but a Final Concord gives the legalistic description of 'one messuage with a stable, gardens and orchard, and an acre of pasture...'.[99]

Susanna, William's widow, earned her own place in Lincoln's history for having been involved in a court case in 1685 for non-attendance at church.[100] Their son, Abraham, was a mercer who had a shop in the parish of St Peter at Arches. In 1703, just two years before his death, Abraham released his interest in no.11 Steep Hill to a group of trustees who all seem to be his fellow Quakers; his brother William made a similar release. The trustees Samuel Everatt and John Frotheringham handed over the trust estate to other trustees in 1716, and in 1718 both no.11 and the Chapter leasehold were handed over to Stephen Long.[101]

The subsequent history of the ownership of this house onwards to the early 19th century follows the pattern of the leasehold succession, but the story of the occupation of the house and its various tenements and outbuildings is perhaps more interesting. In the Willson and Betham Survey of 1828, the tenant was Quarter Master John Paxton of the Royal North Lincoln Militia, and the outbuildings were used as a depot for the Battalion: this was some years before the Militia found a permanent base on Burton Road. By 1841 Captain Francis Kennedy, an Irishman, had appeared on the scene as tenant, living there until the mid-1850s. It is quite possible that the use of this site by the Militia goes back to the period of the Napoleonic War.

One of the outstanding features of the grounds at no.11 was a large chestnut tree which is seen to dominate the hillside in many late 19th- and early 20th-century photographs. This was said by Mr Len Syson to have been planted in 1816 or 1817 in a position just south of the garden gate, from a conker picked up on the battlefield of Waterloo by Capt. Kennedy, then a young soldier aged about 24, who had taken part in the battle. The tree survived until 1962, when a storm rendered it too dangerous to remain standing.[102]

In about 1857 Miss Emma Edman established a Ladies' Seminary at no.11, and it became known as Chestnut House School. The school survived until the 1930s, and towards the end of the 20th century was the home of Mr and Mrs Albert Syson.

ARCHITECTURAL DESCRIPTION

The location of this tenement is of interest in that it has no direct approach by way of the street elevation, unlike others on the west side of Steep Hill. Its layout suggests that it inherited a block of building next to the street and roofed parallel to it, and to the rear an attached long range roofed east–west. The present decorative state throughout precludes any conclusions regarding the development of this property other than to note that no evidence of a timber-framed phase is visible and that the walling generally is substantial and a probable combination of brick and stone. The street elevation rising vertically through three storeys is of brick and of 18th-century origin; the installation of a small bow window c.1820 at a central point on this front was accompanied by the blocking of earlier openings at the same level; this feature presumably also marked associated internal improvements.

It has been shown how, in the case of no.13 Steep Hill, floor levels might be re-organised to meet later requirements and it may well be that something similar was undertaken in no.11, transforming what previously may have been a shop with cellar into a wholly domestic arrangement.

The plans[103] show the main entrance to the house as from the south or garden side. The dividing wall between the street range and the back east–west range is thin, rising through two storeys, and is held to be of brick construction and 18th-century in origin.

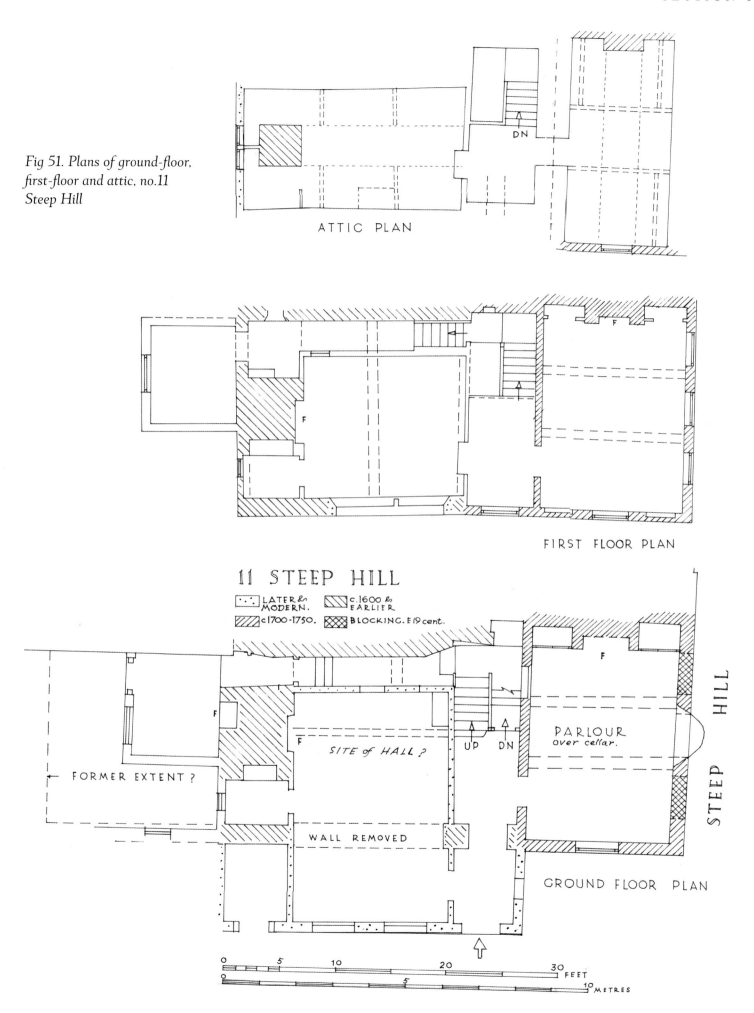

Fig 51. Plans of ground-floor, first-floor and attic, no.11 Steep Hill

ATTIC PLAN

FIRST FLOOR PLAN

11 STEEP HILL

LATER & MODERN.   c.1600 & EARLIER
c.1700-1750.   BLOCKING. E19 cent.

F

FORMER EXTENT ?

SITE of HALL ?

WALL REMOVED

UP   DN

PARLOUR over cellar.

STEEP HILL

GROUND FLOOR PLAN

0   5   10   20   30 FEET
0   5   10 METRES

Fig 52. Street plan, no.10 Steep Hill to no.1 Steep Hill and nos 8–24 Strait

A single-storied modern extension added to the south wall of the back range, appears to account for the removal of the major part of the encroached wall on the ground-floor. The ground plan shows a corridor against the north wall of the back range, a convenience of modern origin, and a feature repeated also on the upper floors. Less easy to explain is the position of the large axial chimney stack at the westernmost extent of the back range, unless one postulates a former continuation of the building westwards and that what one is seeing is the result of an earlier truncation.

The general size and proportions of No.11 presumably reflect those of the tenement it superseded in the 'brick phase'. That which was replaced most likely sported a solar above shops at the street front with a back range of building that included an open hall and further chambers, workshops stables etc. The other interesting aspect is the generous open ground that extends to the south and forms the bounds of no.10 Steep Hill, an area that for a considerable interval has carried no permanent building and is shown as such on Padley's map of Lincoln of 1842.

8–10 STEEP HILL

The sole medieval reference thought to be relevant to no.10 Steep Hill is contained in the same list of properties acquired by Hagin in 1257, as mentioned above.[104] A house in the parish of St Cuthbert, south of one which was owned by Henna, was held by Isaac, brother of Elias Martrin.[105] This reference, however, cannot yet be identified with the same property.

The situation regarding nos 8-9 Steep Hill is even more difficult to interpret for the medieval period. It seems possible that they were both part of an extensive holding, which by the late 18th century[106] stretched back towards the road later called Michaelgate, in earlier centuries often referred to as part of Hungate or the Street of the Parchment Makers. The 1257 schedule is silent as to the parish in which this estate was situated: that portion abutting Steep Hill was undoubtedly in the parish of St Cuthbert, but that portion which fronted onto Hungate/Michaelgate was probably in the parish of St Peter Stanthaket. The boundaries between these two parishes have not been accurately determined.[107] Some of the medieval references to property in St Peter Stanthaket, which may possibly be in or near this area, have yet to be matched up with later leaseholds.[108]

10 Steep Hill

For whatever reason, no.10 Steep Hill emerged from the documentary 'wasteland' of the late medieval period in the hands of the Mayor, Sheriffs and Commonalty of the City of Lincoln, and was leased out in 1569 to the Graceman, Warden and Fellows of the Company of Carpenters for 99 years at a rent of 6s per annum. Also included as a makeweight in the lease was a small gardenstead in the Old Fish Market, charged at 8d pa.[109]

Owing to the length of this lease it may be assumed that it was a 'repairing lease', where the tenants were normally responsible for maintenance and repairs: the site may have been in considerable disrepair, and the Carpenters were presumably in a position to organise the work. This lease was revoked in August 1603; it was stated that the Hall "is suffered to come to great ruin, therefore the lease is forfeit", which does not reflect well on the Guild.[110] Richard Rawe, a pewterer, was to have a lease and make specific repairs, but this arrangement was itself revoked and the Carpenters given a second chance to proceed with the work.[111] By September 1604 they had either not started the work, or had perhaps only just begun it, and they were supplanted by George Carter, a plumber and glazier who lived nearby and was specifically tasked with re-edifying the Carpenters' Hall within 18 months.[112]

Justinian Walwyn, instrument maker, took a reversionary lease in September 1617 and another in 1625.[113] He occupied the premises for a number of years, and one of the rare Commonwealth references to Corporation leaseholds (in 1656) concerned his joint occupation with William Johnson, which was concluded in that year. Henry Bromhead took over at that point, on a 41-year term, still at 5s pa, a sum which was to remain unchanged until 1835.[114]

The lessee in 1738 was John Bailey as trustee for Mary Doubleday of Aubourn; John Armstrong was in occupation, and it was about this time that the house was rebuilt.[115]

The final lease before the enfranchisement of the City leaseholds in 1835 was Thomas Skepper, ironmonger, who was trustee for William Taylor, surveyor, the man responsible for many of the site plans in the Corporation leases which are so useful to the local historian.[116] The plan for his own lease shows a stable at the Fish Hill end of the premises. Taylor purchased the freehold by feoffment dated 24 August 1835 for £96.[117]

In 1841 George Morton, stonemason, and Elizabeth his wife were the occupiers,[118] and two years later Robert Gardiner Hill was living there.[119] He was a surgeon at the

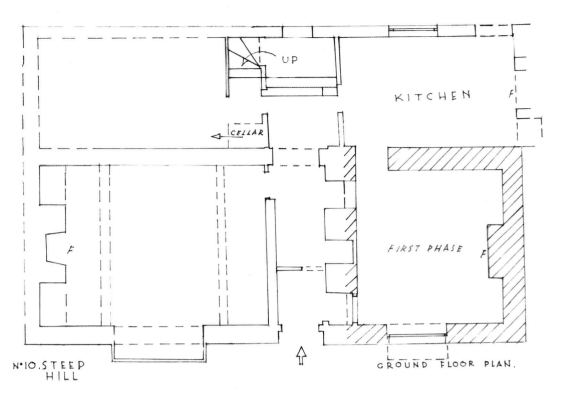

N°.10. STEEP HILL

GROUND FLOOR PLAN.

Lincoln Lunatic Asylum. After him the house was occupied successively by Meredith Redman, MRCS, surgeon and apothecary (c.1850-90), George Mounsey (1891–1901) and later by other surgeons.

ARCHITECTURAL
DESCRIPTION

This is a two-storied brick house with attics, built in two stages: the earlier of the 18th century, and both parts given projecting bay windows fronting the street in the later 19th century, together with other refinements of that period. The steep slope it occupies and its alignment north–south on the west side of the street has permitted the provision of cellars beneath the south end of the house; these are approached both from the street and internally. A vertical joint in the brickwork to the right hand of the entrance doorway rises the full height of the frontage, and internally a corresponding division is visible in the chamber above the kitchen. Of this bi-partite arrangement it can be shown that the north end of the house was rebuilt first; this is marked by a three-course brick plat-band that extends from the straight joint to the north gable end.

Internally the north end floor and ceiling levels differ from those in the south part of the house, and perhaps such levels reflect those of a former dwelling subsequently replaced at its south end. The lean-to against the west side of the northern end of the house would seem to be of a piece with the first half of the 18th-century build. A modest heightening of the outer west wall has allowed a chamber to be formed above the kitchen. What is retained is a long embedded timber plate set on a single brick ledge in the former back wall and to which both the past and present roof rafters were fixed. One may see in this simple duality a small habitable unit, sustained by a back kitchen providing the means whereby persons looking to enlarge by rebuilding their residence could subsist moderately. Precisely how access was contrived to gain the upper floor probably relied on a stair within the ground-floor room in the main range – or perhaps the southern part of the house awaiting rebuilding provided the means of access.

The present plan of the house is centralised about the entrance hall, with heated rooms on either hand and a staircase hall at the rear; the latter, along with the kitchen, are accommodated in lean-to projections. From the staircase hall a narrow stair leads to the cellar, an area sub-divided to store foodstuffs, coal, beers and wines etc.; it has a joisted ceiling that has early reed and plaster attached – its original traditional finish –

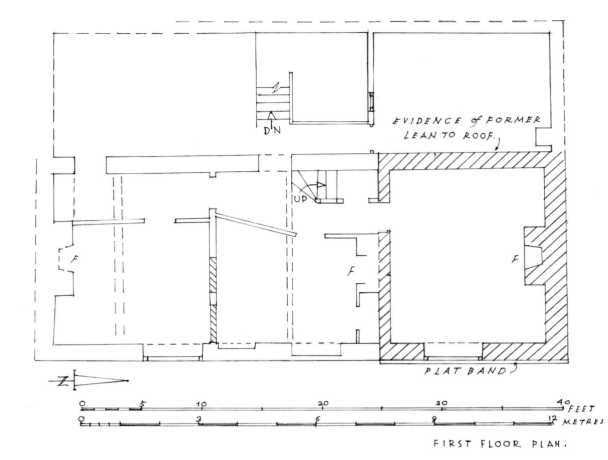

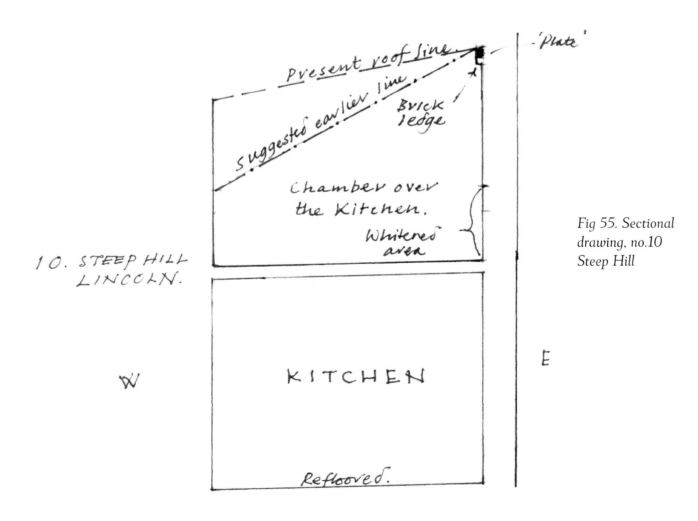

Fig 53. (opposite) Ground-floor plan, no.10 Steep Hill

Fig 54. (left) First-floor plan, no.10 Steep Hill

FIRST FLOOR PLAN.

Fig 55. Sectional drawing, no.10 Steep Hill

75

Fig 56. Exterior photograph, no.10 Steep Hill

and a technique that is found elsewhere in the house. The street door to the cellar is at the extreme south end of the frontage and has a small window or hatch, a short distance to the north, presumably to receive coal deliveries from the pavement. The front wall footings of the house continue a short distance to the north, though whether this is simply consolidation related to the higher ground of the garden to nos 11 and 11A may be worthy of further investigation.

By far the greater number of properties on Steep Hill are roofed parallel to the street and in descent; such an arrangement makes a great deal of sense in terms of drainage and the full economical use of the individual plots. No.13 Steep Hill throws light on how alterations have effectively disguised early floor levels, and evidence of the changes was revealed only when repairs were carried out in the shop area fronting the street in the 20th century. No.13 has a high wall forming its northern side that effectively serves as a revetted boundary marking a considerable change in ground-levels from north to south; the next change in levels may be seen from no.11A to no.10. Both nos 10 and 11A have above ground cellars, an amenity presumably available to earlier superseded houses on both these sites. We have seen how in the case of the Norman House advantage was taken of the fall in ground-levels to provide a long cellar that increased the economical use of its already assured position next to the market place. The former Harlequin perhaps is more typical of exploitation in that access to the ground-floor shops was directly off the street, and the shop divisions followed those of the timber-framed bay intervals overhead. Independence from the main holding is the interpretation that is implied in the suggested shop layout in no.1 Christ's Hospital Terrace, and here it is a matter of regret that more substantial vestiges of how this lower level of the tenement functioned did not survive to supplement the evidence exposed at ceiling level.

8-9 Steep Hill

The evidence for ownership and occupation between the 16th century and the 1790s consists of a single boundary reference (in the leases for no.10) dated 1695,[120] which names Henry Rands of London. Henry was also connected with Nettleham, and married Margaret Scrimshaw, widow of John, at St Peter at Arches Church in 1692, but he was dead before c.1725.[121] It has not been possible to find other documentary evidence for his involvement with this site.

By 1791 the property was in the hands of John Garmston, the attorney, and in that year sold to John Pell, woolstapler, who was related to George Pell, the stocking weaver associated with nos 249–250 High Street,[122] John died in 1800, leaving all his property (unfortunately not listed in detail) in his will[123] to his sister Jane Harvey. It then descended to Jane Flower, nee Pell, probably a niece, wife of George Flower of the Bail.

George was still owner at the time of the Willson and Betham Survey in 1828, and the houses were occupied by Thomas Naylor, staymaker, and Sarah Naylor, described[124] as a milliner and dressmaker. The extensive grounds to the west were in 1831 sub-divided for development into a number of overcrowded courtyards; two tranches of this land were acquired by John Brummitt, ropemaker.[125] William Vickers, the builder, lived at no.9 for a while, the Naylor family staying on at no.8 until c.1850.

William Robert Lilly, son of a miller and baker from Newport, owned no.8 from sometime around 1900 until after 1910. He was an insurance surveyor or inspector, who built up an extensive collection of properties[126] with a view to establishing a Steep Hill Tramway which would run from St Martin's Church up to Exchequergate, partly underground. It was not until 1907 that he started hawking his scheme around the city, hoping for investors but receiving little support.

The Christ's Hospital Foundation Governors expressed initial approval in February 1907, but were apprehensive about possible damage to their buildings on Steep Hill (particularly 46–47 Steep Hill). Lilly was obviously unable to satisfy their demand for an indemnity against this.[127] In 1909 he put his proposals to the City Council, who were unwilling to adopt it or put money into the scheme.[128] This effectively ended his dream, and, having heavily mortgaged his properties, he was obliged to sell them all over the following 14 years, leaving Lincoln sometime during the Great War to live outside Bristol.[129]

1 *RA viii*, no.2274
2 *ibid.*, no.2275
3 *ibid.*, no.2273
4 British Library, Harleian Mss 43A 59A and B
5 *RA viii*, no.2278
6 *ibid.*, no.2280: there are some very informative footnotes in the volume at pp. 90-91
7 See above, p.9
8 *RA* viii, no.2281
9 *ibid.*, no.2282
10 *ibid.*, no.2283
11 *ibid.*, no.2284
12 *Cant* 307-309
13 *ibid.*,310-313
14 *RA viii*, no.2286
15 Bj 2.4, f.92
16 *Cant* 314: see below, p.63 for additional information derived from this grant
17 Bj 2.5., f.137
18 *ibid.*, ff.149v,152v
19 Bj 2.6.2, f.3v
20 *BB*, f.250v no.884
21 Bj 2.10., f.7v
22 Bij 3.16., no.50
23 Bij 3.19 no.4
24 *ibid.*, no.130
25 LCC Admon 1616/253
26 CC 27/152829 2/7, p. 12
27 LL 113/1
28 *ibid.*, 113/2-3
29 LL 113/4-5
30 *ibid.*, 6
31 *ibid.*, 7; LCC Wills 1784/221 and 222
32 LL 113/8
33 CC 32/150910
34 *ibid.*, 150911
35 CC 32/150912 (1831 lease plan): see *Fig* 37 above
36 CC 32/150912; 2CC 9/152947

37 1815 lease plan, CC 32/150911
38 CC 27/152829 2/7, p. 12
39 Bij 3.19., no.105
40 LL 114/1
41 CC 27/152829 5/7, p. 10
42 LL 114/2; Bij 2.8, f.205v (1681); LL 114/3
43 LL 114/6-7; 147/5-7
44 Bij 5.13, p. 511; CC 146 (schedule of leases)
45 Bij 3.19, no.105
46 LL 114/1; see also *Fig* 43
47 *RA viii*, no.2280
48 *CClR* 24 Nov 1255, p. 241; *CPR* 26 Nov 1255, pp. 451, 493; see also the account in Hill, *ML*,228-231
49 *RA* viii no.2280n; *RH*, p. 313; *Cant* 307
50 TNA C85/99
51 See above, p.56
52 *CChR* 1226-57,460
53 *CPR* 1275,88; Jewish Plea Rolls, TNA E 9/20, (1275)
54 P.D.A. Harvey: *A Medieval Oxfordshire Village, Cuxham, 1240–1400*, (OUP, 1965), *passim*
55 *CClR* 1272-1279,501; *Cant* 274-5; Dij 51/1/2,2A
56 *RA viii*, no.2287
57 *Cant* 276-77
58 *ibid.*,278
59 Including part of the range 4-7 Steep Hill: see below, p.79
60 Bj 2.4 *passim*; see also above, pp.15-16, under 46-47 Steep Hill
61 *RA viii*, nos 2280-83
62 *ibid.*, no.2278
63 Bj 2.4., f.92
64 *ibid.*, f.137

65 Bj 5.8.9., f.46v
66 *Cant* 276-77; Dij 51/1/4-6
67 TNA E 9/12
68 TNA E 9/63
69 Record Commissioners, 1805: see pp. 73-76
70 Bij 3.18, no.89
71 LL 117/1
72 LCC Wills 1604 i,18
73 Inv 99/22
74 *ARMH* deeds, Box B
75 *ibid.*, Boxes B and C *passim*
76 Directories; Syson deposit
77 *Fig* 47
78 *Fig* 45
79 *SAH iii*, 79-82
80 *ibid.*, Figs 62-63
81 *SAH iv*, 28, *Fig* 24
82 A 4.7.9; Bj 5.12.9
83 Bij 3. 2: John Grey is named 1572-74, Henry Horner 1575-79, and his assigns from 1580-89
84 Bij 3.18., no.89
85 A discrepancy between lease book entries; LL 117/1 and Bij 3.19., nos 85 and 126
86 LL 117/2
87 Bij 1. 8-9: Fabric lease books
88 LL 115/1
89 *LCL* 5389
90 Will in *LCL loc.cit.*
91 LL 115/2; Hill, *TSL*,182,193
92 *LCL* 5389
93 *Fig* 49
94 *Fig* 50
95 Bij 3.18, no.89
96 L1/3/1 f.167v; see also below, in connection with 4-7 Steep Hill
97 LL 117/2
98 LL 117/3
99 *LCL* 5389: the acre of pasture was a separate holding,

situated off what is now Drury Lane
100 Hill, *TSL*,182
101 *LCL* 5389
102 Letter published in *Lincolnshire Life*, vol 9, no.5,42 (July 1969)
103 *Fig 51*
104 See above, pp.62-3
105 Elias Martrin, who died c.1230, was a former owner of the synagogue site between Hungate and what is now no.262 High Street: see pp.141-2 below
106 cf. L3/722
107 See also under Jews' Court below, p.81
108 e.g. *RA viii*, nos 2300,2302,2310-12
109 L1/1/1/3 f.39v
110 L1/1/1/4 f.26v
111 *ibid.*, f.28
112 *ibid.* f.34; L1/3/2 f.53
113 *ibid.* ff.53,95
114 L1/1/1/6 f.57; Ciij 9.1/117
115 LC Leases 193; MLI 94038
116 LC Leases 693
117 L1/1/1/8 p. 847
118 1841 Census
119 1843 Commercial Directory
120 LC Leases 13
121 Hill 28/1/14/5
122 BRA 1548/4 *passim*
123 LCC Wills 1800/148
124 Pigot's Directory 1828
125 L3/722,858
126 L3/721,722,724; see also under 42-40 Michaelgate, p.38 above
127 LC Educ 10/3/1, pp. 55,59
128 L/1/1/21/2 pp. 326-7,330-31; L1/1/26/1 pp. 435-38
129 See also Hill *VL*, 227n

2–7 STEEP HILL
INCLUDING JEWS' COURT

The 13th-century documentation for this range is limited, but even so we are able to obtain much vital information regarding ownership and occupation of these properties, which has an impact on our understanding of the early history of all the houses in this range. Both Jewish and Christian influences were at work in this area from the late 12th century. Details of property boundaries are minimal in many cases, and a further problem which often hampers reliable identification of people with specific properties is the multiplicity of tenurial levels under the feudal property system of the era.

4–7 Steep Hill

Archaeological investigation in 1974, re-evaluated in 1988, indicated a substantial stone building set at the rear of the site. This building, dated to the 11th to 13th centuries, may well have had an eastward range serving the Steep Hill frontage, apparently replaced in the early 14th century.[1] This agrees with what we know of the documentary history for this site. During the 1260s the name of John of Hampton was associated with it, recorded as living down an alleyway north of the modern Jews' Court (see below). In about 1280, a Jewess named Diei belle, but usually referred to as Diabella, was living in a house north of what is now Jews' Court. She was convicted of an unspecified felony and executed. Her property, simply described as houses, was escheated during the mayoralty of Thomas, son of Robert (1279–80), but put out to farm, her son Benedict being permitted to remain in occupation.

The rent of 10s pa was paid to the City authorities, but they did not account for it to the Escheator, Henry de Bray, until 1285, and only in 1288 did he have his accounts entered into the Pipe Rolls.[2] The houses were later leased to William Goldring and, after the Expulsion of the Jews in 1290, this property was included with the synagogue in a royal grant made to Robert of (North) Leverton, clerk, dated at Welbeck on 27 March 1291.[3]

Because of an embarrassing blunder by the clerks of the Exchequer, William was persistently overcharged for rent to the Crown, it being assumed there that he should also be charged for the synagogue. The Exchequer had been charging 10s for each holding. The same clerks also confused their entries, misspelling Diabella's name and creating a fictitious duplication which was repeated in the Pipe Rolls for many years. It took until 1315 for the situation to be recognised as wrong, and a further three years for it to be properly rectified. Goldring eventually received what amounted to a royal acknowledgment of the error, but only after an Inquisition held at Lincoln on 1 October 1315 and a direct order from the king to the Barons of the Exchequer in 1317[4] was he totally exonerated from the burden of the 10s per annum charge, and the City of Lincoln was acquitted of the same, although the bailiffs still had the 2d pa landtoll charge to pay.

This was not the end of the Diabella story. Despite the exoneration process, underpayments of landtoll relating to Diabella's houses were still being entered onto the Pipe Rolls as late as 1466,[5] written with other out of date entries into the City Charter granted in that year. Diabella's name was also misread as Arabella by the local antiquarian John Ross.[6] To be fair to Ross, he did supply the crucial Pipe Roll reference for the 1317 Order to the Barons which assisted in piecing together the rest of this account!

Goldring continued to live in Diabella's former property, maybe equivalent to the later 4–5 Steep Hill, until his death in 1331. He left[7] his property to his wife Felicia and daughter Lecia for term of their lives, after which it was to be sold. The property boundaries given in the will give us another hint of what was happening in the area. To the west was some property owned by John de Atherby,[8] whose father Gilbert had acquired much former Jewish property in the period around 1300. The synagogue site to the south was described in 1331 as 'late of Roger Bower'. We know from references to the Jew's House that Hugh, possibly the son of Roger, was now tenant there.[9] To the north of Goldring lived William de Ayerminne (otherwise Ermyn, derived from the place name Airmyn, near Goole), another bowyer.

In 1335 William de Ermyn died. 2s per annum in a rentcharge from his lands and tenements in St Cuthbert's parish was to be given to the church of St Cuthbert for the maintenance of two candles there, the rentcharge to pass with the property which was to be sold for masses for the souls of the testator and Agnes his late wife. His executors were neighbours and colleagues, Hugh le Bouwere and John de Rusholme, also a bowyer.[10] It seems from the context of the foregoing documents that Ermyn and Goldring together occupied the whole of the area later covered by nos 4–7 Steep Hill. John de Atherby's plot, of which we know little, may have been the area towards the corner of the Drapery, later called Cavill's Court.

Fig 57. Photograph of street frontage, Jews' Court, from a slide

3 Steep Hill: including Jews' Court

It has been a long-standing tradition that Jews' Court is the site of the former synagogue, although it is noticeable that Sir Francis Hill exercised lawyerly tact and discretion when saying that "the claim of the Jews' Court, while not improbable, cannot be regarded as proved".[11] Of the Jewish historians, Cecil Roth[12] was in favour of the Jews' Court theory, but Joe Hillaby[13] has adopted a more cautious approach.

The main difficulty has always been the quality of the documentation normally associated with this site, which was suggestive but not absolutely conclusive. To make further progress in this, it has been a journey of discovery to analyse and piece together a picture derived from a wider range of sources, notably a number of classes of material from the National Archives now, thanks to the internet, more widely available for study, in addition to the more familiar materials. The result, as presented below, offers a new interpretation of the site we know as Jews' Court.

In the period around 1200, Richard, son of James, son of the Brother,[14] is known to have had a property interest both in this site and another, below the Jew's House in the Strait. His name occurs as the northern bound in a Pipe Roll entry directly relating to the Fee of Maud of Colchester,[15] explained in more detail in the Jew's House discussion to be found below. It is one of those interesting quirks of history that in 1191 Richard was among the foremost of the culprits fined for the infamous assault on the Jews in Lincoln: he had to pay 10 marks.[16] He was the husband of Margery, the sister of Adam, the first mayor. His family had close links with both Kirkstead and Bardney Abbeys, and were also Cathedral benefactors. In 1201 he served as a city bailiff, and in later years was appointed to the position of coroner.[17] Among other property interests were land in St Lawrence parish, held from him by Alan the Goldsmith, and a house in the Hungate area tenanted by Josce son of Ava and later by Peytevin the Jew.[18] Richard transferred his interest in Jews' Court to Thomas of Paris, another influential Lincoln figure who was married to Mary, daughter of Godwin the Rich (for whom Ralf of Colchester once stood surety). By 1205 Thomas and Mary had released this property, described as formerly in the tenure of Benedict of London (*alias* le Jovene), to Bardney Abbey, and it was among the benefactions recorded in the Confirmation Charter of king John issued in that year.[19]

Bardney Abbey held an interesting position in the documentary landscape in this area. In 1264/65 Peytevin, son of Benedict le Jovene, made a quitclaim to Bardney of his interest in this same property, described as a plot of land in St Cuthbert's parish which he held from the abbey for a rent of 22s per annum, situated between land of Henry Bretaldun to the south and the alley where John of Hampton (de Hanttona) used to live on the north. This *starr*, with its Hebrew subscript attestation,[20] was witnessed among others by Osbert son of Giles, one of the two Christian chirographers, and their clerk William le Waleis.

The dating of the *starr* was not precise, but it was within the first year of the mayoralty of William of Holgate, which is now determined to have been Michaelmas 1264 to Michaelmas 1265, a crucial year for Jewish records. The document either survived the storming of the *Archa*[21] by the 'Disinherited Knights', followers of Simon de Montfort, or was deposited in copy form soon afterwards. It is quite certain that this was not the same Peytevin who in 1255 was the proprietor of the synagogue, and fled to France with his son to escape punishment for his supposed role in the murder of the little boy Hugh. The seals of the Jewish chirographers are on the document, wrongly dated as 1272 by Meyr Davis.[22] Mention of the alleyway suggests either a central passageway, such as at the Jew's House or the house of Floria the Jewess,[23] or, as in this case, a passageway between two properties, the synagogue and the houses of Diabella.

For purposes of confirming the identification of no.3 Steep Hill as the site of the synagogue within this plot, the conclusive evidence is in the boundary reference to Henry Bretaldun, alias Breykaldoun, a distinctive name. His property (no.2 Steep Hill) later occurs as the northern boundary of the Jew's House[24] and confirms that Bardney Abbey and Peytevin were involved with the northern portion of what is now Jews' Court. Bretaldun, apart from these two critical references, is otherwise unknown, although a John Bretaldun held a tenancy on land in the North Field of Lincoln in the period before 1250.[25]

At the time of the Expulsion of the Jews in 1290, Robert of Leverton was a royal clerk, working for Robert le Venur, Keeper of the City of Lincoln.[26] Le Venur's status may well account for the grant. According to the initial valuation made prior to the Expulsion and recorded by B.L. Abrahams,[27] Diabella's houses (nos 4–7) were valued at 8s per annum (later increased to 10s pa), which, together with the synagogue, made a total of 20s pa, with a landtoll charge of 2d pa levied only on the houses.

Abrahams, however, missed a crucial entry relating to the synagogue[28] which gives a brief description of it: "...Item the *scola Judeorum* worth 10s per annum paying 1d [landtoll] to the king: two houses in front of the entrance and a ruinous house *in vico scole*". The latter part of this passage we may take to refer not to the synagogue, but to another Jewish property in Scolegate, now Danesgate. The clerk was obviously unaware that the school referred to in the street name was the Dean and Chapter Grammar School, situated in the precincts of the Bishop's Palace,[29] situated at the north end of the street.

There is some inconsistency shown here, not only in the matter of the rentals but also the landtoll charge. Perhaps this is a symptom of the haste with which the king pursued his realisation of the Jewish assets, but there could be an element of fraud in it; in either case it does not reflect well on the Exchequer clerks. The synagogue, therefore, is confirmed as being behind two houses on the street frontage of Steep Hill, and accessible only from the passageway or the rear. It was obviously a special case, as it was not only entrusted to someone high in the royal esteem but the 1291 grant was not registered with others executed on the same day,[30] nor are the proceeds from the sale recorded by Hugh of Kendal, Collector for the king, in his initial accounts.[31] It would appear that various authorities were going to some lengths to conceal the fate of the synagogue.

The synagogue, together with the rest of the site south of Goldring's leasehold, was inherited on Robert's death by his son, also Robert, who sold it on to Peter le Quilter. Peter sub-divided the plot, which may have caused a radical rebuilding of the premises. The area behind the former synagogue site was partitioned off for a marriage portion given to Peter's daughter Sabine on her marriage to Hugh Wolmer; this seems to have been reckoned as a detached portion of the parish of St Peter Stanthaket. In November 1316 Peter granted in perpetuity *the site of the former synagogue*, together with gardens and other appurtenances, situated between the street on the east, land of Hugh and Sabine on the west, land of William Goldring on the north, and other land of his own on the south, to Roger le Bowgher (bowyer).[32] The phrasing with regard to the synagogue implies that the building itself was no longer standing by this time. This deed was not enrolled in the Burwarmote Book until 1344, but we are not informed of the reason for this delay.

There is now a considerable argument for maintaining the long-held assertion that the synagogue lay within the northern section of the property we now call Jews' Court. The actual synagogue only occupied one part of this site, and was probably built on an east–west axis, without a direct frontage on to the street: access would have been via an entrance to the rear. No documentary evidence more specific than this has yet been found, and it is probable that the full text of the 1291 grant would not provide much more useful information than the extracts referred to in the Memoranda and Pipe Rolls.

2 Steep Hill

Jacob Senex is recorded to have held property in St Cuthbert's parish of the fee of Maud of Colchester, who reclaimed it from him in 1204, paying 20 marks and a fine of a palfrey to the king.[33] As shown below, Maud also originally owned the site of the Jew's House, and this strengthens the argument for placing the holding of Jacob and Elias in the plot between the *scola* and the Jew's House. Elias was the son of Jacob *Senex*, possibly the nephew of Aaron, and was hanged in 1255 for his alleged complicity in the death of the boy Hugh. This house of Elias was sold by the king in October 1256 to Thomas de

Beaufou and John Long, along with other property of Peytevin in the parish of St Martin, for a total of 80 marks.[34] What happened between 1256 and 1291 is essentially a mystery, apart from the reference to Henry Breykaldoun. At some point before 1316 it seems to have been acquired by Peter le Quilter. After this there was a sale to John de Blyton or William his son, for which we have no text, and in 1349 a rent charge of 20s per annum was granted from it to Thomas, son of William de Blyton; the house was at that point in the occupation of Nicholas le Furber.[35]

POST-MEDIEVAL OCCUPATION

4–7 Steep Hill

It can be established that for the period 1578–1788 the range of property on Steep Hill between Jews' Court and the lane called Drapery on the north was in sole ownership. In 1578 Henry Stubbes of Grantham, merchant, son of Ralph Stubbes, deceased, made a quitclaim of interest to John Carter, son of Richard Carter of the Close, concerning "a messuage, garden and orchard with the houses and buildings appertaining, situated in the former parish of St Cuthbert and now in the parish of St Michael on the Mount.... between land of the heirs of Paull on the south[36] and a common lane on the north, and abutting the common soil called Pewther Hill[37] towards the west and the Queen's Highway or High Street on the east, and are now in the tenure of William Ellys".[38]

Luke Carter, a vintner from the Bail, was married in 1594 to Alice Maidenwell, who had family connections in her ancestry to Ambrose Sutton.[39] They relinquished their interest in the "messuage or tenement, garden and orchard" on 4 May 1601 to Adam Gartsed, or Garsett, clerk of the parish of St Peter at Arches. Property of William Carter (Jews' Court) lay south, and the common soil of Polter Hill on the west.[40]

The reference to Polter Hill is interesting as it points to a small market area on the corner where the lane turns southward; the segmental area shown on the 1842 Padley plan has some small buildings fronting on to the lane and may be the last vestige of John de Atherby's plot mentioned above. It was sold by later owners of nos 6–7 Steep Hill in 1836 to George Cavill. Dennis Mills, in his work on the people of Steep Hill, noted that Cavill's Yard was one of the poorest areas of the city.[41]

Gartsed died in 1604,[42] and the property was inherited by his wife Alice. In her will dated 1621[43] she left it all to her daughter Ruth. The inventory lists a hall, parlour, chamber over it, linen room, chamber over the hall, store chamber, stable, garth and entry; there was even a beehive in the yard to the rear.[44] By 1657 it was in the hands of John Peachell and Sarah his wife, who conveyed it to Martin Wise, gardener. In his will of 1694[45] he directed that his four surviving children should share in the property. Thomas, one of the sons, bought out his siblings, and it descended to his son James Wise, who, in 1727, together with Rachel his mother, sold it to John Hopton the blacksmith.[46] From Hopton it passed, via William Thorpe, bridle cutter, Mary Ellis and Isaac Wood (who also owned Jews' Court and was lessee of the Jew's House at the same time), to Mary Julian, widow.

2–3 Steep Hill: Jews' Court

In the absence of any title deeds for this historic building from the late 14th century until the late 19th century, only the briefest outline can be given, and we are heavily dependent on boundary references from the leases of the Jew's House. The situation is further complicated by the fact that for the first half of the 19th-century Jews' Court was owned by the representatives of Isaac Wood, who had been declared insane and was

Fig 58. (opposite) Probate inventory for William Carter, 1629

lodged in an asylum at York. His affairs (including several houses in Lincoln) were dealt with by a committee, and there were further issues relating to the dispersal of the remnants of his estate after his death, which were not finally resolved until 1911.[47] What is clear is that nos 2 and 3 Steep Hill were now firmly established as a single property unit.

The earliest name mentioned in the Jew's House leases was John Paule or Paull in 1564; little is known of him. William Carter, glazier, was owner of Jews' Court from c.1601 until his death in 1629. His will[48] mentions several other properties, including what later became nos 10–11 Strait. Jews' Court was his home, and this was bequeathed to William his eldest son. One of his daughters was Elizabeth Paull. His inventory, although sparse as to monetary value, catalogues the contents of the hall, great parlour, little parlour, hall chamber, kitchen chamber, great chamber, kitchen, bakehouse and shop.[49] The second William seems to have left little documentation. He was jointly bound with his mother Margaret to pay a debt to Christopher Randes of the Close, probably in respect of the 'Chirurgeons' holding,[50] and he had a son, a third William Carter, who was left 5s by his grandfather. Margaret in her will[51] left the residue of her estate to her daughter Mary Carter.

The Jew's House leases continue to mention William Carter until 1661, but the 1649 Parliamentary Survey named Mr Lawes as being at Jews' Court; he was related by marriage to the Carters.[52] By 1675 George Carter, plumber, was the owner or occupier,[53] having at one time lived at no.14 Strait, just below the Jew's House. He died in 1681 and his probate inventory has survived; it lists the contents of the hall, buttery, parlour, hall chamber, kitchen chamber, garret, his own lodging chamber, shop, kitchen and yard. The garret implies the use of a third storey above ground-level. Among the contents of the kitchen was a great number of items in pewter, weighing 7½ stone (approx. 47 kg), worth £2 19s, and in the shop was stored over 29 cwt of lead, one hundredweight of shot, 2 lb of solder, four firkins and half a case of glass. He had a glass table in the garret.

After Carter the ownership and occupation at Jews' Court are unknown until 1717, when a Jew's House lease[54] mentions Ralph Mossom. A Mrs

Heneage, of the Hainton family no doubt, was listed from 1728 to 1766, and from 1773 to 1787 William West and others, implying the creation of multiple households within the building and its boundaries. It is suggested that Isaac Wood may have acquired the freehold to Jews' Court at this time. Clement Wood, keeper of the gaol at Lincoln Castle, was lessee of the Jew's House from 1746, and Isaac was lessee until 1794.[55]

By 1851, nos 2–3, which, judging by the position of the original street numbers as seen today, may have been restricted to the basement level either side of the main entry, were in the occupation of William Hammersley, chair maker, and Anne Webster, washerwoman. The rest of the building, together with the back range and maybe a small tenement at the south-western corner of the garden, were divided up between six different households, one being vacant.[56] In terms of numbers of occupants, 1851 was probably the peak year, with 20 individuals counted in the Census. It had been 12 in 1841 and was reduced to 15 in 1861 and 11 in 1881. Some of the tenants were there for many years. Thomas Whitworth Wright, at no.1 Jews' Court, for example, was a painter and glazier, and there were eight in his household in 1881; he had been living there since at least 1857, and he died c.1890. A Mission Room was briefly established under Charlotte Morris at no.2 between c.1877 and 1885. There were still five households in 1913, by which time the building was dilapidated.

In 1911 the lawyers acting for the committee of Isaac Wood finally brought about a settlement of the estate, which then consisted of Jews' Court and nos 8–9 Castle Hill. Various family members were allocated certain proportions of the estate, and E.H. Dodgson of Leeds, one of the solicitors handling the Wood estate, and husband of Frances (nee Pratt), bought out the others, paying a total of £855 for the Castle Hill building and Jews' Court. We are uncertain as to why the estate took so long to be wound up (Isaac Wood having died as early as 1849).

After many years of neglect and decay, the house seemingly of use to Dodgson only as collateral for his two mortgages,[57] he died, leaving to Frances the property of which she had owned half since at least 1886. Lincoln Corporation considered it as ripe for demolition under their extensive slum clearance programme, and this rang alarm bells with the Lincolnshire Architectural and Archaeological Society, who remarked on the situation in their 1928 Annual Report.[58] A year later it was noted that the building had been condemned for habitation, and the Society had put in a formal approach to the Corporation with a view to the preservation of the building. Negotiations between the two bodies ensued.[59]

The Corporation delayed the handover as they were awaiting the outcome of a test case then in the Courts,[60] but in the following year the case was settled, the transfer under way and work permitted to begin on urgent repairs, beginning with the roof, windows and outer walls to ensure it was weatherproof.[61] In 1932, the freehold of the building was acquired for a nominal sum in view of the projected expense, and in order to raise funds for this a lease was granted by the Society to the Lincoln Diocesan Trust and Board of Finance for 15 years, but providing storage and meeting space for the Society. During the same year the Society also acquired the Bardney Abbey site, giving itself a second preservation project.[62]

After the completion of the extensive renovation work in Jews' Court, which had almost entailed the gutting of the building, it was possible to invite the Jewish Historical Society to visit in 1934. After visiting the Guildhall and the White Hart (for tea with the mayor and mayoress of Lincoln, the party were warmly welcomed at Jews' Court by the Society, and Dr Cecil Roth, the foremost Anglo-Jewish historian of the day, read a paper on Lincoln's medieval Jewry and its synagogue, which was later published.[63]

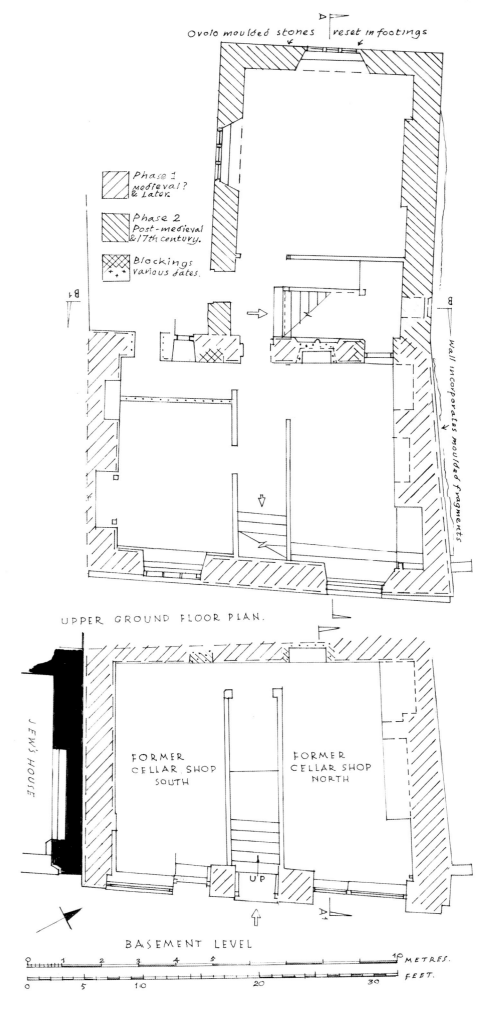

Ovolo moulded stones reset in footings

Phase 1
medieval?
& later.

Phase 2
Post-medieval
& 17th century.

Blockings
various dates.

Wall incorporates moulded fragments

UPPER GROUND FLOOR PLAN.

Fig 59. Plans of basement level and upper ground-floor, Jews' Court

JEW'S HOUSE

FORMER
CELLAR SHOP
SOUTH

FORMER
CELLAR SHOP
NORTH

UP

BASEMENT LEVEL

METRES.

FEET.

85

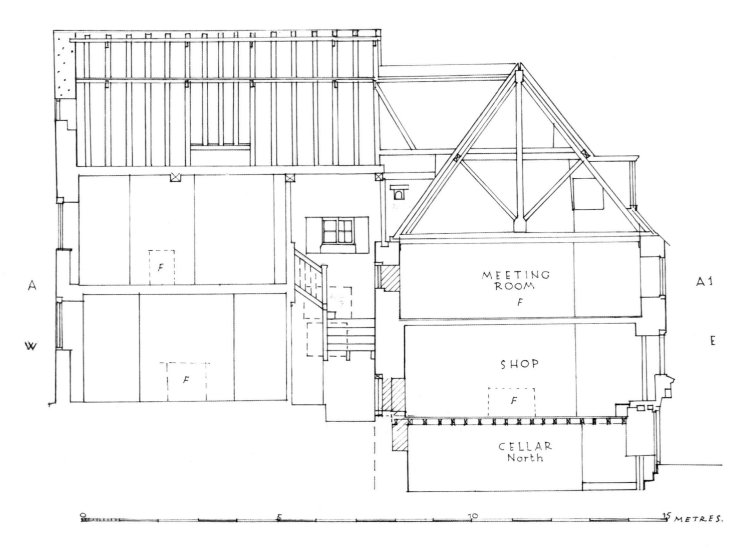

If only one were able to discover an appreciable length of indisputable medieval walling that incorporated worked stones of 12th-century date in the Jews' Court, its structural history would be easier to understand. Carved stone fragments may be distinguished externally in the lower half of the north wall, and some appear to be sections mostly of vaulting ribs (?). The unfinished character of this lower half implies that the present building was raised against a standing structure on its north side; in turn the south wall of the Court abuts the north wall of the Jew's House. At basement level, the west wall has two altered window openings, whose position in what may be read as a back wall would have illuminated what was then possibly an undivided cellar. It follows that the basement windows imply, significantly, a physical gap west of the street range of Jews' Court and one now taken up by a staircase of late 17th-century character.

Setting aside the historical association with the *scola* (synagogue) on site the present impression of the Court is that one is dealing with a stone-built three-storied street range of late 17th-century vintage. A central doorway with a short flight of steps leads directly to a first-floor or elevated ground-floor level. On either hand of the central doorway are semi-basement shops whose low ceilings are formed by the first-floor joists.

Mr Robert Pilling's excellent survey drawings enable one to appreciate the problems in elucidating the building's archaeology and the thick walling at basement level suggests that medieval work, lacking recognisable features, may well be present. One could envisage that the medieval synagogue was a stone building employing fine ashlar masonry whose walls were quarried at a later date for this quality material; what remained after the demise of the synagogue may have been no more than rubble walling and its site lost in later developments thereabouts.

86

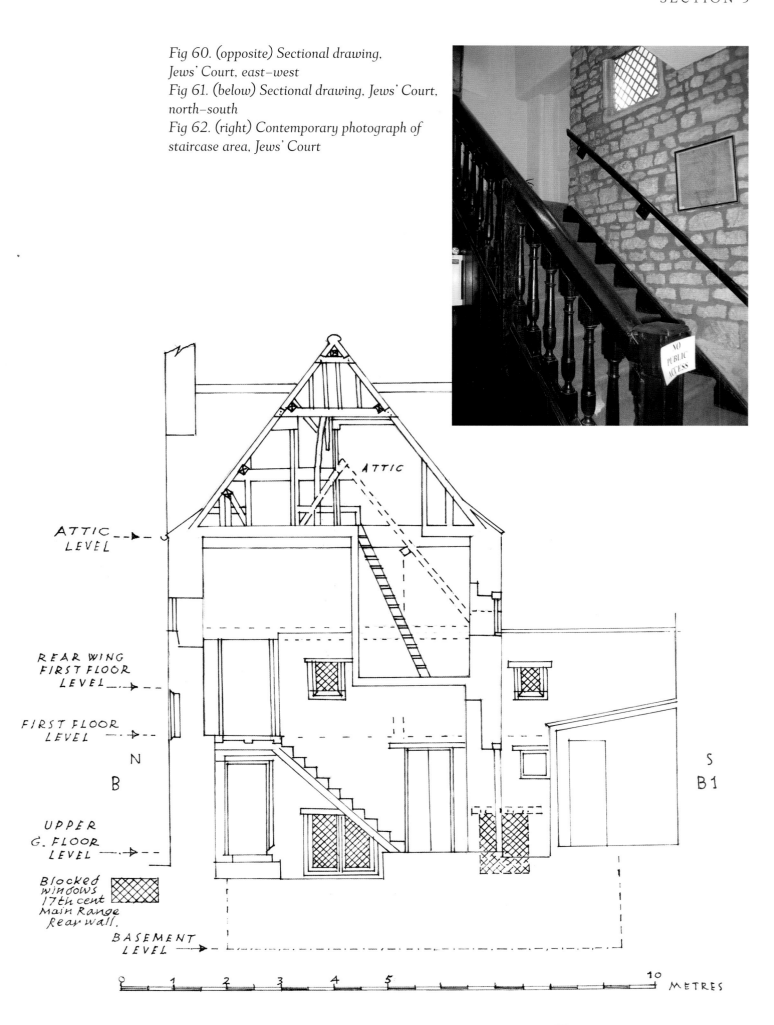

Fig 60. (opposite) Sectional drawing,
Jews' Court, east–west
Fig 61. (below) Sectional drawing, Jews' Court,
north–south
Fig 62. (right) Contemporary photograph of
staircase area, Jews' Court

ATTIC

ATTIC
LEVEL

REAR WING
FIRST FLOOR
LEVEL

FIRST FLOOR
LEVEL

N

B

UPPER
G. FLOOR
LEVEL

Blocked
windows
17th cent
Main Range
Rear wall.

BASEMENT
LEVEL

S

B1

0   1   2   3   4   5   10   METRES

Jews' Court comprises two building ranges, namely one fronting the street and roofed in line with it, the other to the rear and set higher and roofed at right angles to the street range; the link between both buildings is provided by the staircase. That the rear building is an addition is inferable from the blockings in the west wall of the street range. It may be claimed that the staircase provision is to be associated with the rear building[64] and one is aware that the back wing has more generous ceiling heights in both of its main rooms; now suppressed, both rooms were served by a lateral chimney housed in the north wall.

15 STRAIT AND 1 STEEP HILL
JEW'S HOUSE

The earliest years of the Jew's House have for long been shrouded in mystery because of a perceived lack of direct evidence. Nevertheless, recent researches have shown that we do indeed possess some relevant documentation which provides some clues to its origins and development.

From the Dean and Chapter Accounts for the period after the establishment of the Thornton and Gare Chantry in 1312 we know that for some reason the Jew's House, described often as houses in the Cornmarket, was paying an outrent or rent of assize of 6d per annum to the Vicars Choral of the Cathedral. There is no apparent explanation for this regular payment in the charter of Ordination or Constitution of the Chantry,[65] but we know from the Chapter accounts that it continued until at least 1450.[66]

On referring back to the deeds which document the process by which the property came into the hands of the Chapter, there is no reference to this payment, but if we look further back to the period around 1230 a connection begins to emerge between the house, then owned by Adam, son of Adam of Colchester, and at various times in the occupation of Benedict le Jovene and Peytevin of London, his son, and the Vicars Choral. This took the form of a grant of an annual payment, not originally of 6d in cash but of a pound of wax, which it is now thought was commuted to an annual cash payment to the Vicars at the time (1312) when the property came into Chapter ownership.

Benedict, who died before 1228, was one of the foremost Jewish leaders in Lincoln, and it was his son Peytevin who made the grant of wax to Adam.[67] This payment of wax for a candle was granted by Adam to William de Burgo, who was Clerk of the king's Wardrobe under Ranulph Brito.[68] There was a clause in the grant which makes William subject to the jurisdiction of the Chapter on pain of a fine of 10s payable to the Fabric of the Cathedral. The Vicars are not mentioned either in this document or its sequel, a quitclaim of dower right by Maud, mother of the grantor, who around this time also renounced dower rights regarding Prebendal property in the High Street,[69] although the fact of the enrolment of the grant in the Vicars' Cartulary seems to confirm a connection. The clause about the Fabric of the Cathedral suggests a connection with the Cathedral so early that the documentation has not survived, although the wax payment is recorded annually in the rent repayments section of their accounts, as will be noted below.

As the payment was being made in 1230 to someone in the royal household, it suggests that a number of entries in the Chapter Accounts for the period 1304–1310 now make a degree of sense. These annual payments of wax are all made to an attorney for the earl of Lincoln for the same amount, one pound in weight, valued for the sake of the accounts at between 6d and 8d, but usually 7½d.[70] The payments in wax then ceased, but were replaced in the year 1312/13 by payments of 6d per annum, as noted[71] above.

This scenario indicates a link between the Jew's House and the Colchester Fee, and literally throws new light on the origin of the house. What it does not totally explain is the link with the Cathedral, but it is known that the Colchester family had such a connection through their holding of the Prebend of St Martin. It is also worth mentioning that in 1322/23 the Jew's House, described on this occasion as being 'near the Bulstake', was in the occupation of the Vicar of St Martin's Church.[72]

We are accustomed to the familiar outline of the Jew's House, with its asymmetrical appearance of two bays south of the entrance passage and one bay to the north.[73] Other important Jewish properties, however, have a more central position for the passageway, and it is necessary to enquire whether the original plan for the house could have extended further north to take in no.2 Steep Hill.

It has already been established above that no.2 was not linked in tenure with the synagogue site at no.3 until after the Expulsion, but equally there was the fact of common ownership of the two holdings (no.2 and the Jew's House) by Maud of Colchester in the period between c.1170 and 1230. There is, however, no foundation for a physical integration: the architectural plans show that there was a double-thickness wall between the two from an early date.

There is a crucial entry in the Pipe Rolls for 1204[74] which shows that Maud "owes 20 marks and a palfrey for holding land which Jacob *Senex*, Jew of Lincoln, held of her in the parish of St Cuthbert, situated between two lands of Richard, son of James...". This Maud was undoubtedly the widow of Ralf of Colchester, who was active in the period around 1175 when it is thought the Jew's House may have been built.[75] As there is no known link between Richard and the Jew's House, it is easily possible that this Pipe Roll entry relates to both houses, the fine of 20s being a great deal of money purely for the smaller property. The lengthy entry on the Roll also constitutes a sign of an important transaction. Jacob *Senex* was tenant of both properties until his death not long before the Pipe Roll entry, but afterwards the properties had a separate tenemental history.

The history of the Jew's House in the late 13th century is informative, but also tragic. During the 1270s Belasset of Wallingford was the owner. As Sir Francis Hill made clear in his study of the Jews,[76] she is not the Belasset (or Belassez) whose daughter was famously betrothed in 1271. Jewish forenames are used liberally: we know of at least three Belassets, and 40 people with the name Benedict in Lincoln during the 13th century. It is often very difficult to disentangle them, or even reconstruct family histories.

Belasset of Wallingford, who also seems to have had property in Stamford, was arrested, along with several hundred other Jewish householders, in early 1279, for the alleged offence of coin-clipping, i.e. debasing the currency by snipping off bits of silver to recycle, usually as plates.[77] Having gone to Wallingford Castle to take refuge with her husband, Josce of Germany (*de Allemania*), the Justices for the Jews sent an order to the Sheriff of Oxfordshire to arrest both of them, together with one countess (*Comitissa*) of Oxford, a Jewess. The order was enrolled not long before Easter 1279.[78] She was hanged, according to entries relating to her property in the Pipe Rolls, probably in April or May 1279, supposedly along with 292 other Jews or Jewesses, victims of this pointless pogrom, of which the king himself tired during the year.

Belasset's houses were, as was the custom, escheated into the king's possession. Pipe Rolls for several years after 1299 record this, valuing them at 19s 6d pa, even though the Jew's House was sold (finally) in 1291. It would appear that the landtoll charge of 2d pa, exactly as had been the case with the houses of Diabella (see above, under Jews' Court), had not been paid after 1291, when Walter le Fevre of Fulletby entered into possession. The City Bailiffs were required to pay the arrears, but perhaps the upheaval caused by the deposition of the mayoralty caused them to forget, or perhaps there was some peculation involved!

The king's volte-face on the subject of hangings[79] came too late for Belasset. The question which arises at this point is: why was the Jew's House not sold in 1279? Why delay until 1291? The answer is not clear but maybe the king's change of heart made a sale politically incorrect, or perhaps the fact that the synagogue was practically next door inhibited him from selling to a Christian. It was probably leased to one of the Jews on a short-term basis.

The sale to Walter le Fevre was made by a royal grant dated 20 February 1291.[80] Le Fevre, who from his name was a smith, was likely to have been in the king's service at some time. In February 1310 he leased two shops south of the passageway to Roger le Bowier, late of Newcastle, at the nominal rent of 1d per annum. The shops measured 6½ × 5½ royal ells, approximately 26' (E–W) by 22' (N–S)/7.9 m × 6.7 m, measuring from the stone gable of Walter's house towards the High Street. This may indicate that there was an east–west hall and lodging range behind the rear wall of the shops.[81]

Only a year after this lease was arranged Walter died, and his brother and heir William granted all his messuage and buildings here to Master William de Thornton, a Canon of Lincoln Cathedral. This grant[82] had additional property details: '...situated in length and breadth between land once of Henry Breykaldoun on the north and land of William de Lounesdale and land once of Adam Acke on the south, abutting the High Street east and the road called Draperie on the west...'. Henry[83] was the tenant of the southern portion of what is now Jews' Court, so his property appears as the link between the Jew's House and the site of the synagogue. Lounesdale and Acke seem to be associated with the properties now represented by nos 13–14 Strait.

Quitclaims were issued by Lecia, daughter of Walter le Fevre, and by Roger le Bower, soon after this grant to Master William, so the way was now clear for him to establish the endowment for the Thornton and Gare Chantry in the Cathedral, constituted in January 1312,[84] supported not only by this house but also nos 262 High Street and 27–28 Strait, both of which were also former Jewish possessions and extremely important acquisitions, as well as being in a tolerable state of repair.[85]

The Jew's House seems to have been awarded the soubriquet of 'the Great Houses in St Cuthbert', mentioned in 1329/30 when repairs costing £11 14s 8½d were made,[86] whilst the building was in the hands of Hugh le Bower, probably a son or other relative of Roger. Further smaller sums were recorded in various years after this.[87] Entries in subsequent years tend not to be very informative.

<table>
<tr><td>

POST-MEDIEVAL
OCCUPATION

</td><td>

Although the Dean and Chapter leases for the Jew's House only survive in lease book format to begin with, from 1564, some earlier references have been traced through analysis of the early Board Rentals, which include a number of former chantry properties retained by the Cathedral after the Reformation. It is fortunate that some leases of the Jew's House also included a small piece of ground on the east side of Danesgate, now part of the Usher Gallery site, which connection has enabled two pre-Reformation lessees to be identified: John Fawbord in 1489 and Thomas Crosfeld in 1529.[88] John Clarke, a later lessee, is mentioned in the same series of rentals from 1591, paying the same rent as Crosfeld, who may belong to the family of bowyers found in this area of Lincoln.[89]

</td></tr>
</table>

Laurence Braker, yeoman, was granted a lease in 1564. As usual the description of the holding in the lease book is very sparse: "a tenement situated between a tenement in the occupation of John Paule on the north and a tenement of Richard Roberts on the south...". The rent for the 40-year term was 8s per annum with an additional rent of 2s for the little close in Danesgate.[90] He either died or had assigned the lease before 1591, when John Clarke's name began to be noted in the rentals. In 1601 Clarke, a joiner, obtained the lease, again for 40 years. William Carter and George Carter were his neighbours to the north and south respectively.[91]

John Clarke died in March 1622, and his will describes a partitioning arrangement for the house. Margaret, his widow, was to enjoy the house, except for the parlour next to

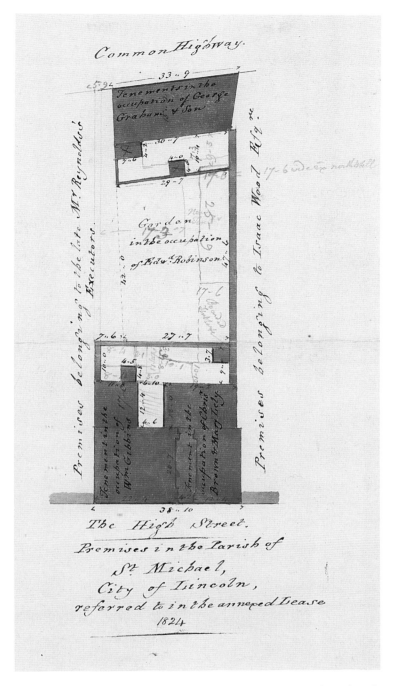

*Fig 63. Ground plan
from 1824 lease,
Jew's House*

the street and the chamber over it, the kitchen where Jane Thickstone his daughter lived, and the chamber over that. Margaret would have a 12-year tenancy provided that she remained unmarried, paid the rent and kept the premises in repair. Antoninae (maybe a variant of Antonia) and Elizabeth Clarke, two other daughters, were to have tenancy of the aforesaid parlour next to the street and chamber over it, for the same term. Jane would have to pay her mother 5s pa towards the rent. Residual rights under the main lease would, after this 12-year term, be divided among such of the daughters as were then living.[92] Unfortunately no probate inventory has been found to accompany this remarkable description.

In 1634 Antoninae (written as Antinyno in the text) and John Fisher, painter, were given a joint lease for 21 years at the old rent; this lease and its counterpart are the first to survive in the usual cyrograph format on parchment.[93] The Parliamentary Survey clerk also had difficulty with Antoninae in 1649: when noting this lease he put her down as Anthony! The description of the house given in 1649 is again very useful towards an understanding of the architecture of the Jew's House: "...all that tenement in St Michael's

91

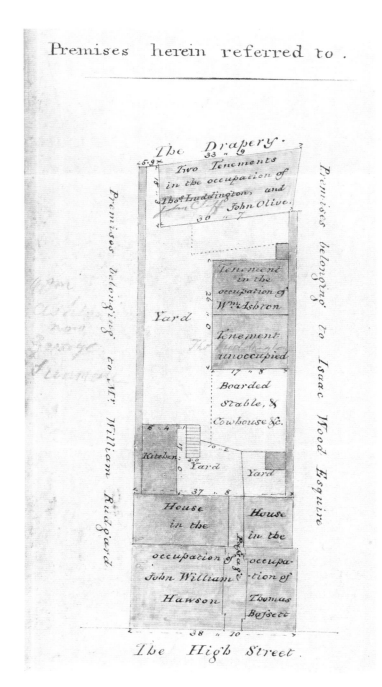

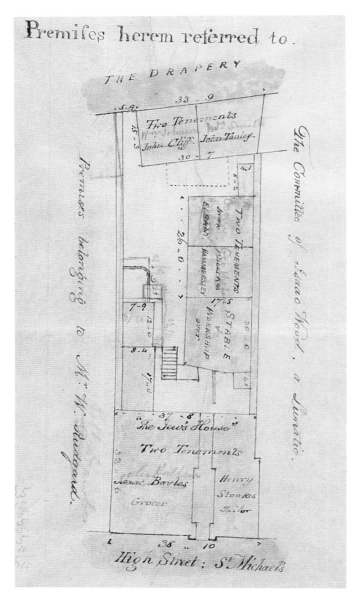

Fig 64. (left) Ground plan from 1831 lease, Jew's House
Fig 65. (above) Ground plan from 1845 lease,
Jew's House

parish consisting of a hall, a kitchen, an old parlour, two shops next to the street, four chambers with one other parlour and chamber over it; also one other room to lay fuel; with a small backside. The building of rough stone, part covered with thatch, part with tile, abutting the street east, Common Chamber lane west and Mr Lawes on the north...". A memorandum attached to the entry runs: "This house in time of the wars stood under the Works and suffered much spoil and waste by the soldiers".[94] John Fisher was lessee again in 1661 and 1675;[95] by 1675 the small close was no longer leased with the house.

Clement Wood, keeper of the gaol in Lincoln Castle, was lessee in 1746 and 1753, and his daughter Frances Randes, widow, was his devisee in 1766. In 1773 Isaac Wood, gent., son of Clement, succeeded to the leasehold, and Friskney Clark, cordwainer, and a Mr Wolf were his tenants;[96] Isaac Wood's final lease was granted in 1787[97] and he was dead by 1791. In that year the leasehold was temporarily split into two holdings, for the purpose of developing the land to the rear, which was assigned by Messrs Parkinson and Hallifax, Wood's executors, to Alderman Joshua Morris.[98] Morris had already bought up several other properties or portions thereof further down the Strait for the same purpose, but found that there was little extra space for tenements in the back yard of the Jew's House; by 1787 some additional tenements had already been erected there, occupied by James Abraham, Hugh Maples, William Hawson and Robert Jinks.

By the time that Alderman Morris and Thomas Mason took out the next lease in 1794 the occupiers were James Abraham, William Hawson, Mason and George Bilton.[99] Ground plans on the leases from 1824 to 1852 show some of the later development of the site.

The Pickering family operated a furniture business in no.15 Strait from c.1855 to 1907, in the latter years incorporating an antiques business which also spread to no.1 Steep Hill in about 1897. The ownership of the premises as a whole was retained by the Ecclesiastical Commissioners in 1870, instead of being enfranchised. In 1873 Euan Christian reported a survey to the Commissioners, noting its dilapidated state but saying: "the front is of so much beauty and interest that it ought to be restored at least to a state of safety ... to estimate the cost of such work is almost impracticable as it will require to be dealt with stone by stone...under a Clerk of Works of knowledge and experience." It was only in 1951 that the Jew's House was finally sold to the City Council.[100]

SUMMARY   The building is deservedly famous from several viewpoints with the emphasis on: (i) that of its remarkable preservation since the late 12th century; (ii) the retention of evidence throwing light on the lower half of its street elevation and the original and later shop openings; (iii) the close resemblance of plan and access features to those embodied in the Norman House on Steep Hill; (iv) that its roof, a post-medieval affair, has re-employed an impressive number of primary roof timbers, including three tie-beams. Documentary evidence, as a former Dean and Chapter property, notes former occupants and others with an interest in it, though no absolute indication to date as to who may have built the house.[101]

The visual impact of the Jew's House may be said to depend entirely on its street elevation, its carved ornamentation culminating in the robust intricacy of the entrance doorway and the delicate detailing of the two first-floor arched window openings. That which lies behind the frontage is plainer and more utilitarian, there being no inclination whatever to adorn the three doorways at the rear of the building, all of which are integral to the original structure.

The house is two-storied, having at first-floor level originally a probable layout of two unequal sized rooms, the larger of which was heated from a fireplace in the front wall; the prominent projection of its chimney shaft above the entrance doorway is a feature it has in common with the Norman House.[102] The primary ground-floor plan from north to south consisted of a shop, entry passage and two further shops. Low segmental arches topped the shop openings, each with their individual voussoirs being joggled throughout; the springing point for each arch was from a short attached moulded shaft, a near complete example being preserved for the south side of the northern shop. For the two low arched openings south of the entrance a central masonry pier would have provided similar springing points of equal height. It is also apparent that each arch had a continuously moulded external arris that was carried through to the central pier. It is held that the pier served both to provide narrower spans for the shop arches and a point overhead in which a heavy transverse ceiling beam was lodged. It may be argued, plausibly, that this beam had the additional role of providing an essential component by topping a dividing partition wall between the shops. Access to the individual shop when in possession of its arched opening may have required the entry from the street to be at a central point. If adequate headroom was an essential factor, then this may be a possible pointer to a lower floor level than exists at present.

In the north wall of the northern shop a long shallow arched recess probably held a

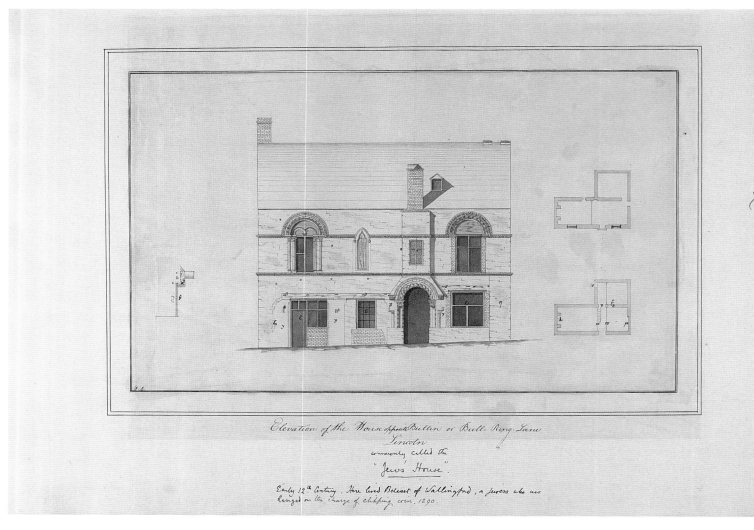

Elevation of the House opposite Bullen or Bull Ring Lane
Lincoln
commonly called the
"Jews' House".

Early 12th Century. Here lived Belaset of Wallingford, a jewess who was hanged on the charge of clipping coin. 1290.

Fig 66. Street elevation, Jew's House, c.1790

cupboard associated with early activities; the voussoirs are chamfered, not joggled, and its jambs show signs of having been re-ordered. In the south wall of the southern shop the installation of a radiator in the early 1970s[103] revealed the springing of a similarly recessed locker with joggled voussoirs, but unfortunately a 19th-century fireplace and chimney breast have obscured or destroyed the remainder. Presumably the middle shop may have had the equivalent of the stone locker installed in the convenient form of a large timber ark.

With shop evidences in mind as at no.1 Christ's Hospital Terrace, could one see the shops at Jew's House being similarly sub-divided, with each having a small storeroom to the rear? For the northern shop a round-arched doorway in its west wall provided access to the western part of the shop's sub-division; here again there would appear to be a close parallel, in part, to those ground-floor arrangements outlined in the Norman House uphill.

The Banks Collection drawing of the east front of the Jew's House, made c.1790, is particularly useful in showing a later phase of shop openings that still maintained the triple divisions. What is particularly commendable is the careful delineation by the draughtsman of the superseded springing points of the former shop arches, these being shown with their carved capitals and a hint of the generous use of billet/pellet ornamentation, a decorative element used profusely in and about the mouldings of the arched entrance doorway. Just as reliable a guide to the development of the façade is a drawing by William Twopeny and engraved by Orlando Jewitt, reproduced in the first volume of Turner Parker's series *Domestic Architecture of the Middle Ages* (Oxford, 1851).[104]

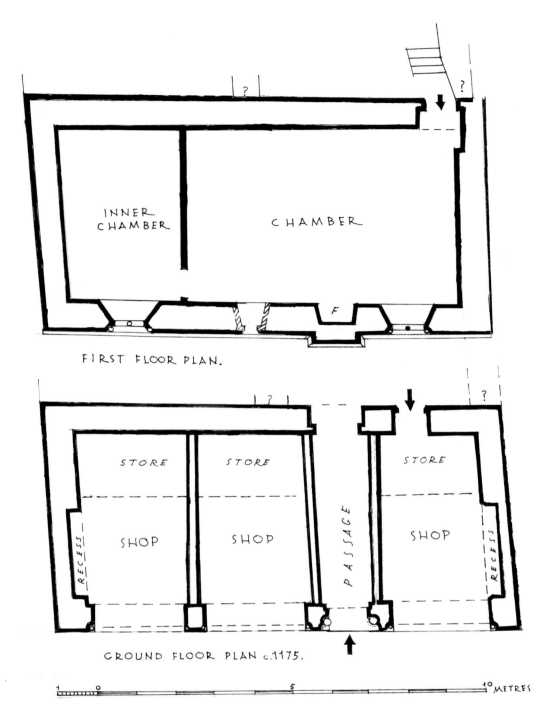

INNER CHAMBER

CHAMBER

FIRST FLOOR PLAN.

STORE   STORE   STORE

RECESS   SHOP   SHOP   PASSAGE   SHOP   RECESS

GROUND FLOOR PLAN c.1175.

1   0   5   10 METRES

Fig 67. Sectional reconstruction of original shop layout, with chamber above, Jew's House

The substitution of a more severe and robust stone framework in lieu of the sensitive arched openings may perhaps be ascribable more to fashion than to possible structural failings of the frontage. This would seem to be borne out by the present front of the northern shop in the Banks drawing, where the straight vertical joints, defining the limits of the second phase shop opening, are topped by a timber lintel, a chamfer on the lintel's arris lining up with the deep splay of the south jamb's chamfer. This precise relationship between lintel and deep splayed sides of the other shop fronts is such as to convince one that this intervention was based on contemporary exemplars rather than a repairs programme. One obvious point to note is that the new shop fronts probably provided higher headroom, although, as with the primary shop arrangements, there would have to be the means of securing such openings with shutters and an associated frame.

In terms of circulation in the building, one is on familiar ground regarding access to the upper floor. This was first appreciated at the Norman House (46–47 Steep Hill, above),

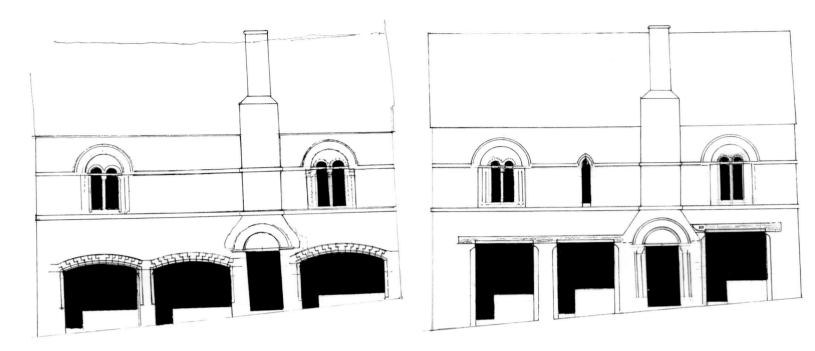

Fig 68a. (above left) Reconstructed street elevation, Jew's House
Fig 68b. (above right) Reconstruction of 14th-century re-design of street elevation, Jew's House

where the rear doorway has its checks opening into the eastern half of the building, and hence is securable against entry by unauthorised persons using the passage from the street. At the Jew's House a later two-storied medieval building made against the northern half of the rear elevation has, in turn, indications of having been reduced in size. It covers the entry to the cross-passage and a stair flight leading to the original entry on the first-floor; it also has a small round arched doorway that leads back into the northern shop, noted earlier. This small door, contrariwise, has its door checks on the shop face; note the flanking doorways in comparable positions at the Norman House. Whether the rear building to the Strait house has superseded a structure in timber framing, and which may have been more extensive in its coverage of the main range, as implied in the case of the Uphill house, is uncertain. Certainly one might argue that the virtual blind west side of the house is a factor in supposing that a further building was intended to complete the layout; its function, other than that of providing a ground-floor hall, is uncertain. The later rear wing addition would seem to provide substantial protection for the original openings and the stair approach on the west side of the house – replacing what, if anything?

As with the majority of houses covered in the current and earlier surveys, the provision of kitchens seems to have come into its own and to be recognised as such from the 16th century onwards. This may be further qualified by excluding the canonical residences where cooking rooms can be identified, and these not always convenient to the main dwellings. Presumably the cooking facility for the Jew's House lay to the rear and was intended essentially for those persons who were installed at first-floor level; the tenants of the individual shops fended for themselves, and probably resorted to cook-shops in the immediate neighbourhood.

It was during a period of refurbishing at first- and attic-floor levels in 1978 that an opportunity arose to examine timbers and rafters comprising the roof trusses in the entire length of the Jew's House. In its present form the roof is of clasped purlin type and incorporates as re-used material rafters and tie beams held to be of 12th-century origin.[105]

The accompanying drawing of a typical truss of the primary phase is based on dimensions taken from timbers now pressed into service as flooring joists and the majority of rafters also re-allocated to the present roof. In its entirety the original roof

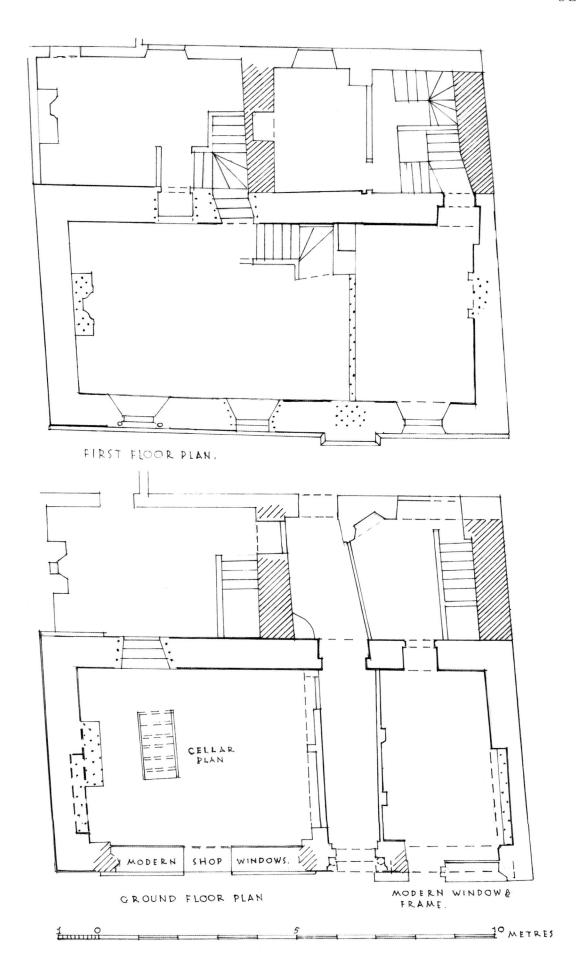

FIRST FLOOR PLAN.

CELLAR PLAN

MODERN SHOP WINDOWS.

GROUND FLOOR PLAN

MODERN WINDOW & FRAME.

1 0 5 10 METRES

Fig 69. Ground and first-floor plans, Jew's House

Fig 70. Restored cross section of main range at rear of shops, Jew's House

comprised a series of close-spaced tie-beams, each supporting a collared rafter couple. At its junction with the tie-beam the rafter is lap-jointed to it and the joint pegged; in turn, the tie-beam appears to have been notched over a raised fillet on a now missing wall-plate.[106]

This particular lap joint has in the past received much publicity in papers dealing with buildings having roofs of comparable age. The creation of an attic c.1700 could not have incorporated the original roof with its forest of close-spaced rafter couples, nor could the small-sectioned tie-beams have provided sufficient strength to carry a floor without additional support.

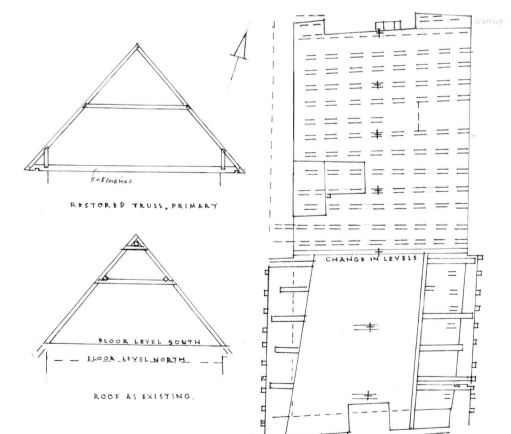

5+5inches

RESTORED TRUSS, PRIMARY

FLOOR LEVEL SOUTH

FLOOR LEVEL NORTH

ROOF AS EXISTING.

CHANGE IN LEVELS

Fig 71. (above) Photograph of springing point for joggled arch, to south of shop opening, no.15 Strait, Jew's House

Fig 72. (centre) Photograph of springing point for joggled arch to north of passageway, no.1 Steep Hill, Jew's House

Fig 73. (right) Photograph of blocked arched recess in south wall of no.15 Strait, Jew's House

METRES
FEET

Fig 74. Plan of the roof space, Jew's House

99

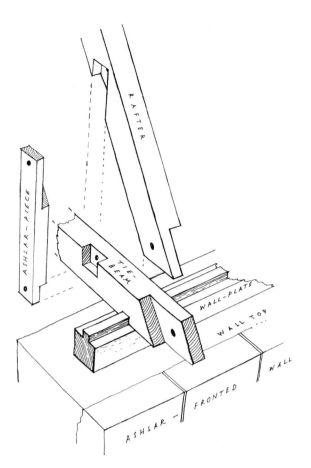

Fig 75. (left) Roof detail, Jew's House, showing
tie-beam and wall-plate arrangement
Fig 76. (above) Photograph of passage doorway,
Jew's House

Fig 77. Photograph showing internal passage-way, Jew's
House, from the back doorway of no.15 Strait, from a slide

Fig 78. Photograph. Jew's House, from rear of shop,
no.I Steep Hill, looking eastwards

Fig 79. Engraving of the Jew's House by William Twopeny, c.1850

One rafter had two lapped joints for collars that were set in close conjunction and this would seem to imply that the roof may have been completed by hipped ends. The present ends of the roof are of brick that on the evidence of the 19th-century engraving by Jewitt are later impositions.

It is assumed that, as built, the Jew's House abutted properties to the north and south. This would have obviated the need for any decorative finish at such junctions, the ornamentation being confined exclusively to the street front.

Fig 80. Photograph of exterior, Jew's House, from a slide

101

13–14 STRAIT

Only a few medieval references have been established for these properties, despite their proximity to one of the most important Jewish houses. Richard son of James is noted in 1205, and Samuel the Long, a Jew, or possibly Sampson, son of Mattathias, occurs c.1230.[107] John le Furber appears in a document of 1310[108] as the south boundary of the Jew's House; his property is said to be in the parish of St Martin, which confirms that the parish boundary with St Cuthbert's lay between nos 14 and 15. In the next deed in the Jew's House series[109] dated 1311, the south bound has two names, William de Lounesdale and Adam Acke. The latter was also named in 1290 as the beneficiary of a rentcharge of 9s pa for a house belonging to Hagin son of Benedict, also in the parish of St Martin;[110] whether it is the same property is unknown. It is possible that Adam held no.13, which has the Jew's House as its northern bound to the west of no.14.

14 Strait

No.14, which seems to have been formed from a larger plot, the remainder of which is no.13 Strait, was from the mid-16th century owned by the City of Lincoln. The earliest historical trace of it in the post-medieval period is a memorandum of a lease dated 15 January 1586 to Reginald Morres, cook; he was given a 21-year term, but the rent is not recorded.[111] His successor was George Carter, plumber and glazier, lessee from 1604, with a 25-year term:[112] Carter had a number of freehold properties elsewhere in the Strait and Steep Hill. No further leases are known until September 1656, when Henry Tutty, baker, who had other premises on Steep Hill, began his tenure. His rent was 3s 4d per annum, and the lease was renewed in 1676 for a further 21 years.[113]

William Rudgard, a merchant and brewer who had numerous waterfront properties in the city, became lessee of no.14 in July 1835[114] and became one of the first to take advantage of the Corporation's enfranchisement programme, by purchasing the freehold a month later for £96.[115] Among the later occupiers were Joseph Halman, a general dealer (1897–1905), and Francis Smith, carver and gilder (1907–1911).

13 Strait

The only references before 1835 to this freehold property are from the bounds to the leases for no.14; the grounds behind it stretched round to the west of the leasehold. Joshua Morris, who had the garden to the west of no.14 for his development scheme (1797 and 1814), Robert Reynolds and William Rudgard were successively owners in 1814 and 1835.[116]

12 Strait

Like no.13, this property is also very poorly served by documentation, and we have to rely on the 1828 Survey, Census returns and street directories for most of our knowledge. John Hawson, pawnbroker and dealer in musical instruments, was the owner at his death in 1834; his will begins an abstract of title that charts the descent of the property through his family line until 1847.[117] Elizabeth Hawson (d.1847) was a pawnbroker, listed in the 1841 Census and the 1842 directory.

10–11 Strait

These properties appear to have been jointly owned since at least the early 17th century, when William Carter, glazier, divided his impressive portfolio of properties among his family in his will of 1629.[118] He left to Ellen Archer of Washingborough a house or tenement divided into two tenements, situated near the Green Hill, upon the backside of

his house, in which Robert Mitchell and Elizabeth Muncaster lived. This properly relates to a separation of the Strait frontage from the two tenements which backed onto the back lane, which at that time was known as the Greenhill.

81 Contemporary photograph, no.10–14 Strait

In 1681 George Carter, plumber, also referred to this site in his will: Penelope Dowager of Aisthorpe, another Carter relative, was to pay an annuity to Penelope Smith, widow, mother of the testator so long as she did not disturb John Harryman or his heirs in peaceable possession of a house in St Martin's parish which the said John had lately purchased of him (i.e. nos 10–11).[119] Penelope Dowager also succeeded George to the tenancy of some property on the south side of Bull Ring Terrace which belonged to the Governors of Christ's Hospital.[120]

John Harryman, a cordwainer, and Jane his wife, had no children. At his death in c.1710 Jane and some nephews and nieces, who lived elsewhere in the county, sold off this property, then in the occupation of John Pearson, to Thomas Lund of Lincoln, carpenter, who had a number of property interests in the city.[121] In the mid-18th century Peter Fisher, tailor and cap maker, was owner; he made his will in 1761, although he did not die until 1778, leaving the property to his daughter Salina, wife of William Dixon, tallow chandler, and their family. It was later purchased by Robert Reynolds.[122]

John Hall was the owner in 1828,[123] with Margaret Carratt and Hannah Armstrong as occupiers. From c.1840 to 1855 the Morehead family held both premises; at no.11 was Mary Anne's straw hat and bonnet business, and John plied his trade as an engraver at no.10. After this period the two shops were run by separate concerns.

103

1. *Lincoln Archaeology* 1, 1988–89, City of Lincoln Archaeological Unit
2. TNA E372/133, Pipe Roll 15 Edw 1 (1287/88), m.31: Accounts of Henry de Bray, Escheator *citra Trent*, for the years 11-13 Edw1
3. A partial transcript of this grant is entered in the Lord Treasurer's Memoranda for the year 12 Edward II, TNA E 368/89, m.38 d.; see also Pipe Roll for 11 Edward II, TNA E 372/163, m.32; the original enrolment of this important grant has yet to be discovered.
4. TNA E 372/163, *loc.cit.*
5. Hill, *ML*,58, 235; W. de Gray Birch, Royal Charters of the City of Lincoln (1904),137ff
6. John Ross, *Annales*, vol. 3, 252-53; noted in Maureen Birch, *Lincoln's Medieval Jewry and Uphill Norman Houses* (Lincoln, 2005), ch.10,51
7. *BB*, f.126, no.346
8. *Lincoln Archaeology* 1, 1988–89, City of Lincoln Archaeological Unit
9. Bj 2. 5, Chapter Account Book, Expenses on Houses (*Cust' Dom'*), 1329/30 and succeeding years
10. *BB*, f.129v, no.371
11. Hill, *op.cit.*,237
12. Cecil Roth, *Medieval Lincoln Jewry and its Synagogue*, in *Essays and Portraits in Anglo-Jewish History*, JHS (1934); his account is largely echoed by Maureen Birch, *op.cit.*, ch.5
13. Joe Hillaby, "Beth Miqdash Me'at: The Synagogues of Medieval England", in *J.Eccl.Hist* vol 44 no.2 (April 1993),182-198
14. His full name is found associated with 261 High Street: see p.156 below
15. *PRS, Pipe Roll 6 John* (1204), NS vol.18,78
16. *PRS, Pipe Roll 3 and 4 Ric 1*, NS vol. 2,15-16,242-3; Hill, *op.cit.*,397
17. Hill, *op.cit.*,388-9
18. Sempringham Charters, *The Genealogist* vol.xv, 5 ; *Book of Fees i*, 365
19. Inspeximus Charter, *CChR* (1327-1341),1331,242; *Rot. Chartarum*, 149
20. *WAM* 6729: photograph of the *starr* at Lincolnshire Archives, *MCD* 994
21. This took place in May 1265 and resulted in the burning of the chest and its charters: Royal permission was granted afterwards to make copies – see *CPR* 1258-1266,510
22. MD Davis, "The Mediaeval Jews of Lincoln", in *Arch. Jnl* XXXVIII,198
23. For the Jew's House see below, and for the house of Floria, see under 27-28 Strait below, p.119
24. *Cant* 282
25. *RA ix*, no.2453
26. *LRS* vol. 36 (1944),267; TNA E 179/69, m.2
27. Abrahams, *op.cit.*, p. 96, entry no.65: the 1290 valuation (from E 101/249/27) listed by Abrahams ignores the fact that the houses had for some years been in Royal possession.
28. TNA E101/249/30, m.3d (AALT IMG 0311)
29. This street name has confused many historians, and has mistakenly led some to think that a third synagogue existed
30. It does not appear in the published Calendar of Patent Rolls, nor in the *Abbreviatio* of the Originalia Rolls, or the transcript of this at the British Library: BL Lansdowne MS 826/5, transcript 4, ff.28-64
31. TNA E 159/64, *King's Remembrancer's Rolls* 1291/92, m.13
32. *BB*, f.168, no.544
33. Davis, *op.cit.*,186
34. *Welb*, 50; CFR 40 *Hen III*, m. 2, *no*.1172: see www.finerollshenry3.org.uk
35. *BB*, f.189, no.613
36. i.e. Jews' Court
37. Otherwise, Poultry Hill
38. L1/3/1 f.171
39. See above in connection to 11 Steep Hill, p.68
40. L1/3/1 f.196v
41. L3/1532; D.R. Mills, *The People of the Steep Hill area of Lincoln about 1900: an illustrated social study*, (Lincoln, 2005), pp. 29-30
42. Inv 99/100
43. LCC Wills 1621 i,192
44. Inv 125/144
45. LCC Wills 1695&6, 413
46. L3/1532: Hopton was connected with no.195 High Street, see below, p.173
47. L3/680
48. LCC Wills 1629/400
49. Inv 135/188
50. See above, p.9
51. LCC Wills 1630/418
52. CC 27/152829 3/7 p. 17
53. LL 116/4
54. LL 66/3
55. 2CC 21
56. Census Returns 1851
57. L3/680: mortgages of 1911 and 1919
58. *LAAS* vol.39: Report for 1928, p. xi
59. *ibid.*,: Report for 1929, p. lxxxvi
60. *LAAS* vol.40: Report for 1930, p. viii
61. *ibid.* : Report for 1931, p. lxviii
62. *LAAS* vol. 41: Report for 1932, p. vii. Both properties are now cared for by the Jews' Court and Bardney Abbey Trust.
63. Cecil Roth, *Medieval Lincoln Jewry and its Synagogue: a Retrospect and a Reconstruction*: JHS (London, 1934) copy at Lincolnshire Archives; the paper was also published in the Diocesan Magazine; *LAAS* vol. 42: Report for 1934, p. vii ff
64. *Fig 64*
65. *Cant* 73; Dij 74/3/8
66. e.g. Bj 2.7, f.12v, Bj 2.15
67. For this Peytevin, see also Welb. 50
68. *VC* no.288; CLR 1,161
69. *VC* no.289; *RA viii*, no.2319
70. Bj 2.4: *redditus solute*, ff.3 (1304/05),14 (1305/06),24v-25 (1306/07),34v-35 (1307/08),44v-45 (1308/09),55 (1309/10)]
71. *ibid.*,f.95
72. Bj 2. 5, f.56
73. E.g. 262 High Street, 27-28 Strait
74. *PRS, Pipe Roll 6 John*, NS vol. 18,78
75. Cf.*RA viii*,no.2316, note, and 2336; Jacob son of Senex may have been the Jacob who was a nephew of Aaron
76. Hill, *ML*, pp 235-36
77. H.G. Richardson, *The English Jewry under Angevin Kings* (London: Methuen, 1960), 217-219; Robin R. Mundill, *The King's Jews: Money, Massacre and Exodus in Medieval England* (London: Continuum, 2010),90-92
78. TNA E 9/26, m.6: AALT IMG 0013
79. *CClR*,1272-1279, 529-30
80. *Cant* 290
81. *Cant* 281
82. *Cant* 282
83. See above, p80
84. *Cant* 73, 292; Dij 74/3/8
85. No major expenditure on repairs is recorded until 1319/20: see Bj 2.5.,f.23
86. *ibid.*, f.116. A dendro-date range of 1321–52 was obtained for the lintel above the door and window of no.1 Steep Hill: see *Vernacular Architecture* vol. 25 (1994)
87. *e.g. ibid.*, ff.165,173v,181; Bj 5.1
88. Bj 1.2 and 1.3
89. Bj 1.1.7ff
90. Bij 3.16., no.32
91. Bij 3.19., no.80
92. LCC Wills 1621 i,123
93. LL 116/1-2
94. CC 27/152829 3/7, p. 17
95. LL 116/3,4; see also Canon Featley's notebook, 2 CC 8/152941, p. 118
96. LL 116/10
97. 2 CC 21/150888 1/3
98. Civ 95/1
99. 2 CC 21/150888 2/3
100. *BNLW* 4/11/71; L3 list at LA has a note by Joan Varley; no deeds deposited
101. See the historical account above
102. *Fig 66*
103. *Fig 73*
104. *Fig 79*
105. *Fig 74*
106. *Fig 75*
107. Pipe Roll reference as for note 15 above; *VC* no.288: there is no reference to which boundary was north or south
108. *Cant* 281
109. *Cant* 282
110. Abrahams, *op.cit.*,94-96
111. L1/1/1/3 f.154v
112. L1/1/1/4 f.34
113. L1/1/1/6 f.58v; Ciij 9.1/45
114. LC Leases 745
115. L1/1/1/8 p. 847
116. See the references to Corporation leases under no.14 Steep Hill above
117. *ARMH* deposit, bundle 299 (uncatalogued)
118. *LCC* Wills 1629/400
119. *LCC* Wills 1681 ii, 420
120. *LCL* 5079 *passim*
121. *Misc Don* 1097/1
122. Boundary reference in St Martin's Parish lease for nos 8-9 Strait, 1794
123. Willson and Betham Survey: St Martin's parish

5–9 STRAIT

The medieval documentation for the area, which centres on no.7 Strait, is lacking in quantity but most rewarding with regard to its historical and topographical evidence. When the later records for these sites are analysed, the material contained in just three documents of the 14th century may be more fully explained.

Among the unpublished charters of the Dean and Chapter are two deeds, one of 1335 and one dated 1336, which deal with the acquisition of a messuage (no.7 Strait), situated between the king's way on the east and the king's street called Pulterie or La Pulterye on the west. The first is a lease for 14 years dated 14 September 1335 from William Russell, a merchant, and Isold his wife, to Roger Brydok, draper, at the rent of 24s per annum.[1] The north bound in this deed is a messuage of William de Blyton. This, according to the later leases and other documents for the site,[2] comprised both nos 8 and 9 Strait, which stayed in common ownership until well into the 20th century. The south bound in the 1335 deed consisted of another property owned by the Russells and a shop of William de Blyton.

Using again the story told by the later documents for this area, it is clear that this was another case of conjoined tenements, true at least for the 17th–18th centuries and probably originating in the medieval period. Blyton was an important figure in 14th-century Lincoln, and would have preferred to own the more spacious double-fronted messuages which characterised other parts of the Strait and the upper High Street: Jews' Court, Jew's House, 10–11 Strait, and on the other side of the street, nos 16–18, 25–26, 27–28 and 33–34 Strait. It seems clear that the archetypal narrow burgage plot was not the general rule in the central part of the city, and it was only in the later medieval period that many properties became subdivided.

The 1336 document is a quitclaim issued by Isold Russell, now a widow, to Roger Brydok on 30 November 1336, of her interests in no.7.[3] Presumably a formal conveyance

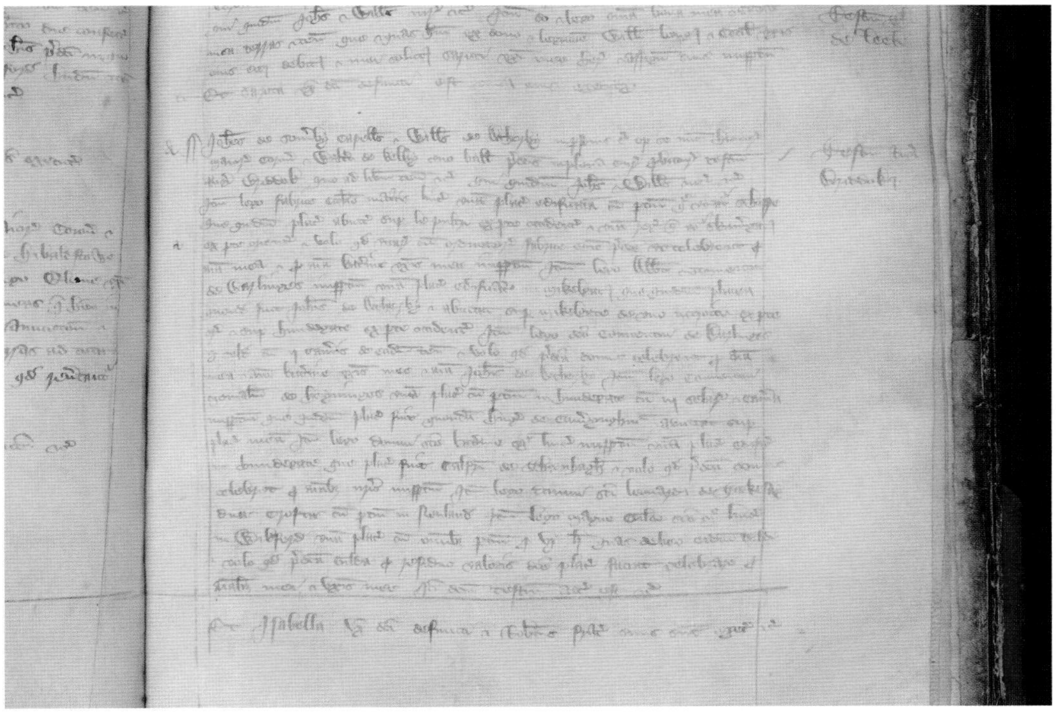

Fig 82. No.7 Strait: will of Roger Brydok, 1349, from the Lincoln Burwarmote Book

of the freehold predating the quitclaim was lost at some point. The north bound (Blyton) was just as before, but the Russells' other messuage to the rear of nos 5–6 had already been granted to Richard, son of Adam Fitzmartin, member of another leading city family; John Shipman, poulterer, was the occupier. This property, described as two shops with two solars and one little garden in the Poultry, was left by Richard to his wife Isabella for life, with a reversion to his son Philip, in 1345.[4]

The third document in the series concerning no.7 is the will of Roger Brydok, a copy of which was registered in the Burwarmote Book.[5] Like so many others, it was proved in the fateful year of 1349. Brydok had two executors: his wife Isabel and brother Robert. Two other people saw to the probate of the will: John de Somerby and William Atherby. In the will, which includes a bequest to the Cathedral for the use of the Fabric, the plot or shop is said to abut on le Pultri on the west side and the king's way called Skinnergate on the east side. This is rather confusing, as the skin market was originally elsewhere, to the north of Hungate. A second problem is the later assignment of the property by the Chapter to the Board Rents[6] rather than to the Fabric Fund. Brydok stipulated that the *Ordinator Fabrice* (Master of the Fabric) was to celebrate masses for his soul and that of his first wife, Catherine.

8–9 Strait

The Resurrection Gild at St Martin's Church was the point of receipt for a number of property bequests in the late medieval period. Some tenants of this property in the period around 1600 are mentioned in an early volume of churchwardens' accounts preserved among the Corporation records.[7] William Goone, who also owned houses in the parish of St Michael on the Mount,[8] paid 4d per annum c.1595–1601, and John Birks from 1601 to 1633. In 1612 the rent increased from 8d pa to 3s. Audrey Bradshaw, widow, is recorded as tenant c.1672 according to the north bounds of a Chapter lease for no.7. She died in 1685, bequeathing the bulk of her estate to her son Robert, a baker.[9]

*Fig 83.
Contemporary
photograph,
nos 8–9 Strait*

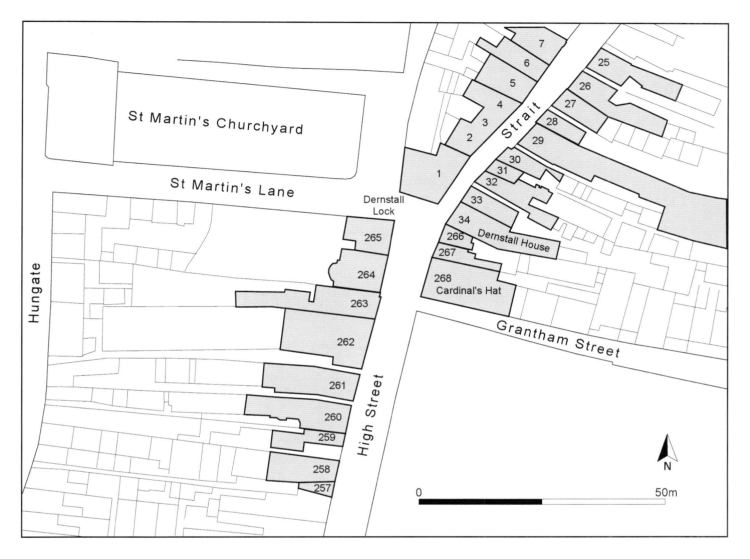

St Martin's Churchyard

St Martin's Lane

Hungate

High Street

Dernstall Lock

Strait

Dernstall House

Cardinal's Hat

Grantham Street

265
264
263
262
261
260
259
258
257

266
267
268

7
6
5
4
3
2
1

25
26
27
28
29
30
31
32
33
34

N

0   50m

In 1755 the parish lessee was Alderman John Willson, and the tenements were occupied by Edward Hunton, painter, and Widow Bee. The parish, in addition to the main rent, also charged a quit-rent of 'one large fat roasting piece of beef or 5s pa'.[10] Mary Julian, who was also connected with 4–7 Steep Hill as mentioned above, had a lease here from 1794, when there were four tenements on the site, two facing the Strait and two fronting the Green Hill at the rear. There was a paddock here, intermixed with freehold land owned by Alderman Joshua Morris.

As was the case with nos 10–11 and several other houses in the Strait, these houses soon formed part of the property 'empire' of Robert Reynolds. He was a cordwainer by trade, and had obviously prospered, with contracts on behalf of Christ's Hospital to provide boots and shoes for the boys.[11] In later life he was styled 'gentleman'. His widow Mary kept on the lease here, and was recorded in that capacity in the 1828 Survey, with Anthony Swales and Thomas Turner, joiner, in occupation.

As with other shops in the Strait, these changed hands regularly in the Victorian period. As shopkeepers progressed in their trades they often aspired to move further down the road and into the prime retail area of the High Street. The Strait and Steep Hill became the entrepot for second-hand clothing and furniture broking, a synonym for pawnbroking. Fred Beecham Morris was one of the furniture brokers, and he had a sideline in antiques. He occupied no.8 c.1877–1882. James Hallifax, also a broker and dealer in gold and silver, operated from no.9 between 1866 and 1882. Alfred Groundsell, who started his career as a blacksmith, also became a furniture broker and antiques dealer; he was at no.9 from 1891 until the period of the Great War.

Fig 84. Street plan, nos 7–1 Strait, 25–34 Strait and 257–268 High Street

107

7 Strait

This is one of those properties for which no direct post-medieval references are found prior to the Civil War period. The first surviving Chapter lease is dated 1672, given to Joyce Darby, widow.[12] The plot dimensions were mentioned in the description, a rare occurrence in this area of the city: 22 yards long by 6 yards wide / 20.1m × 5.8m. In 1662 Canon Featley mentioned in his notebook[13] that Joyce, née Whittaker, had previously been married to someone named Ellis, later identified as Simon Ellis, who had died in the 1640s. She had married William Darby, labourer, c.1650, and they were both reportedly "...Anabaptists or some other sect of Separatists...".

The original lease to Ellis[14] had expired, and William Graves accused William and Joyce of concealing the 'purchase' of a house, garth and cottage occupied by Richard Mumby. William Darby was presumably still alive at the time of Featley's survey (1660/61), but no new lease appears to have been issued at this time. Board Rentals, sporadic at best for the pre-Reformation period, are preserved only from 1700.

Elizabeth Ringstead, widow, was lessee 1696–1703.[15] Her son John, a tailor but described in his will of 1705[16] as an innholder, also had a short-lived tenancy.[17] James Pink, carver at the Cathedral, lived here from c.1770 until his death in around 1812, succeeded by his widow Catherine.[18] In 1820 Benjamin Carrington, furniture broker, took over the leasehold. He was probably responsible for building a tenement in the yard, occupied in 1828 by John Maginly and in 1837 by Richard Lilburn. Carrington sublet both parts of the leasehold in 1837 to William Howitt, eating-house keeper, Edward Howitt, confectioner, and George Howitt, butcher, for 14 years at £27 10s per annum; they were to reinstate any conversion work at the expiration of the lease.[19]

Benjamin Carrington junior, a cabinet maker, and Roger Hiley, currier, executors of the elder Carrington, were joint lessees of no.7 in 1841 and 1848. Carrington alone held the lease for some years afterwards[20] and was followed by the Swallow family of furniture dealers and paper hangers who occupied the premises c.1861–91; later occupants were in a similar line of business.

5–6 Strait

This was a freehold property, situated immediately south of a Chapter leasehold. By the early 16th century, it is understood that the tenements here had deteriorated. In 1527 Christopher Wymbyssh leased them to John Huchinson, cordwainer, for 61 years at a nominal rent of 6d per annum, on what must have been a repairing lease. At this point in the history of the site Wymbyssh owned both the frontage to the Strait and the property adjacent to the lane on the west, described as 'the backside of Dernstall Lock'.[21]

Documentation for the period 1528–1672 is non-existent, and until the early 18th-century we have to rely on boundary evidence from Chapter leases of no.7, described as 'void ground' in 1527. The earliest reference thereafter is to a William Daniel, owner or tenant here c.1672. He also held land near the Old Fishmarket in the parish of St Michael, which was known as Daniel's Garth.[22] In 1696 Isabel Long, widow of Stephen Long and also connected with the Garth and no.11 Steep Hill, was the owner of nos 5–6 Strait. It may be that she remarried, as an Isabel Archer was noted there in 1703.[23] Peter Basford was the next known owner, recorded in the 1730s and 1740s; he also had land off Michaelgate, and his name was still used (anachronistically) in lease boundaries until 1806.

Around 1750 Edward Holland, plumber and glazier, acquired the property and left it in his will to trustees for the benefit of his wife Ann for life. The freehold was to be put into the hands of devisees for sale (John Garmston and Richard Barker), who were authorised to sell after Ann's death, which may have occurred c.1763.[24] By this time the property had become divided into two tenements, although still under single ownership,

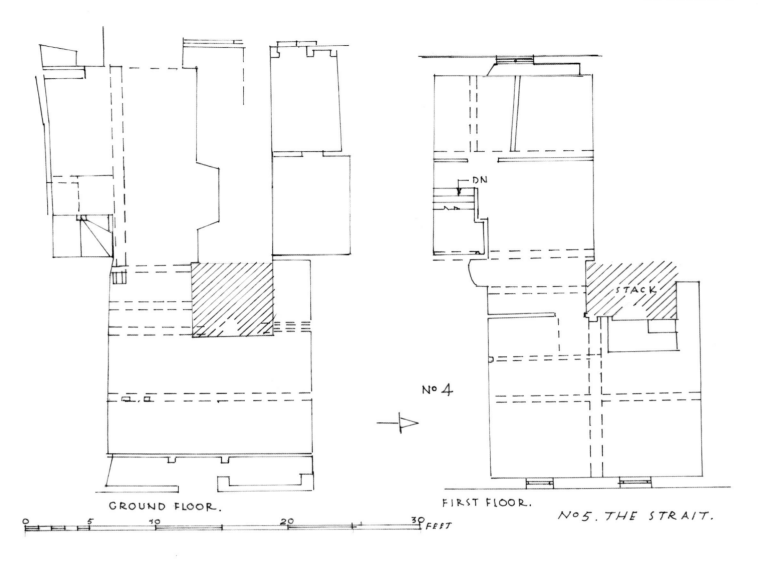

GROUND FLOOR.

FIRST FLOOR.

No 4

STACK

DN

No 5. THE STRAIT.

0 5 10 20 30 FEET

Fig 85. Plans, no.5 Strait, from a slide
Fig 86. Contemporary photograph, nos 5–7 Strait

and there were in addition two cottages at the rear of the premises fronting onto the Green Hill. John Woodhall, a gardener who held other properties, including Chapter and Christ's Hospital leaseholds in several areas of the city, purchased the whole estate for £140.[25]

The Woodhall family later made a partition between the frontage on the Strait and the rear properties, which went to Ann his wife. Thomas, his son, retained nos 5–6 Strait. In the 1828 Survey Robert Medley, also a gardener and married to Ann Woodhall, was proprietor of no.6 and Rebecca Woodhall owned no.5. Robert and William Medley, brazier, effected a Common Recovery of part of the premises at no.6 in 1832. Ann Jane Medley of Southwell sold no.6 in 1836 to George Bishop, watchmaker, and two years later it was purchased by William Parry, victualler, who died in 1877.

At no.5 the majority of the occupants in the 19th century were furniture brokers or similar traders, including Matthew Smith, described as a mattress maker and upholsterer and listed in the directories from 1856 to 1863.

ARCHITECTURAL
DESCRIPTION
(5 STRAIT)

A small 'L'-planned building, stone walled, excepting the north gable, and of two stories throughout.[26] The roof, partly visible, is inaccessible unfortunately but is of clasped purlin type above the street range at the south, of which may be seen a tie-beam buried in the end wall there. There is no evidence for attics or of any use of the roof space. At ground-level a through passage may be inferred from the filled-in area north of the back wing of the 'L', and from a blocked window on that side in the same wing. The shop ceiling joists originate from cut-up roof rafters etc. with notched joints of late 13th-/early 14th-century character.

A point of some interest is the way in which the back wing overlaps the adjoining tenement to the south (no.4) by what appears to be the width of a further passage from the street. The common wall at this junction is of stone extending through to the street and is unplastered where exposed in the roof void. A closer examination of the roof might reveal the original arrangement of the front upper wall towards the Strait, which, at present, is of early 19th-century brickwork. A probable date for the house in its present form is of the later 17th century. It is worth noting that the re-use of earlier material could point to a superseded house being its immediate source.

1–4 STRAIT

POST-MEDIEVAL
OCCUPATION

This wedge-shaped block has proved very difficult to elucidate, as the surviving records are few in number. Nevertheless it is possible to show that there were several different holdings in the late 15th and early 16th centuries, and these have assisted in making an informed guess as to the precise location and nature of Dernstall Lock, a feature which has occasioned as many theories as variants in spelling.

In the south-west corner of the plot in February 1475 was a shop with a room built above it, owned by John Barwyke, a merchant, situated between property belonging to the Prior and Convent of St Katherine's outside Lincoln, on the north, land and a tenement of Henry Byngley, mercer, and late belonging to Robert Knyght, merchant, on the east, the highway of Dernstall on the west and 'the highway at Darnstalloke' on the south. Barwyke granted this to Thomas Hall, William Hall and Robert Emsale, Merchants of the Staple at Calais.[27] It is uncertain whether this was a straight conveyance or a trust deed. This document seems to limit the range of Dernstall Lock to the east–west frontage of the shop.

Contrast this with the lease of 1527 described in the passage on nos 5–6 Strait above as being situated between a tenement of Christopher Wymbyssh on the south (nos 1–4)

and void ground of the Dean and Chapter on the north (no.7). The backside of Dernstall Lock was to the west, so the Lock at this point covered the lane to the west, between the south-west corner of no.1 and the northern extremity of no.4.

The third document relevant to Dernstall Lock concerns the Henry Byngley who lived at the south-east corner of the site in 1475. He lived there until the 1520s, and made his will,[28] leaving the house at 'Darnstall lok' (*sic*) to Alice his wife for life, then to be sold. Hamon Pay, brazier and Alice's executor, acquired this property in 1526. Byngley's tenement comprised all the property on the east side of the range, from the corner northwards to the boundary with no.5 Strait.

Sometime after the Restoration part of this range, i.e. what is now nos 2–4 Strait, was leased by an unidentified owner to John Scrimshire, gentleman, who it is thought came here from the Grantham area and had properties of his own in Swineshead, Frampton, Gosberton, Boston, Heighington and Wellingore, all mentioned in his will, proved in 1686.[29]

His estate was left to his wife Hannah, with reversionary interests in this leasehold to their daughters Sarah, Hannah and Margaret. Margaret's second husband was John Lobsey, Alderman of Lincoln and twice mayor of the city. His name and the year 1737 are engraved on a tablet once fixed to the wall of the Butter Market, now incorporated into the north wall of the Central Market, City Square. Lobsey was also a philanthropist and left a generous legacy to Christ's Hospital in his will of 1748.[30]

In 1726 Lobsey purchased the various interests of his wife's relatives in this property, described as being at Dernstall Lock, which Scrimshire had sublet before his death to

Fig 87. Contemporary photograph, nos 1–4 Strait

William Darby, Widow Jackson, Thomas Hammond and Robert Hodgson.[31] At some point before 1726 the freehold of the property had been acquired, but the deed for this has not been located. After Lobsey's death the property remained involved in a family trust presided over by Taylor Calcroft, an attorney who lived in the Close and was also related by marriage to Lobsey. This trust was wound up in 1764/65 when the various family interests were bought up by Gervase Gibson.[32] Gibson died in 1789, leaving his City properties to Clifton Wheat of Timberland, a cousin.[33] Wheat soon sold nos 2–4 to Alderman Joshua Morris for £640. Morris also acquired no.1 Strait, for which there are no separate earlier deeds.

Nos 2–4, at one time two cottages, were used together as an inn called the White Lion, in the tenancy of John Wade, from c.1764, but this name had been dropped by 1789, when Widow Peacock was the tenant. Morris sold nos 2–4 to John Peacock, watchmaker, in 1795.[34] For some years afterwards these properties were in the hands of John Steel, one of the partners in the doomed financial business of Messrs Sheath, Steel and Wray, which collapsed c.1814. Their assignees in bankruptcy sold nos 2–4 to John Walker, gentleman, who died in 1833. His descendants sold them in 1894 to John Mills.

No.1, the corner property, has left us few records except for the references to Joshua Morris around 1800. Daniel Hill Davis, the baker, who had property on the other side of the Strait,[35] apparently owned and occupied no.1 c.1816.[36] Thomas and Mary Skepper lived here consecutively from c.1828 until the late 1860s, followed by the ironmongery business of John Elliott, which occurred c.1877–1901, although Richard Swallow had a lock-up shop here in 1891. From 1907 to 1913 Charles Foulds had a music warehouse. Charles Beard, saddler, lived at this address in 1918: a fire insurance policy for 'Dunston Lock House' includes provision for musical instruments and music books.[37]

1   Dij 75.2.12
2   See below
3   Dij 75.2.19
4   *BB* f.170v, no.551
5   *ibid.*, f.198, no.661; see *Fig 82*
6   LL 123 *passim*
7   L1/5/12
8   L1/3/1 f.209
9   LL 123/1; LCC Wills 1685 ii,32
10 Lincoln St Martin parish 8
11 *LCL* 5082
12 LL 123/1; Bij 4.2 no.85
13 2 CC 8/152941,p.190
14 This has escaped all attempts at discovery, and thus may cast doubt on Featley's informant, William Graves
15 LL 123/2
16 LCC Wills 1705/251
17 LL 123/3
18 LL 123/8-10; Bij 5. 6 f.69v; 5.7 ff.5v, 250; 5.8 p. 594
19 Sills and Betteridge, Leases and Agreements, uncatalogued
20 Bij 5. 12 p. 453; Bij 5.13 p. 281; 2 CC 9/152947
21 Lancs RO, O'Hagan Mss K/12/18
22 *LCL* 5389; *DEG* 7/2
23 LL 117/2-3
24 LCC Wills 1756/86
25 *Misc Dep* 478/2/1
26 *Fig 85*
27 L1/3/1, f.35v
28 *Ibid.*,f.107-107v
29 LCC Wills 1686 ii,172
30 *LPC* 1/18/7
31 Hill 28/1/14/5
32 *ibid.*
33 LCC Wills 1789/77
34 Hill 28/1/14/1; *Misc Don* 522/3
35 See below, p.123
36 Hill 28/1/14
37 4 *DEG* 3/1/2/1

16–26 STRAIT

16–18 Strait, including some references to property further eastwards

Existing information we have relating to this range of properties in the medieval period points to a high-status area dominated by large plots which were later subdivided. One such plot was that which was later split into nos 16–18 Strait and nos 2–4 Danes Terrace. This was even larger at one time, as archaeological investigation has indicated that the building line originally came much further west, at least five metres into the current roadway. The Strait, therefore, was narrow all the way between Danes Terrace and Dernstall House, thoroughly justifying its name.

Unfortunately no medieval documents directly relate to this northern section of the range, but the fact that it was still under single ownership well into the post-medieval period argues for it being an important site. Of similar status were two nearby properties, one of which, situated to the east, covered the corner bordering Flaxengate and Danes Terrace. A Dean and Chapter tenement, this was described in the Parliamentary Survey of 1649 as: "...a piece of ground ... wherein did stand a fair house ruined by the wars...", i.e the siege of May 1644.[1] Four 13th-century deeds, printed in *Registrum Antiquissimum*,[2] relate to this site, which also received a comment in Bob Jones' work on the Flaxengate excavations of the 1970s.[3]

The property immediately south of this corner plot was the home of one of the leading citizens of the early 13th century, Robert son of Ywein (Eudo). In c.1215–20 it

DOCUMENTARY HISTORY

Fig 88. Photograph showing archaeological excavations, nos 16–18 Strait, c.1973

was described as his *curia*, and was therefore in all probability his main residence. Robert at various times filled the offices of bailiff, mayor and coroner. One vital question, which may not be answerable, is whether his *curia* extended all the way from Flaxengate to the Strait (should this ever be proved, it would relate to nos 19–24 Strait). Robert is known to have acquired one messuage in Lincoln which had belonged to Aaron the Jew and was in escheat to the king. Robert's debt of 10s per annum on this house was recorded in successive Pipe Roll entries for many years between 1228 and 1299.[4] It is possibly the same house, once of Roger Peppercorn, which Aaron acquired not long before his death in 1186.[5]

Described as 'three mansions or tenements together', nos 16–18, together with other tenements abutting Bull Ring Terrace (later Danes Terrace), were owned until 1513 by Edward Browne, jeweller, one of the leading lights in the city at this time, together with several other properties elsewhere. After his death his grandson John Sutton ejected a number of other feoffees and set up a new trust under John Pykerd (Pickard) and the Town Clerk, Richard Hunston.[6] By 1518 Robert Wymark was the sole surviving trustee and, instead of perpetuating the trust, devised the properties in his will[7] to Robert Turnour, chaplain and chantry priest of the chantry of Alexander FitzMartin in the parish church of St Laurence, which had been established for over 200 years. Wymark died in 1523, and his will and codicil were enrolled in the City's *White Book* in 1526.[8]

After the dissolution of the FitzMartin chantry, this and other former chantry properties were granted by Edward VI in May 1549 to Sir John Thynne and Thomas Throgmorton, and transferred by them a few days later to John Broxholme Esq. and Thomas Burton Esq.; the tenant of the Strait properties at this time may have been Peter Carter, whose family, as seen earlier in this volume, had extensive property interests in the city.[9] Later in the same year Broxholme conveyed his moiety to a group of city Aldermen for £124 12s 4d,[10] although what happened to Burton's share is unrecorded. Nevertheless, a boundary reference from the St Mark's parish property deeds in 1550, relating to nos 19–24 Strait, gives us the names of Thomas Wymbyssh Esq. of Nocton, who himself had a number of city holdings,[11] and William Rotheram, who sold the property to the south to St Mark's parish.

The next reference to this range occurs in a St Mark's parish lease of 1617,[12] where the holder of property to the north is named as Alderman George Dickinson, who also at this time owned the property immediately to the east of this site along Bull Ring Terrace, acquired by him in 1614 from Edward Griffin, lessee of the "fair tenement" owned by the Dean and Chapter on the corner of Flaxengate. This site of Dickinson's was sold by him to Christ's Hospital in 1619,[13] William Bunce was also associated with part of the site, which was later referred to as Tailors' Hall, occupied by John Todd in 1667.

Ellen or Ellinor Cawton (nee Bracewell) is thought to have retained the Tailors' Hall site until her death, when it was left to Eleanor and Elizabeth Standish, daughters of Thomas Standish, deceased. The main part of the plot was sold to her sister Ann Dailes at some point before July 1667.[14] Ann died in the autumn of 1668, leaving this property, along with other tenements near the South Bail Gate, mentioned earlier in this volume, to her son John, who was already in residence.[15] John and Ruth his wife died without issue, their property passing to the children of his sisters Ann Bayley (later Ann Charles) and Elizabeth Taylor. As there were numerous offspring in both families, it made for a potentially complicated arrangement, not resolved until 1713. The Bayley heirs were Jane, wife of John Story, a Lincoln schoolmaster, and William Bayley of Grantham, fellmonger, and the Taylor heirs were Ann, wife of Lewis Dickinson of Grantham, joiner, Elizabeth, wife of Joseph Bullock of London, pattern maker, and Susanna and Bridget Taylor, also of London.[16]

They were all bought out for £30 by Ellen Seely, another sister of Ann Bayley and

Elizabeth Taylor. Ellen was the widow of John Seely, the founder of the Lincoln baking dynasty, who died in 1710.[17] Ellen died in 1735, leaving this property, described as a house or tenement near Bull Ring Lane, to William, their son, also a baker, who held it until his death in 1750.[18] Some partitioning of this extensive site seems to have been made during the middle part of the 18th century: another William Seely left four tenements in 1784 to Ann his wife, in trust to sell, as by this time the bakery business had moved downhill into the parish of St Peter at Arches. The property in the Strait was purchased for £110 by Charles Foster, a local mason; the occupants in 1784 were John Glew, John Cook, William Spicer and Mary Bellamy.[19]

This range, now five houses and a common yard, was bequeathed by Charles Foster in his will of 1799 to his son Thomas, also a builder; there was a partition of Charles' estates in 1822, and a schedule was made of the various holdings. In 1839 Thomas left the property to his son, another Thomas, who left it to his sister Martha Dixon in 1852; the Dixon family retained ownership until the early 20th century.[20]

19–24 Strait

On the Strait frontage, the area until recent times listed as nos 19–24 Strait was in the later medieval period owned by Barlings Abbey, although, like several other inner-city properties, it was not recorded in the abbey cartulary.

In 1546 the king granted various properties, including these houses (described as three tenements or cottages), to John Broxholme and John Bellow, agents for many such disposals. The cottages, in the occupation of John Denton, Robert Holand and Edward Thorpe, were granted on to William Rotheram, and in 1550 sold by him to Edmund Atkynson, Alderman of Lincoln, for the sum of one farthing.[21]

The document by which Atkynson transferred ownership to the parish of St Mark

Fig 89. Photograph of demolition work, rear of nos 23–24 Strait, c.1931

R. E. LEARY,

PRINTER, BOOKBINDER, AND STATIONER,

19, STRAIT, LINCOLN.

LETTER-PRESS PRINTING.

R. E. L. has at considerable expense added a Patent Locomotive Printing Machine, also a superior Iron Press of large dimensions, and a considerable quantity of new and fashionable types and ornaments, by which means he is enabled to execute all orders in Pamphlets, Posting and Hand Bills, Grocer's Wrappers, Chemist's Lists, Labels, &c., with despatch and at prices hitherto unknown in Lincoln.

COPPER-PLATE PRINTING.

R. E. L. has entirely re-constructed his Copper-plate Press, and by the addition of Iron Rollers, Regulating Screws, and using the best of Inks, he is enabled to execute all orders in this branch of his business in a superior manner.

BOOKBINDING

In the best manner and on moderate terms.—All books sent to bind on or before Saturday, will be returned home on the Saturday following, or earlier if required.

Fig 90. (below) Plan of parochial leaseholds, nos 19–26 Strait, c.1830
Fig 91. (left) No.19 Strait: advertisement from street directory, 1877

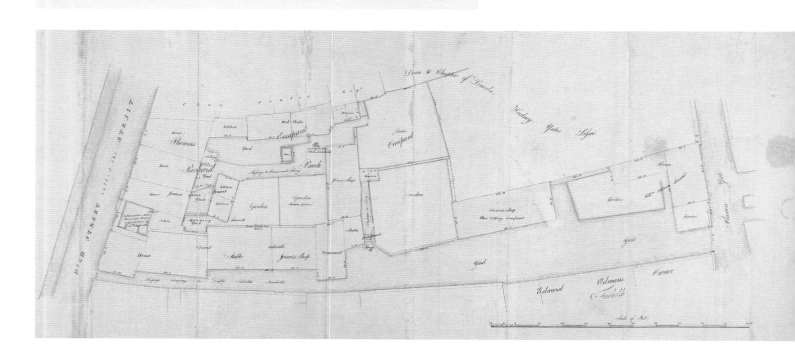

Fig 92. Photograph of the east side of the Strait, nos 16–26, c.1900

has not survived, but leases were being issued by 1573 for two leaseholds created from the original three tenements; the northern section consisted of one, and the southern portion had two. It is difficult to suggest which of the Victorian-era tenements were in the northern section. Details for all known lessees and occupiers for each section may be found in the disk accompanying this volume. Robert Duffield, one of the northern lessees, left an inventory in 1621 which described a simple room plan of a kitchen, hall, parlour and two chambers, one next to the garden at the rear.[22]

From the early 19th century, if not earlier, the parish reorganised the management of these properties to avoid a situation where lessees could sub-let on a rack rent system. Individual tenements were therefore rented out by the parish: some of the rental books have survived.[23] The street numbering for the Strait was occasionally altered during the first half of the 19th century, which may cause confusion to anyone trying to follow up the history of particular tenements.

There are occasional glimpses into the problems of maintaining run-down tenements. No.20 was given a new bow-fronted window in 1833, along with an oven and grate in the front room and a grate over the cellar window. In 1842, Mr Howitt, proprietor of a mill behind neighbouring properties, paid an acknowledgment of 7s 6d for having road access, past the City Arms (23 Strait), to his mill.[24] T.J.N. Brogden, in his report and valuation of 1855, commented that rents were in many cases below the actual site value. He recommended that George Draper at no.22 should have a kitchen with a chamber

117

over it, which would justify a 5% rise in his rent. One further remark is symptomatic of the acquiescence of landlords to the prevalence of overcrowding: "at present the accommodation afforded is miserable and the sleeping accommodation so stinted as to be prejudicial to health, and will soon be hurtful to the morals of your residents".[25]

25–26 Strait

Just within the medieval parish boundary of St Cuthbert, later absorbed into St Michael's parish, was the twin property known as 25–26 Strait. This has left few medieval traces, although there is some boundary data from nos 27–28 (see below). Before 1299 this property was described as land once belonging to William de Grymmesby, and by 1310 was in the hands of Adam de Grymmesby, skinner, who then granted it to Thomas Smethe, clerk, c.1324.[26]

Although we know that this pair of tenements was in the ownership of St Swithin's parish as early as 1550, no parish leases earlier than 1834 have been preserved, so this is another site where the historian is fairly heavily dependent on boundary evidence and occasional probate material to provide clues on the history of the site before 1828. The parish churchwardens' accounts from 1735 assist somewhat by quoting some names of tenants.[27]

The first known tenant, probably also a lessee, was Alderman Robert Bartholomew, fellmonger, who died in 1652.[28] He was also associated with the Corporation leasehold of St Laurence's Churchyard in 1635.[29] The Dry family of bakers lived here in the early 18th century, Mordecai Dry also being a lessee of the St Mark's property to the north. Faith Dry, his widow, stayed on until 1735, when John Lamb started a lengthy tenancy. He was a bricklayer and had properties both free and leasehold in the city centre area. In his will of 1779 he was able to style himself gentleman.[30]

From 1852 St Swithin's parish followed the lead of St Mark's in adopting a system of separate tenancies and rents. William Mitton, the wireworker or wire-drawer, who had been an occupier of no.25 in 1851, was recorded as tenant at £12 pa and George Footitt held no.26 at £24 pa. In 1856/57 both properties were rebuilt at a cost of £550.[31]

1	CC 27/152829 2/7, p. 24		*MCD* 161	21	FL St Mark's Parish 3/1
2	*RA viii*, nos 2267-2270	12	FL St Mark's Parish 3/2	22	FL St Mark's Parish 3/2-9; Inv

1   CC 27/152829 2/7, p. 24
2   *RA viii*, nos 2267-2270
3   *LAT vol xi-i: Medieval Houses at Flaxengate, Lincoln Archaeological Trust*, 1980,5-6
4   e.g. TNA E 372/72: Pipe Roll 11 Hen III
5   *Book of Fees* i,365
6   L1/3/1 f.97
7   *ibid.* f.104v-105,106-106v
8   cf. *LRS* vol 12,48-51
9   L1/3/1 f.119-120v
10   *ibid.*f.120v-121v
11   cf. his rental of 1537, ref.

   MCD 161
12   FL St Mark's Parish 3/2
13   L1/3/1 f.209; *MCD* 794/2,f.20v
14   See also the will of Ellen Cawton, LCC Wills 1668 i,312
15   LCC Wills 1668 ii, 354
16   L3/2326/1-2
17   LCC Wills 1710 i,82; L3/2326/1-2
18   LCC Wills 1750/153; L3/2326/3
19   LCC Wills 1784/189; L3/2326/4-6
20   L3 *ibid.*, 7-13

21   FL St Mark's Parish 3/1
22   FL St Mark's Parish 3/2-9; Inv 124/135]
23   Lincoln St Mark's Parish 8/1, 15/5/1; see also a plan of the Strait properties among the plans held at Lincoln Central Library, no.585 (*Fig 90*)
24   See below, p.123
25   Lincoln St Mark's Parish 8/3
26   *Cant* 286-289
27   Lincoln St Swithin's Parish 7/1
28   LCC Wills 1652/385; Lincoln

   St Mark's Parish 3/12
29   L1/3/2 f.115
30   Lincoln St Swithin's Parish 7/1; LCC Wills 1779/132
31   Lincoln St Swithin's Parish 7/1

SECTION EIGHT

27–28 STRAIT

One of the most extensive and certainly most intriguing of the former Jewish properties in Lincoln is the messuage of Floria, daughter of Josce, sometimes referred to as Floria of London; this was situated in the parish of St Martin. The site has now been identified because of the excellent chain of documentation in the Chapter records.

Her properties, both here and in the parish of St Cuthbert (as yet unidentified) were among those registered in 1290,[1] at around the time of the Expulsion, and also listed in B.L. Abrahams' table of the Jews and their assets.[2] The description of this property stands out from the other entries in the schedule: "*optima domus cum duabus shopis et pulcro exitu*": a top-quality house with two shops and a magnificent entrance passage.

The reader may be forgiven for thinking that this is estate agent-style hype, but this is very close to the truth, as the scheduling of the properties was part of the king's programme for calling in the assets of the Jews and selling them off for the best possible price. Hugh of Kendal was deputed to raise a maximum return from the forfeited properties in Lincoln and Stamford, as well as elsewhere, so the description could well have been used to appeal to prospective purchasers. On 27 March 1291 a grant was given by the king to William de Tame, cordwainer, of Lincoln,[3] who paid £20, a considerable sum and

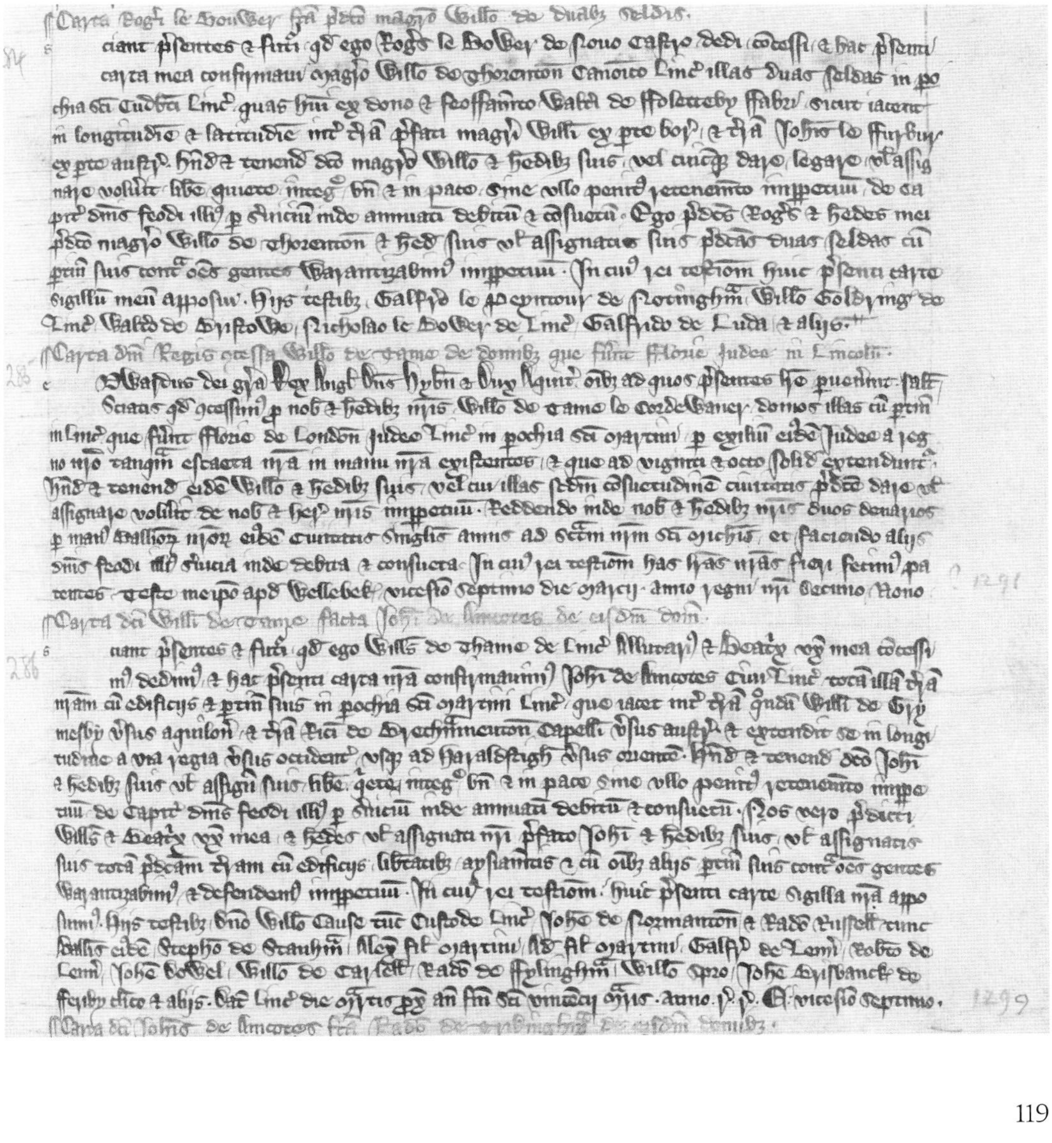

Fig 93. Nos 27–28 Strait: entries for the house of Floria the Jewess, from the Chantries Cartulary

DOCUMENTARY HISTORY

comparable to the 20 marks raised from the sale of the Jew's House, one of several sold by Kendal and reported to the king in June 1291.[4]

The house in the Strait was, in Abrahams' schedule, in the occupation of William le Belliget, more usually referred to as William le Belgetter (Bellfounder), who had property in the parish of Holy Trinity in Clewmarket, near Silver Street.[5] Floria and four of her siblings (Leon, Breton, Benedict and Bon) were among the last Jews left in Lincoln, and were sent into exile in France in November 1290. William de Tame was to pay 2d per annum landtoll charge to the king for this double tenement (it was rated at 1d in the original schedule). The 'magnificent entrance passage' was the central corridor, common to many of the Jewish houses, and the forerunner of the courtyard called, at various times in the next 600 years, Strait Passage, Carrington's Passage and Dickinson's Passage.

In January 1299[6] William de Tame and Beatrice his wife sold the property to John de Amecotes, who was bailiff of the city in 1300/01[7] and served as mayor in 1308/09.[8] John granted it in November 1310 to Ralph de Trikyngham, servant to Master William de Thornton.[9] Ralph in February 1311 granted it to Thornton; to the north was land once owned by William de Grymmesby and to the south land owned by Richard de Brecham, or Brechamneuton, chaplain, and land once owned by Alice de Rande.[10] Thornton received a royal licence to alienate this and other properties into mortmain, i.e. to the Dean and Chapter for religious uses, to endow the chantry which he was establishing.[11]

The last document in this medieval series is an agreement between Thomas Smethe, clerk, and the Chapter in May 1324 concerning water drainage between their properties,[12] Smethe had received a grant from Adam de Grymmesby of what is now nos 25–26 Strait, and there was some argument about responsibility in the matter, which was resolved.

Some references to repair work carried out on this property and others of the Chapter may be gained from their account book, all dating from between 1333 and 1340, when Roger de Kele was tenant: 6d was spent in 1333/34, 8s 3¼d in 1335/36, 4s 11d in 1337/38 and 14s 11d in 1339/40 – relatively minor expenditure perhaps suggesting that the Jews had looked after their properties fairly well.[13]

As a surviving chantry endowment, there are some references in the Board Rentals of the Dean and Chapter, in which the Thornton and Gare properties were normally included. A William Batty was paying 6s 8d rent per annum in 1529,[14] an amount which seems not to have changed in later years.

In the years prior to 1588 John Barnes was tenant, but in that year a 40-year lease was registered to Nicholas Crosfeld, yeoman, doubtless related to the Richard and Edward Crosfeld who successively held the Cardinal's Hat between 1572 and 1588, and another Edward, a bowyer who was associated with no.265 High Street in 1542.[15] The description of the property in 1588 was, as usual, sparse in the extreme, so we have no way of knowing whether there were any remnants of the 13th-century fabric.

This was still an important site, with potential for development, as it had retained the frontage to the former Haraldstigh, later Flaxengate, to the east. This area had not retained the population it had in the 13th century, and several plots away from the main streets were now orchards or gardensteads. The Wymbyssh rental of c.1527[16] shows several 'waste' tenancies where no rents were recoverable.

Crosfeld was here for only a few years, as the rentals include payment by Peter Willson in 1591 and 1598 for a tenement and orchard. Edward Taylor, baker, took a lease in 1614, followed in 1633 by George Becke, fishmonger,[17] Amid the disruption of the siege of Lincoln in May 1644 Becke lost his lease, and many of his other belongings and goods. There is a good description of the property in 1649 at the time of the Parliamentary Survey:[18] "a tenement in St Martin's, consisting of a hall, a parlour, a kitchen, a buttery, two lodging chambers, one stable with a hayloft over; the building of rough stone, part tiled and part thatched, with a garden and orchard by estimation 1 rood and 20 perches, abutting a common lane east, the high street west, St Swithin's church land north and Mr White's land on the south".

Precentor Featley noted in 1662 that it had lately been in the occupation of Edward Friskney, gent., "with the shop, chambers and other buildings to the same belonging".[19] Becke renewed the lease in 1668, by which time there were now five lodging chambers instead of two; his term had been adjusted to 21 years.[20] Sometime after 1668 Richard and Mary Howrobin became occupiers; Richard died in 1681, leaving this house to his son George after his mother died.[21] His probate inventory[22] adds some detail to what we know of the house at this period, cataloguing the contents of the parlour chamber, boarden chamber (wainscotted?), chamber over the kitchen chamber, brewhouse chamber, little parlour, great parlour, cellar, kitchen, brewhouse and stable. Most of his net worth was tied up in bills, bonds and debts owed to him. In the stable he kept a horse and two pigs.

Mary Howrobin took a new lease in 1682 and promptly assigned it to George.[23] Dr Edward Legh succeeded in 1692 and his son Richard, a clergyman in Leicestershire, followed in 1714. It was the subject of three further assignments, latterly to Hadnah Yates, tailor in 1767. Yates died in 1794 and his son, another Hadnah, was given a new lease at that time.[24] He also took over the Cardinal's Hat holding soon afterwards (see below).

At some point between 1808 and 1815 Francis Mansford, grocer, became involved with this property. Mansford also held leasehold shops at 263 and 257/8 High Street,[25] and his grand plan was to redevelop the Strait property and nos 257/8; he went bankrupt in the process, but not before removing any vestiges of the medieval buildings in the Strait. New houses were erected at nos 27 and 28 Strait, with three other buildings behind the former, the beginnings of a courtyard development. Mansford may have been one of the unfortunate investors caught up in the Sheath, Steel and Wray bankruptcy fiasco, and by June 1815 he was reduced to living in one of the courtyard tenements behind no.27.[26]

Because of the redevelopment and Mansford's collapse, the Chapter property was split into four separate leaseholds in 1815:

No.27 with three tenements to the rear
A paddock behind no.27 which also took in land to the rear of nos 25–26 (later Edman's soap factory)
A tenement and yard south of the paddock behind
No.28 with premises for Carrington's furniture business at the rear and right of way through a passage to Flaxengate: this passage was later developed

The new premises at no.27 were leased in 1815[27] to James Bass Topham of Mavis Enderby, farmer, and Charles Vessey of Lincoln, butcher. By 1843 there were five tenements to the rear, along what was now called Carrington's Passage. The front premises were described in the auction particulars[28] as "a good dwelling house and shop, with two bow windows and a door in the centre". No.28 was leased to Benjamin Carrington and included land for his business, carried on initially with John Hawson. Carrington, a staunch Methodist, moved to Scarborough and then to Hull.[29] His son, another Benjamin, carried on the business but let out no.28 to Thomas Spencer, boot and shoe maker, who occupied the house until c.1861. After 1843 both buildings were let to a succession of small businesses, ranging from baking to phonographs.

29–32 STRAIT

Historical evidence for any of these properties before 1485 is minimal and largely confined to boundary references. The geographical layout of these plots may throw some light on their relative importance in the early post-medieval phase. Bob Jones, in his work on the medieval properties in Flaxengate,[30] thought that there had originally been an extensive holding covering nos 28–32, situated between the Strait and Flaxengate. If a slight adjustment to this model is allowed for no.28 Strait to have belonged with no.27, as shown above, there is a good argument for continuing to link nos 29–32.

Whether this range actually connected through to Flaxengate (Haraldstigh in the earlier period) cannot now be determined, as the 1842 Padley plan[31] shows a north–south property boundary creating a division at the midway point behind no.29, and another at a point further west behind the other properties. This shows up again on the OS Town Plan and Bob Jones' reconstruction diagram. No.29 appears to have been the key holding, with nos 30–32 forming a sub-group. Looking more closely at the OS plan, no.31 seems to be an infill of some kind, perhaps masking an earlier entrance passage.

For no.29 there are only two surviving medieval references which are relevant, both as south boundaries to the former Jewish property at nos 27–28. In 1299 this was land belonging to Richard de Brechamneuton, chaplain,[32] and in 1310 belonging to Richard de Brecham and Alice de Rande.[33] Nothing further is known of either, unfortunately.

It is known from boundary evidence contained in leases of nos 27–28 Strait for the late 16th and early 17th century that the area covered by no.29, if not also nos 30–32, consisted of a stable and orchard belonging to the 'heirs of Wymbyssh'. The Wymbyssh family of Nocton owned several properties in Lincoln, some of these in the parish of St Martin being very ruinous, according to the 1527 rental.[34] This particular site could be the piece of ground occupied by John Howe, skinner, in 1604 when the estates of Richard Towneley, previously of Edward Wymbyssh, were assigned to trustees for sale.[35]

At some point in the first half of the 17th century this property came into the hands of a Mr White, and his name was perpetuated in boundary references as late as 1808. This was possibly Alderman Richard White, who is known to have left property in the parish of St Martin to his son Richard in 1641/42.[36] By 1815 the owner of no.29 was Benjamin Carrington, the cabinet maker who also held no.28, although the eastern portion of this site (no.29), extending to Flaxengate, was in the hands of Daniel Hill Davis, baker, who had been one of the sheriffs in 1812. Carrington's son Benjamin still held this property and probably also no.30 in 1851, with George Goodwin (maybe related to Jane Goodwin, housekeeper for Carrington, a widower), proprietor of the land to the rear.[37]

Nos 31 and 32 were owned c.1828 by Peter Rook, baker, who also held nos 33 and 34. He took over from a Samuel Lloyd, whose occupation is unknown. By 1841 Rook had sold out to Benjamin Carrington, and he died in 1847.[38]

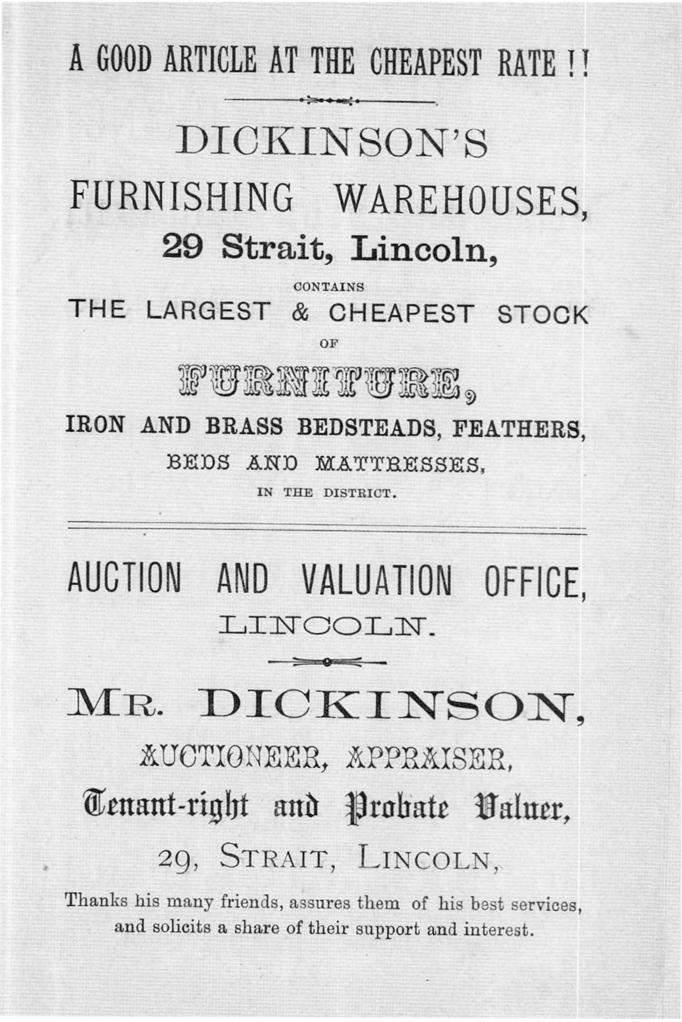

Fig 94. No.29 Strait: advertisement from street directory, 1904

A GOOD ARTICLE AT THE CHEAPEST RATE !!

DICKINSON'S
FURNISHING WAREHOUSES,
29 Strait, Lincoln,
CONTAINS
THE LARGEST & CHEAPEST STOCK
OF
FURNITURE,
IRON AND BRASS BEDSTEADS, FEATHERS,
BEDS AND MATTRESSES,
IN THE DISTRICT.

AUCTION AND VALUATION OFFICE,
LINCOLN.

MR. DICKINSON,
AUCTIONEER, APPRAISER,
Tenant-right and Probate Valuer,
29, STRAIT, LINCOLN,

Thanks his many friends, assures them of his best services,
and solicits a share of their support and interest.

33–34 STRAIT: DERNSTALL HOUSE

For a complex which has survived as long as this timber-framed gem undoubtedly has, it deserves a better-documented history than the extant records will allow us to discover; this is why the architectural evidence is so important in this case.

If we assume that the grant of the Cardinal's Hat to John de Welbourne, Treasurer of the Cathedral, in 1361, encompassed the two smaller tenements to the north, now nos 266–267 High Street, then it is feasible to suppose that the northern bounds of that grant, identified in the text as belonging to Walter de Poynton and Robert de Thymelby,[39] relate to holdings north of no.266, i.e. nos 33–34 Strait and a more extensive area of property going eastwards behind the Strait frontage.

Both Poynton, who lived in Canwick, and Thymelby are known from other sources to have been of the merchant classes. Thymelby, with its variant spellings, was a prominent family name in the city from the late 12th to the 16th centuries. Robert had property in the parish of St Cuthbert,[40] bequeathing it to his children. His will was proved in August 1361, just a few weeks before the grant to Welbourne. His main residence was in the suburb of Thorngate, between the Witham and Sincil Dyke, and he also had land in St Michael's parish.[41]

Poynton had property in St Mary le Wigford parish,[42] and his widow Oframinna held land further down the High Street in 1383, just south of the Little Gowt Drain and abutting the city wall to the east; incidentally this is one of a select few references to a wall in this area.[43] As the property to the north was freehold, and early modern boundary references to nos 266–267 High Street lacking before 1693, it has so far proved impossible to unearth any owners or occupiers of this site before that particular date, when William Dean is found as occupier.[44] Nothing is known of his occupation, although he may have been a baker, as that trade was followed at no.34 Strait from or before 1708 until c.1861. In 1708 the tenant was a Mr Coulson,[45] and he was followed by George Brooks, who also had connections with nos 249–250 High Street.[46] George died in 1719, leaving his house in St Martin's parish to his wife Elizabeth, then to William his brother, a cordwainer.[47] William's son George inherited his uncle's chamberlain's gown and silver-headed cane; George senior had probably been the Chamberlain for the North Ward of the City.

After the death of Elizabeth Brooks, who was here in 1722, there is a gap in the boundary evidence until 1736, when William Johnson was the occupier.[48] He was still in residence in 1749, followed by Jonathan Durance in 1763.[49] The Durance family continued in ownership until 1815, with Thomas Hill (to c.1800) and Ann Hayes in occupation.[50]

From 1815 onwards there are two groups of title deeds which help to tell the story of the building. In 1815 Mary Durance, spinster, bequeathed it to Daniel Hill Davis, gent., who presumably was related to the Thomas Hill mentioned above. Davis and another baker called Peter Rook, who between them already had interests in the land behind nos 28–32, were here, although Davis dropped out of the partnership within a few years. Rook purchased the freehold of the two dwelling houses with the bakehouse, yard and buildings behind it, which were subject to a mortgage.[51]

Peter Rook sold his business and property to John Edman, miller and baker, in 1841, and made his will in 1844; this was proved in 1847.[52] Edman sold on the property and business to Edward Howitt, a miller with new ideas. Instead of using a post mill up in Mill Furlong, he decided to install an 8hp steam engine for grinding the corn to make his flour, although to carry through his plans the mortgage was increased by £400. He also had to buy another plot of land behind nos 33–34 and 266–267 High Street, with access to Grantham Lane, and another piece of land just west of the access point was leased from Rachel Yates, lessee of the Cardinal's Hat, who stipulated that "no steam boiler or other apparatus" was to be used in these premises.[53]

Howitt's plans appear to have foundered, and the whole property sold to Richard Mason, the solicitor, with the stables, granaries, piggery and outbuildings. Mason died in 1862, and Thomas Howden, baker, took over as owner. The business was too heavily burdened by mortgages to be successful, and Howden too joined the ranks of the business failures. Katherine Hebb, spinster, took over the mortgages, and with Edmund Curtis, cabinet maker, managed to sell up completely in 1875 to Albert Wingfield Hall, a grocer who was becoming established in city trade: he was to be associated with no.262 High Street and the Cardinal's Hat in addition to nos 33–34 Strait. Hall was owner here until 1913.

ARCHITECTURAL
DESCRIPTION

The principal interest of this tenement is its jettied two-storied timber-framed range aligned in length with the street. The upper storey is claimed to have contained one long chamber of three bays whose south wall, full height, is of rubble construction and is corbelled/jettied out in the same profile as the timber frame. In the restoration and repair of this building the original robust profile of the wall has not been followed, as may be observed in comparing earlier frontage photographs before work started. The tendency to tidy up in this instance has resulted in a diminishing somewhat of the building's character and that of its immediate surroundings; it would be of interest to learn of the justification for this alteration.

Use has been made in this account of the survey drawings of the building before restoration, including an isometric produced by the architect John Roberts and his colleagues, and we are grateful for permission to use their survey to illuminate the structural arrangements of Dernstall House. The dire structural state of the building was such that a decision was made to carefully dismantle the framework and replace, where appropriate, certain rotten timbers. It is noticeable that at a later phase in the building's history the first-floor studs and posts had been subjected to a severe vertical paring in order, presumably, to accept new wall surfaces/finishes. With the exception of the inverted wall braces in the street wall the stud work, present before restoration, was related to the insertion of sash windows at first-floor level.

An inspection of the tenement was afforded to Dr W.A. Pantin, the architectural historian, before stripping out commenced; he came to the conclusion that of the two conjoined rear wings only the northern one was the earlier yet considerably later than the street range, whose crown post roof clearly impressed him. The final product of the repair and restoration undertaking clearly did not heed Pantin's conclusion and framed up both wings with a common but misleading timber pattern. The earlier wing in question has a clasped purlin roof truss and the southern wing is clearly much later. Pantin quite correctly pointed to the possibility of the rear wings having replaced a ground-floor open hall that would have complemented the street range.

The description of this renovated property is based on two visits made after its completion, together with an examination of the survey drawings produced by the architects John Roberts and Associates of James Street, Lincoln. Briefly, the timber-framed building parallel to the Strait is aligned roughly north–south and had two conjoined wings to the rear (east). The street range is two-storied, three bays long, and is jettied to the Strait at first-floor level. A substantial party wall of rubble construction forms the south end of the range and projects streetwards to conform roughly to the jettied profile of the timber frame. Internally the same wall has a high placed offset, presumably intended to accommodate a collar beam of the crown post and collar purlin roof that survives above the range to the north; it is also conceivable that this end wall may have served an earlier structure in the same capacity.

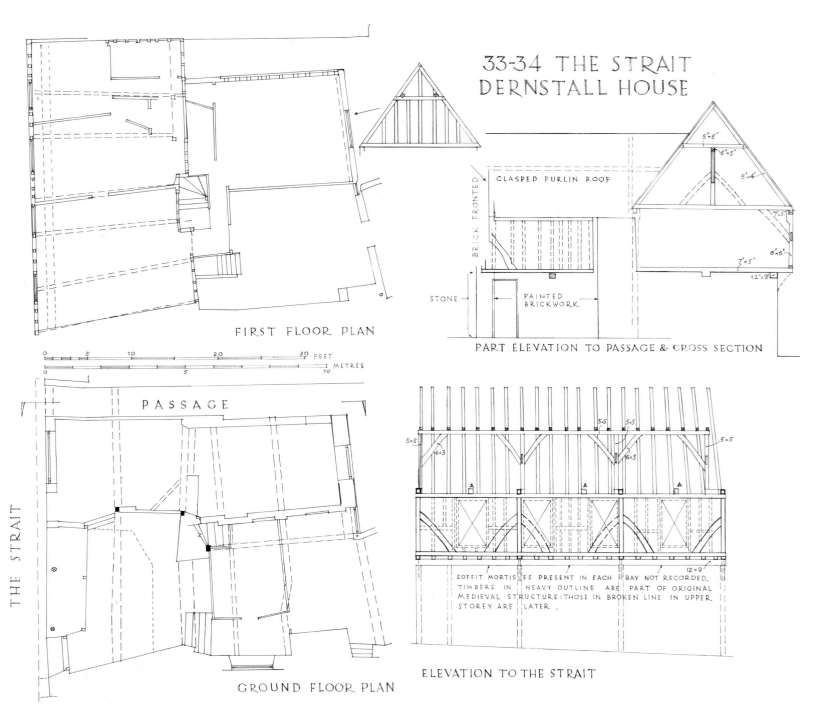

33-34 THE STRAIT DERNSTALL HOUSE

FIRST FLOOR PLAN

PART ELEVATION TO PASSAGE & CROSS SECTION

CLASPED PURLIN ROOF

BRICK FRONTED

STONE

PAINTED BRICKWORK

PASSAGE

THE STRAIT

GROUND FLOOR PLAN

ELEVATION TO THE STRAIT

SOFFIT MORTISES PRESENT IN EACH BAY NOT RECORDED. TIMBERS IN HEAVY OUTLINE ARE PART OF ORIGINAL MEDIEVAL STRUCTURE: THOSE IN BROKEN LINE IN UPPER STOREY ARE LATER.

Of the former pair of two-storied conjoined rear wings, only the northern unit had preserved its timber framing. Both wings had clasped purlin roofs; the framed east gable end had a lower storey of rubble, and both this and the unit to the south were ridged east–west: the latter had earlier been modernised. It is usual to expect that buildings to the rear of front ranges of this distinction and age would have functioned as open halls. Unfortunately the north wing that retained the features appeared to have been built as a fully storied unit and both this half and its counterpart may well have occupied the site of a superseded hall.[54] It is of interest to note that the entry from the street is at the north end of the tenement, giving access to the rear of the property; a similar location has been proposed for an entry, now suppressed, at the Cardinal's Hat (268 High Street: see below).

Was this north end entry a pattern for tenements on this side of the Strait and the adjoining High Street? One can be reasonably certain that a north end entry had served the tenement south of no.34 because a large window on the south side of the south

Fig 95. Plans and elevations, Dernstall House, nos 33–34 Strait

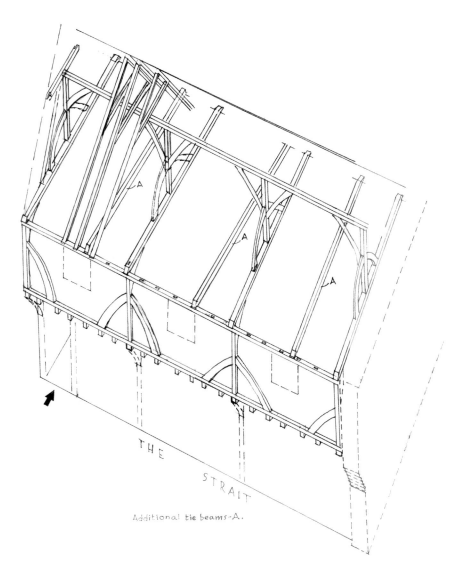

Additional tie beams-A.

Fig 96. left) *Isometric drawing of timber structure, Dernstall House*
Fig 97. (above) *Pre-restoration photograph of street façade, Dernstall House*
Fig 98. (below) *Post-restoration photograph, showing internal timber work, Dernstall House*

wing was made in the stone party wall there in order to obtain natural lighting from the adjoining yard. No.34 had served as a bakery from 1708 and seemingly throughout the 19th century, when it comprised a 'dwelling house, baker's shop and oven, yard, stable, granary, cart shed, piggery and outbuildings'. In no.33 it appears that a bakehouse had occupied the wing to the rear of the shop and from the lease evidence it would seem that the whole tenement had been engaged in baking for more than two centuries.[55]

For the street range, with its early roof form, a conservative date is likely to be in the second half of the 14th century; for the timber-framed rear wings a probable origin in the first half of the 16th century may be more appropriate. It is feasible that each of the three bays in the street range at ground-level may have served as individual shops and conceivably had no access to the chamber(s) overhead. Though now concealed externally in Dernstall House, the bold use of large inverted braces in timber framing as expressed at the Harlequin, Steep Hill, and the Cardinal's Hat, High Street, was widespread, as witness its employment in York and Coventry buildings, and whose use spans the period 1350–1550. It would be customary to expect that a chamber of three bays' length in the Strait house would have been sub-divided to provide two-rooms, and the division to be made on the line of one of the roof trusses, giving a one-bay inner room. The architect's survey drawings unfortunately do not divulge the building's archaeology, and such interpretative features as there are are hinted at but not recorded.

Archaeological excavations and investigations made at the angle between the Strait and Danes Terrace in 1974 exposed substantial stone walls of medieval date held to be of 12th/13th-century date and reliant in some instances on Roman walling that was then still upstanding.[56] Some in their alignments had been used in part by later tenements; these and their cellar provision in a 19th-century development of that section of the Strait resulted in a considerable loss of material. By way of compensation, observation of service-trenches dug in 1975 in the same area revealed the street frontages of the medieval buildings as being approximately 16.5 ft.(c.5m) further west of the site excavated; this early encroachment serves to emphasise both the confines of the medieval Strait and its mix of house types.

266–268 HIGH STREET
INCORPORATING THE CARDINAL'S HAT

From analysis of the 19th-century lease plans[57] and the ground plans prepared by W.A. Pantin,[58] as well as the context provided by the documentary evidence, it is now thought that these properties were all once part of the same complex. Nos 266–267 were for some years in the 14th century separate, although occupied by relatives of the owners of the main tenement, and it seems also that it expanded to the east along Brancegate in the years after 1291.

Members of the Anglo-Jewish community lived here and in many other houses along Brancegate, now Grantham Street, not only in the section of it within St Martin's parish but also in the further range on the far side of Haraldstigh/Flaxengate, in the parish of St George. As early as 1228 Jacob son of Vives, Samuel son of Vives and Elias *Grossus* had already suffered confiscations of their property,[59] and similarly in 1256 after the Little St Hugh inquisition Peytevin, Abraham, Samuel the son in law of Leo, Vives of Norwich and probably also Vives of Northampton were also stripped of their properties in this street.[60] It seems justified to assume that some of these Jews lived in the houses towards the corner of Haraldstigh on the north side of Brancegate, which were investigated in Bob Jones' work on the Flaxengate site.[61]

MEDIEVAL
DOCUMENTATION

The messuage known as the Cardinal's Hat (so named from the 1520s onwards) was, we find from the surviving documents, originally a combination of two houses: one large tenement on the corner of Mikelgate and Brancegate, and the other immediately to the east, combined into one holding in 1291. This is at variance with the story of the building put forward by Pantin in the 1953 booklet, which suggested two narrow east–west plots, but does not rule out a later rebuilding phase.

As a result of the confiscation in 1256 of a substantial number of Jewish properties in the city, the king recorded a fine or agreement made with Thomas de Bellofago, otherwise known as Beaufou, and John Long, both citizens of Lincoln. They were to purchase from him, among other properties, certain houses owned by Peytevin the Great, proprietor of the synagogue, who had been outlawed for fleeing from the inquisition set in motion by the king during the Little St Hugh episode.

One of the properties owned by Peytevin was a house situated in Brancegate between land of Alan the baker on the east and land of Josce of Colchester (the corner property) on the west, of the fee of the nuns of Sempringham.[62] Thomas de Beaufou transferred his interest in this house to John Long, who in turn would have passed it on in his family line to Osbert le Lung, or Long, and his son Richard.

In November 1290 the Jews throughout the country were expelled and their remaining properties confiscated by the king, appraised for sale and parcelled out to a variety of people, mostly those who had served him in some capacity. Among the lucky recipients of favour, although he had to pay £24 for the purchase, was Walter of Gloucester, who at this time was the clerk to John Dyve, Sheriff of Lincolnshire. Walter was granted in February 1291[63] a group of three houses in Brancegate formerly of Benedict of London, a house in the parish of St George, previously the property of Manser de Bradeworth, and, more significantly, some tenements also in Brancegate, described as "well built with two chambers",[64] which had formerly belonged to Josce of Colchester, valued at 12s per annum. This Josce was possibly related to the Josce of 1256, and is referred to in the Jewish Plea Rolls in 1268 and 1275.[65]

Walter sold these houses on the corner of Mikelgate in April 1291 to Osbert le Long and Richard his son, and added to the sale the three houses formerly owned by Benedict in Brancegate, whose exact location has not been determined.[66] The combined property stayed in the Long family until 1342. Richard Long's will was proved in October 1341: according to it the properties were to be sold separately, but Richard de Kele and Matilda his wife bought both of them. The north–west portion of the site, which later became nos 266–267 High Street, was partitioned off prior to the sale, Margaret Long, widow of Richard, taking no.266 and Alice, presumably their daughter, no.267. Margaret made a quitclaim of her interest in the property not long afterwards, thus reuniting the various properties.[67]

In August 1361 Richard de Kele made a grant of these properties and a garden, situated between Mikelgate and another messuage belonging to Richard, acquired from Peter Wodecok, on the east, abutting a tenement of Walter de Poynton and another belonging to Robert de Thymelby, on the north, to John de Welbourne, Treasurer of the Cathedral, who was gathering a portfolio of city properties to form the endowment for his chantry, founded in 1366.[68] Wodecok and Roger de Kele were tenants of the Chapter in Mikelgate, c.1323–39, and in Skynnergate (the Strait), c.1333–45, respectively.[69]

POST-MEDIEVAL OCCUPATION

266–267 High Street

These two properties appear to have been leased out by the Chapter separately from the Cardinal's Hat for a considerable length of time, certainly from the mid-16th century onwards. Before 1572, according to the Fabric rentals, they had been leased to Stephen Christopher, then to his widow, who remarried someone named Byron, and in 1573 to another Stephen Christopher. From 1577 to 1579 Thomas Tompson paid the rent of 2s 4d pa, and he was succeeded in 1580 by Henry Christopher, who appears in the rentals until 1592. At this point there is a gap in the records, but in 1616 the name Thomas Christopher appears. Peter Christopher is recorded from 1618 to 1632.[70]

After the Restoration the Fabric rentals still name Peter, but no rent is recorded as being paid. It is possible that no lease was issued until 1693, and when the name Elizabeth Parish first appears in that year, the property is described as "late Newall's". Poor record keeping by the Fabric accountants has robbed us of useful information for the intervening period in a number of cases.[71]

The lease of 1693 shows these two tenements demised to Elizabeth Parish of the Close, widow, and in the occupation of George Beck and Mary Brown, widow.[72] In 1708 and 1722 she renewed the lease, the occupants being John Hicks, chandler, and James Beverley respectively.[73] William and Mary Burgess successively held leases from 1736 to 1763, when Hadnah Yates, tailor, took over as lessee and occupier.[74] He was succeeded in 1794 by his son, another Hadnah, who remained here until 1822.[75] There is a brief description of the premises in 1822, with a sketch plan: "a cellar and kitchen in the basement, parlour and shop chamber over the parlour, a ware room over the shop and a garret over all".

Fig 99. Photograph of roof timbers, nos 266–267 High Street

Rachel, his widow, had this property included in her lease of the Cardinal's Hat in 1836,[76] and she sublet nos 266–267 in 1841 to Thomas Atkinson, stay maker, at £2 per annum.[77] In 1847, after her death, the lease was taken over by family representatives until it was assigned in 1870 to Albert Wingfield Hall, who purchased the freehold along with that of the Cardinal's Hat in 1872.[78] The Grimsby Fish Supply Association, which became the Grimsby Fish Co., occupied no.266 during the period between 1890 and 1914, and no.267 was used for a variety of trades at this period. A no.267A is recorded from 1909, marking a further subdivision of the holding.

An opportunity in October 2011 to inspect the interior of this building was accepted and what was evident on entry was its overall modernisation. The only area of interest was the roof space of three and a half bays, which contains trusses of clasped-purlin type and whose rafters are mostly re-used.[79] In its present form the roof is probably late 17th century in origin. The north wall at this level is that belonging to Dernstall House and is of coursed rubble. Given its location, it is a matter of regret that alterations to its fabric went unrecorded.

268 High Street: the Cardinal's Hat

William Barker was named in the Fabric rental of 1521/22 "for le Cardynal hat",[80] which in an earlier entry of 1520/21[81] was listed as a *hospicium* or inn. Thomas Wolsey, who had been bishop of Lincoln in 1514/15, was made a cardinal in the latter year, so the connection is fairly obvious. Barker was listed again in 1536, but the early series of rentals ends there. John Crosfeld was given a lease in 1560, with Richard Smith as occupier.[82] The rental sum of 26s 8d per annum is very high, and quite distinctive in the rentals, where the Welbourne Chantry properties are often listed in a separate section.

Crosfeld occurs also in 1572, and was in 1576 succeeded by Edward Crosfeld, who stayed until 1588. Robert Smyth paid the rent between 1589 and 1592.[83] Thomas Stirropp, Notary Public, was both lessee and occupant in 1601, according to an entry in the lease book; the property was then described as "one messuage set lying and being within the parish of St Martin, late in the tenure of Richard Smith or his assigns, and now in the tenure of the said Thomas Styrropp, and all manner of houses and buildings, orchards and gardens belonging to the same".[84] Sir Francis Hill was unable to prove that this was the same Richard Smith who founded the Christ's Hospital School in Lincoln.[85] William Marrett, innholder, took over in 1609 with a 40-year lease,[86] but he died in 1616. His very informative probate inventory[87] was interpreted and printed in the 1953 booklet.

John Morton was in occupation of the inn at the time of the next lease, given in 1621 to Jeffrey Wilson, pewterer, who had a *fundus* or smallholding tucked away between the Drapery and what is now Michaelgate. This lease[88] was still in force when the Parliamentary Survey was undertaken in 1649, when Robert Holland was in occupation.[89] By this time Wilson had already assigned his lease to Edmund Shuttleworth, who had other property across the road at 265 High Street.

According to Hill's documentary notes in the 1953 booklet, the inn suffered during the Civil War, necessitating £100 in repair work, and was regarded as ruinous. In 1650 George Walker acquired the freehold, after the abolition of the Chapter, and it was purchased by John Oliver, who in 1654 sold it to William Legate for £103 12s. In 1660, when the Chapter recovered its leaseholds, Legate managed to recover his main purchase money, but had to pay for seven years' worth of arrears in 1662, a total of £9 6s 8d, as well as his entry fine of £20. He carried on at the Cardinal's Hat until 1674, when he died. In his will[90] Legate awarded his son in law Henry Craven a shilling "which in regard of the unkind usage I have had from him is more than he deserves, or could have expected". He left the residue of his estate to his friend William Walker, instrument maker, who was appointed executor.

Craven took over the task of paying the rent, making an initial payment to cover 18 months, but thereafter failed to pay even a shilling, clocking up a total of seven years' arrears before his name was expunged from the records. No entry was made for the inn between 1683 and 1687, a sign that the inn was in a state of disrepair.[91] Hill records a lease of 1685 to William Willerton for the term of the lives of his three children, but this seems to have fallen through on his death; his widow Ann was given a lease of the 'Cardinal's Cap', as it was to be known until the late 19th century. Trustees (William and Richard Burnett) were to act for her daughter Mary. The term was again for lives, a practice found usually only in the uphill part of the city.[92]

From 1687 to 1696 the rents were actually paid in by John Routledge, a near neighbour; between 1697 and 1699 they were paid by Mr Routledge and Mr Hesslewood. The latter, now occupier, paid from 1700 to 1706 and from 1708 to 1717. In 1708 it was the Assigns of Ann Willerton who were recorded in the rental.[93]

John Arnold of Deptford, gent., was the next lessee, entering in April 1718.[94] This lease continued in force until July 1741, when Thomas Sympson took a lease for the lives of himself (aged 39), and his sons Thomas and Joseph (aged 14 and 10 respectively).[95] Sympson, the noted antiquary, assigned the lease in 1748 to Ann Kitching, widow, and Ann, later wife of Thomas Mattkin, joiner, further assigned it in 1756 to Noah Straw, maltster, who continued as lessee until his death in 1782.[96]

In 1795 Hadnah Yates and his trustee Thomas Hill, and 'baker' took an assignment of the lease, and thereafter the inn remained in the family until 1843. Rachel Yates sublet the Cardinal's Cap in 1841 to Griffin Parish, who briefly established a Temperance and Commercial Hotel, but reverted to a previous trade of butcher and confectioner until 1863.[97] As described for nos 266–267, Rachel Yates' representatives took over the property in 1843 and retained it until 1870, when it was assigned to A.W. Hall.

Hall purchased a reversionary interest in both the Cardinal's Cap and nos 266–267 in 1872 from the Ecclesiastical Commissioners, and he continued to hold the premises until the Edwardian period.[98] No real preservation work or large scale repair was carried out on the main building during this time; it became a storage area, awaiting eventual rescue by the St John Ambulance Brigade and a band of local historians in 1952/53, when it seems to have recovered its original title of the Cardinal's Hat. The story of the restoration is told in the booklet mentioned elsewhere in this account, and also in an article printed in *The Builder* in September 1953.

ARCHITECTURAL
DESCRIPTION

Described as being in a ruinous state in the later 17th century, the property then underwent a drastic facelift involving the removal of its oriel windows, the defacement of its moulded timbers and the resetting of its south-facing gable; this facilitated the introduction of new-style windows and a wholesale rendering in order to conceal the underlying timber frame. One can be reasonably confident in ascribing this transformation to a Mr William Willerton of the Close, who was excused his fine of admission on condition that he repaired the tenement at his own expense.[99] The work can be placed in the period 1686–1700, and an early 19th-century drawing of the High Street by the artist William Henry Brooke that includes part of the frontage of the former inn, shows both the plastered frontage and the coeval windows that were introduced;[100] there was, understandably, no attempt to disguise the jettied projections of its main elevation. It is fortunate that a photographic record of the building's exterior to the street was obtained before restoration and repairs were undertaken in 1952.[101] This confirms the main lines of the earlier drawing as reliable evidence for the appearance of the former inn; in turn, the survey drawings, produced by the architects, of the surviving timbers in the main frame make it clear where the 'new style' windows were located, and, of equal importance, the degree to which, miraculously, the frontage had preserved evidence of its original fenestration and timbers formerly embellished with moulded profiles.[102]

The Cardinal's Hat, in the recent past, has received attention from two architectural historians, the late Drs William Pantin and David Roberts, whose analyses and conclusions merit closer study.[103] For the building to have functioned as an inn, Roberts suggested that the adjoining tenement no.267 High St may have provided the main wagon approach to the rear courtyard; however, the Parliamentary Survey of 1649 for the inn refers only to a small yard and notes no.267 as then being in separate occupation. Both writers make use of a detailed probate inventory – that of William Marrett, innkeeper, compiled in 1616[104] – to flesh out the arrangements in the establishment, with Pantin's interpretation being the earlier and lengthier version. It is clear, however, that Pantin's investigations were made after certain significant features had been removed, e.g. the chimney stacks in the street range. The restoration work, however, revealed sufficient information to enable him to indicate that a vertical subdivision of the street range had existed at all three levels. Unfortunately evidence for the ground-floor division which dovetailed neatly with the inventory is now either concealed or destroyed. A simplified ground plan accompanying Pantin's paper was also used by Roberts in his interpretation. From both descriptions one is made aware that the modernisation of the structure has left gaps in an understanding of how the former inn functioned, and its later usage.

The plan of the tenement in 1952 at ground-floor level comprised, as now, a long two-storied stone range of building aligned roughly east–west and extending along the north side of Grantham Lane; this contained the hall, cross-passage, and service elements of the early house in a west to east progression. It is claimed that post-medieval alterations saw the insertion of a floor in the open hall, the removal of its early roof structure, the blocking of former window openings and a modest heightening throughout. The manner in which the hall range intrudes into the timber-framed west end of the building would seem to imply that originally it may have continued through to the High Street as a wholly stone-built structure. Reference to the plan shows the opposite north wall of the hall range apparently integrated with a chimney stack that served the north end of the timber-framed block; it is also evident on plan that this particular stack appears to fill a gap that existed between the north wall of the hall range and the north wall of the framed block. This gap may have marked the alignment of a through passage, leading from the High Street to the rear premises of the inn in an earlier phase. The principal chimney stack shown against the east wall of the street range had a winder stair against its north side and provided hearths for both the hall range and a parlour fronting the High Street; it is reasonable to assume that the bipartite nature of the street range might have had a stair located either within or without the building for access to each floor; if internal then such access would have required trimmed openings for ladder-type stairs; if external this would possibly take the form of an attached timber turret . The architectural survey by Pantin describes the hall stack in 1952 as 'later', from which one infers it to be a post-medieval improvement. There is now no way of determining whether the timber-framed range was originally heated; for the hall Pantin claimed this to have been open, i.e. single-storied and presumably served by a hearth made on the floor. Somewhere on site and probably situated at the east end of the hall range there would have been a kitchen giving a total of two hearths for the medieval phase. A near parallel, but more complete, is the timber-framed Governor's House in Stodman Street, Newark on Trent, a building dendro-dated to 1475, and where an integrated chimney stack and stair serves both rear hall and street front block; the Newark hall is flat ceiled at a great height and chambered over, the latter extending to a kitchen chimney bay at the extremity of the hall range.[105]

The Parliamentary Survey of 1649 records the leaseholder Edmond Shetlworth and 'all that messuage in parish St Martin called or known by the name of the Cardinal's Hatt inne in the occupation Robert Holland, undertenant, consisting of a hall, 3 parlors, 1 Kitchen, 1 cellar, pantry and brewhouse with a low room to lay fewell in, 5 lodging chambers with two garretts, a garden and smal yard, two stables with haylofts, the scite and seat by estimation 30 perches (built part of wood and part of stone, the covering of tile, abutting high street west and Grantham Lane south and on Peter Christopher north)'.[106]

Two hearths serving the ground-floor of the street range would imply a sub-division of that space but one cannot know now whether the hearths were staggered in date or coeval impositions; both were removed in 1952. Both before and after the stack introductions the divided area provided parlours at ground-level; note that there is an absence of any reference to shops throughout the available earlier lease material for the former inn.

David Roberts in his analysis of the Cardinal's Hat proposed that the timber-framed street range had been heightened by the addition of the present top storey and that prior to this the structure may have sported a crown post and collar purlin roof. What may have misled him is the clearly rebuilt and reset south gable which, on closer inspection, retains sufficient evidences to demonstrate its original medieval arrangement, as the following description will, hopefully, make clear. A plaster cove raised on curved brackets was attached to the soffit of a now-removed and formerly forward-set tie beam. An interval at a central point in the coving accommodated an oriel window, itself set on brackets and whose mullions were tenoned into the soffit of the removed tie-beam. Dowel holes for the brackets supporting the plaster cove and those of the removed oriel are plainly visible on this, the south side studding. Such a cove would have tied in neatly with that at eaves level, now restored, along the High Street elevation. The roof of the street range is of clasped-purlin type and is original. It comprises two main bays, subdivided at mid bay by collared common rafter couples forming the two garrets of 1649; confirmation of this is the fact that the central roof truss has an original stud partition, complete with a doorway.[107]

It is perhaps the symmetry of the street elevation of the timber-framed range that is most striking, having as its principal feature a central oriel, flanked by a continuous series of carved unglazed windows at first-floor level. Internally their window sills, where unrestored, preserve evidence of how such unglazed openings were closed by shutters. On the same front the second floor had planted-on oriel windows, now restored, for its two chambers, plus another at the south end gable, as noted earlier. At ground-level no street framing has survived save for two sections of its bressummer that retained early colouring, recently spoiled;[108] such alterations at street level presumably reflected what was modish for shop fronts from the later 17th century onwards, with the final clearance of any earlier arrangements occurring with the installation of plate glass windows c.1900. Pantin, in reference to earlier alterations to the inn, c.1600, noted that 'a great chamber was formed out of the two front first-floor rooms'.[109] The structural evidence for this original sub-division is unmistakable, and it is clear that the street end of this division did not bisect the oriel projection but permitted a gap sufficient for access between the rooms at that point. The removed partition was close-studded, as is the present second-floor division, and at this latter level the east wall can be shown to have had large inverted braces as stiffeners in the framing.

Alterations to the west end of the hall at its junction with the timber-framed range have not helped the interpretation of the arrangements of the house c.1500. Critical to this is the location of the large south side window lighting the hall interior. Usually such an important window would have been in a close relationship to the dais or high table in the hall, whereas at the Cardinal's Hat, assuming that the latter was likely to be positioned backing onto the east wall of the street range, there is a more than generous interval

1952. WEST ELEVATION. RESTORATION STAGE.

CARDINAL'S HAT
268 HIGH STREET.

SOUTH ELEVATION.

Fig 100. West and south elevations, the Cardinal's Hat, no.268 High Street

between these points. The ovolo mouldings of the large window could well belong to an earlier phase than the late 16th/early 17th century, as suggested by Pantin. As noted above, a case could be made for the newly raised timber-framed block to have inherited a layout that derived from an earlier stone-built tenement which, in turn, may also have terminated in a framed structure fronting the High Street. Prof. David Stocker has drawn attention to this form of stone and timber combination in certain of Grantham's domestic buildings, where the timber frame is adopted for the solar or upper end of the dwelling exclusively.[110]

Questions of access to inn courtyards must necessarily involve an approach that (a) is either able to accept a wheeled vehicle, i.e. a coach or wagon, or (b) a wide enough passage for foot traffic and baggage. The cross-passage off Grantham Lane was of the latter category and perhaps the Lane saw more the stowing of wagons, but with their draught animals stalled in the inn's stabling? The alternative, that of accessing the rear premises through no.267 High Street, as proposed by David Roberts, may now prove difficult to demonstrate, given its total makeover post-1952, and for which no known detailed surveys survive.

The former sub-division of the ground-floor of the street range into two parlours, a function confirmed in the 17th-century inventory, is unusual in that one might have expected the junction of High Street and Grantham Street to have been seen as an ideal location for the establishment of shops.

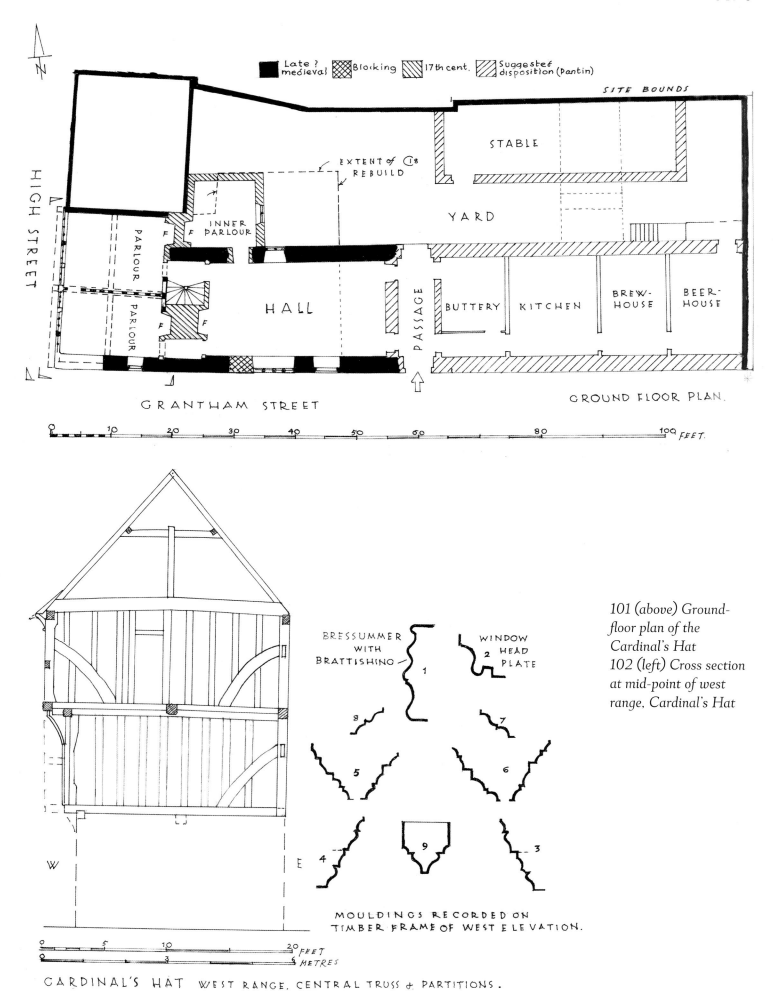

Late ? medieval | Blocking | 17th cent. | Suggested disposition (Pantin)

SITE BOUNDS

STABLE

YARD

EXTENT OF C18 REBUILD

HIGH STREET

INNER PARLOUR

PARLOUR

PARLOUR

HALL

PASSAGE

BUTTERY | KITCHEN | BREW-HOUSE | BEER-HOUSE

GRANTHAM STREET

GROUND FLOOR PLAN.

0 10 20 30 40 50 60 80 100 FEET.

BRESSUMMER WITH BRATTISHING

WINDOW HEAD PLATE

MOULDINGS RECORDED ON TIMBER FRAME OF WEST ELEVATION.

W   E

CARDINAL'S HAT WEST RANGE. CENTRAL TRUSS & PARTITIONS.

0 5 10 20 FEET
0 3 6 METRES

101 (above) Ground-floor plan of the Cardinal's Hat
102 (left) Cross section at mid-point of west range, Cardinal's Hat

135

Street View looking down Lincoln Hill to _____ Gate 14 Nov 181

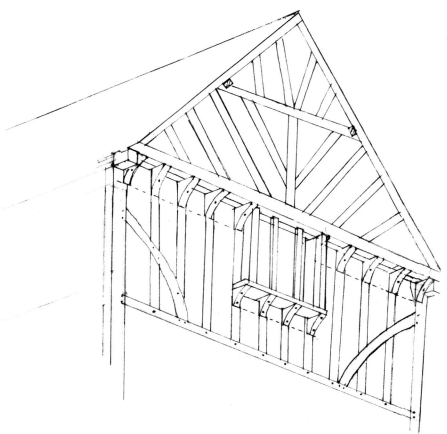

Fig 103. (left) Restored south gable
end, Cardinal's Hat
Fig 104. (above) Drawing by
W.H. Brooke showing the Cardinal's
Hat c.1818

Fig 105. (above)
Pre-restoration
photograph of west
range, Cardinal's Hat
Fig 106. (left)
Post-restoration
photograph of west
range, Cardinal's Hat,
from a slide
Fig 107. (above left)
Cardinal's Hat,
no.268 High Street:
advertisement from
street directory 1899

1   *Abbreviatio* (1805), rot.19, p. 74
2   B.L. Abrahams, 'The Condition of the Jews of England at the time of their Expulsion in 1290' in *TJHSE* 1894/95,76ff: here it was valued at 30s pa, but different sources (the *Abbreviatio* and the Lansdowne transcript) have 28s. There are several inconsistencies of this kind between documents produced at this time
3   *Cant* 285; *Fig 93*
4   TNA E 159/64, *King's Remembrancer Rolls*, 19 Edward 1, m.13; for the Jew's House, see above, p.90
5   Dij 75/3/14; 77/1/44
6   *Cant* 286
7   Dij 82/1/28
8   Dij 79/2/20
9   *Cant* 287
10 *Cant* 288
11 The other properties alienated at this time were the Jew's House and what is now 262 High Street: *Cant* 292,73
12 *Cant* 289
13 Bj 2.5, ff.115v-181 *passim*
14 Bj 1.1/3
15 L1/1/1/2 f.2v; for the other properties, see below in their respective sections
16 *MCD* 161
17 Bj 1.1/7-8; LL 120/1; Bij 3.20 no.203
18 CC 27/152829 3/7, p. 12
19 2 CC 8/152941, pp. 55-56
20 LL 120/2-3; Bij 4.1, no.48
21 LCC Wills 1681 i, 415
22 Inv 182A/61
23 LL 120/4-5
24 *Misc Dep* 38/3,9
25 *LPC* 1/16/2; also see below,

p.162
26 Exley: ts. of draft lease in Civ 95/1
27 Civ 95/1
28 Padley 3/52
29 Bij 5.8, p. 846 (1815); Bij 5.11, p. 529 (1836)
30 Lincoln Archaeological Trust, *The Archaeology of Lincoln, vol xi-I* (1980), *fig*. 42, Block E
31 *LRS* 92,50
32 *Cant* 287
33 *Cant* 288
34 Lancs RO Townley MSS I/11; transcript at LAO *MCD* 161
35 L1/3/1 f.198v
36 LCC Wills 1641/413
37 Census returns HO 107/2105
38 LCC Wills 1847/335
39 *Welb* 57
40 *BB* f.246v. no.867
41 *ibid*. f.236, no.825
42 *Welb* 146; Dij 76/3/30
43 TNA, Ancient Deeds v, 52
44 LL121/1
45 LL121/2
46 BRA 1548/4
47 LCC Wills 1719 i, 21
48 LL121/3-4
49 *ibid.*, 5-6
50 *Misc Dep* 159/1; *Misc Dep* 38/6,8,13-14
51 *Misc Dep* 159/1
52 LCC Wills 1847/335
53 *Misc Dep* 159/3; *Misc Dep* 38/20
54 *Figs 95-96*
55 See historical account above
56 *Fig 88*
57 *LRS* 92 *passim*
58 Published in 'The Cardinal's Hat', 1953
59 *BFees* i,365
60 *Welb* 50; RH i, 321,322; *CChR* i, 1257,460; *CFR* 40 Henry III, 20 October 1256, (www.finerollshenry3.org.uk)

no.1263
61 LAT, *op.cit.*,3-6 *passim*
62 *Welb* 50
63 TNA *Kings Remembrancer's Rolls*, E159/65 m.1; and 159/66, m.53
64 See the summary of the grant in the *Abbreviatio.*, rot. 20, p. 74; Abrahams, *op.cit.*; TNA E101/249, 27 and 30
65 TNA E9/9, 20 and 21
66 *Welb* 51; there was some earlier connection with the Cathedral as this property, as described by Abrahams, paid an out-rent of 21s 4d per annum to the Chapter
67 *op.cit.*52-56; *BB* f.149v, *no.486*
68 *Welb* 57 and 367-370
69 Bj 2.5., *passim*
70 Bij 3.2; Bj 1.7
71 Bj 1.9
72 LL 121/1
73 *ibid.*,2-3
74 *ibid.*,4-6
75 *Misc Dep* 38/6,8
76 *ibid.*,16
77 *ibid.*,17
78 *ibid.*,21-23,26,30
79 *Fig 99*
80 Bj 1.5
81 A 4.7.9
82 A 3.9, f.9v
83 Bij 3.2
84 Bij 3.19, no.27
85 Booklet 'The Cardinal's Hat'
86 Bij 3.20, no.77
87 Inv 118/244
88 LL 122/1
89 CC27/152829 3/7 p. 23
90 LCC Wills 1674/212
91 Bj 1.9
92 Bij 4.4, f.68
93 Bij 1.10
94 LL 122/3
95 *ibid.*,4

96 *Misc Dep* 38/1-2,7; LL 122/5-7
97 *Misc Dep* 38/10, 12, 12A, 15, 16; Commercial Directory 1843
98 *Misc Dep* 38/19,22,26,29-32
99 Bij 4.4, f.68
100 *Fig 104*
101 *Fig 97*
102 *Fig 100*
103 W.A. Pantin, 'Architectural history of the Cardinal's Hat', in the 1953 brochure; see also his article on the restoration work in 'The Builder', 4 September 1953,343-346; D.L. Roberts 'The Cardinal's Hat, 268 High Street, Lincoln' included in the Programme of the Summer Meeting at Lincoln of the Royal Archaeological Institute, 1974,84-86; see also S.R. Jones 'Ancient Domestic Buildings and their Roofs' *ibid.*,49-53
104 Inv 118/244: published in the 1953 brochure
105 Unpublished survey report by Guy St. John Taylor Associates, Newark (restoration architect: Philip Siddall)
106 CC 27/152829 3/7, p. 23
107 *Figs 101-103*
108 *Fig 101*
109 1953 brochure, p. 15
110 D. Start and D. Stocker 'Early Secular Buildings of Grantham' in *The Making of Grantham: the medieval town* (Sleaford, Heritage Trust of Lincolnshire, 2011), ch.13, pp 1-24 and reviewed in *Antiquaries Journal*, vol. 92, 2012, p. 482

262–265 HIGH STREET

A good starting point for this review would be the estate of the Prebend of St Martin, which was endowed with a significant group of properties on the west side of Mikelgate, south of the churchyard of St Martin. Geoffrey, the king's chaplain and holder of the prebend between c.1154 and his death in 1165, made a grant to Ralf of Colchester and his heirs of a messuage belonging to his prebend in the parish of St Martin, together with shops held by Walter, son of Redwi, as tenant, and another shop which Wiger the canon held; the rent was to be 30s per annum. The ancestors of Maud, wife of Ralf (Fulk, Richard his son and grandsons, and Walter son of Redwi, who gave the messuage to Ralf as a marriage portion with his daughter) had held the property by right of Geoffrey's predecessors, and Ralf, according to the grant, had re-edified and improved the building.[1]

Where, then, was this portion of the prebendal estate? Given the long-standing connection with the Colchester family, which is evident in the number of references to be found in this account, all published in the same volume of *Registrum Antiquissimum*,[2] the estate almost certainly occupied the eastern portions of the sites now occupied by nos 262 and 263 High Street, and maybe also no.261, given the shape of the property boundaries in this area. It is tempting, not altogether unreasonably, to suggest that the mansion itself was on the site of no.262 High Street, where some 12th-century arcading was found in the fabric of the north wall during restoration work in 1871[3] and rediscovered in the late 20th century.

A: Properties facing Hungate

From the structure of the deeds preserved in the archives of the Dean and Chapter,[4] the western portions of these properties, i.e. those facing Hungate, were, during the second half of the 12th century, the property of William son of Warner, of whom we see traces both in the earlier deeds in the series relating to nos 262 and 263 and in the records for the Vicars Choral holding to the west of no.264. There is also good evidence to show that William's estate reached northwards to the churchyard entrance, and was therefore probably also originally held as part of the prebendal estate.

William son of Warner made a grant, the equivalent of a lease for a rent of 10d per annum, to Richard Belot and his heirs around the year 1190. Richard was to have a certain piece of land in Hungate on the east side, in length and breadth as Belot his father held it, from the entrance to his house as far as the churchyard of St Martin.[5] This grant therefore incorporates the plot west of nos 264–265 High Street (of which the Vicars Choral later held a portion), and probably also the Hungate frontage west of no.263, which came to the Chapter in the 14th century.

Between 1255 and 1265 Adam, son of William son of Warner, granted to Ralph Bok a small area of land south of the churchyard at the west end of the plot now represented by no.264. It was bounded on the east by land then occupied by Peter the Cordwainer (Peter Allutarius) and on the north by property of his tenant William son of Thomas de Paris.[6] It owed an outrent of 32s to the prior of Torksey.[7] Bok, who had other interests in the Dernstall area, soon passed on this property to Richard de Southwell, chaplain and Vicar Choral, who arranged for it to be assigned to the Vicars' estate. Ralph made a quitclaim, as did his son.[8]

The Belot holding, by 1233 × 1245 confined to the site south of Adam's property, was relinquished to the Dean and Chapter. At the Hungate end, Sybil, daughter of Gilbert Belot, made a quitclaim of her interest to the Chapter, from whom she had already been renting the eastern moiety of the site.[9] Godfrey Toche is mentioned as occupant here c.1255–1265, after which it may have come into the hands of the Scarlet family, probably connected with the dyeing business just upstream of the High Bridge.

WEST OF NO.263
HIGH STREET

Walter de Bredham and Matilda Scarlet his wife granted in February 1313 a plot of land in Hungate to Master Richard de Stretton and Harvey de Luda, rector of a mediety of Tansor. This plot, to the west of the present-day 263 High Street, was situated between the land of the Vicars Choral on the north and land once of Elias Martrin, Jew, now the property of the Cathedral, on the south. Albreda and Margaret, the daughters of Matilda Scarlet, made quitclaims a few weeks later.[10] Richard and Harvey transferred the property to the Dean and Chapter, including a revised description of the south boundary: "next to land of the Dean and Chapter which they have by gift from Master William de Thornton and which was of Gilbert de Atherby and where used to be situated the *scola* of the Jews".[11]

John de Thornhagh, who was receiving an outrent of 2s 6d per annum from Walter de Bredham from this property, also made a quitclaim of it to the Chapter, although not until 1324.[12] These deeds are listed with others relating to the Thornton and Gare Chantry, yet there is no mention of the property in the 1324 Augmentation deed.[13]

WEST OF NO.262
HIGH STREET

The main problem over the precise location of the Jewish *scola* or synagogue associated with no.262 High Street has always been the difficulty inherent in working out where on this long plot it might have been situated. From earlier discussion about the Steep Hill synagogue[14] it seems impractical to place it directly adjacent to the street. In this case the options are limited because there are streets at either end. After consideration of the deeds for both the Hungate and High Street properties[15], it is quite obvious that the documents for the Hungate frontage hold the more specific and compelling references to the synagogue, which was probably situated just behind the street range. The main documentary discussion on this property is to be found below.

B: Properties facing High Street

NOS 264–265
HIGH STREET

Evidence for this plot from the end of the 12th century onwards is confined to boundary references as there are no charters directly dealing with it. In 1195 or 1196 the Lady Maud, widow of Ralf of Colchester, held it, as referred to in a lease to her of no.263 (see below): "next to land of the said Maud".[16] During the early 13th-century tenure passed to William, son of Thomas de Paris,[17] when another charter for no.263 described the property to the north as "formerly of Ralf of Colchester".[18]

William de Paris was still being quoted as tenant here in charters as late as c.1250,[19] then between 1259 and c.1265 he was followed by John Coker, who was from c.1273–1282 described in the past tense.[20] In the Hundred Rolls, certain land with buildings in the same parish which formerly belonged to Peytevin *parvus*, Jew of Lincoln, held by the wife of John Coker, after Coker was escheated in 1250, worth 40s per annum.[21] As control of no.263 reverted to the Chapter in 1285[22] there are no further medieval references to this site to be located.

NO.263
HIGH STREET

In the period c.1180–90 Belot held this property, presumably from Ralf of Colchester, and by 1195–96 his tenure had descended to his grandson John of St Bartholomew, who leased it to Lady Maud, widow of Ralf of Colchester; an outrent of 8s 6d was payable to the Chapter.[23] From a different source we have a glimpse of what was happening at a lower tenurial level. Sometime between 1190 and 1200 there is a boundary reference in a grant of no.262 which gives the north bound as: "land which Abraham son of Aaron holds from the Hospital of Lincoln".[24] This important linkage implies that a financial transaction of some kind was in force, as we have seen before.[25]

Abraham was involved at one point with Bardney Abbey over a quitclaim of property in St Andrew's parish, on the hill.[26] He and his brother Vives, both formerly Aaron's business partners, held a bond on land owned by Roger Peppercorn; this was not resolved until 1202.[27] Abraham owed £6 for a golden mark, to enable him to hold debts,[28] and was implicated with Elias Martrin in 1205 over clipped coins found in his chamber. He was still alive in 1228, when he gave a house in Lincoln to the nuns of Halliwell.[29]

Lady Maud's holding passed to Adam of Colchester, her son, in the early 13th century. Adam was to pay the 8s 6d rent to the Chapter[30] and his son, another Ralf, together with Maud, released their tenancy to the Chapter, who leased it in c.1228 to Gilbert Belot; his daughter Sybil also held the land to the west of this property. She also made a quitclaim to the Chapter[31] in the 1230s. The Chapter then leased no.263 to Peter the Cordwainer for a rent of 32s per annum. Future lessees in the period before 1285 included Maud le Scheyer,[32] mother of Michael le Cutler; she also had a shop near the South Bail Gate.[33] Some references to this property occur in the Chapter Accounts of the early 14th century. Canon John de Wythington, lessee here from as early as 1281/2, is mentioned as former tenant as late as 1335, when the house of Geoffrey de Hagham was repaired at a cost over two years of 46s 9¼d.[34]

Alfred de Hadington, who, as Professor Major noted, was on a Grand Assize in 1202,[35] made a grant to Hamo, son of Lambert, who was a smith, in or before the last decade of the 12th century. Hamo's rent was to be 3s per annum.[36] He, or perhaps his son, received another grant of this property c.1240.[37]

NO.262 HIGH STREET

Elias Martrin, mentioned in a later boundary reference,[38] belongs to a period much earlier than 1313. We have already heard about the clipped coinage found in 1205, and he is found quite often in Jewish records until (and after) his death c.1230. He is recorded as making a contribution to the Bristol tallage in 1223.[39] Debts amounting to 170 marks were due to him by c.1220[40] and this list had grown by his death to £480, which his heirs Isaac, Peytevin and Dyaya were forced to hand over *seriatim* to the Crown from January 1233 onwards.[41] This raft of debt was still being chased in the Pipe Rolls as late as 1280,[42] and was a main cause of the eventual escheat of the property into the king's hands.

In November 1249 the king granted to Hagin, son of Master Moses, Jew of London, a messuage in the parish of St Martin, which the heirs of Elias had held, for an annual payment of 5s. Hagin was excused from paying the sum of 22 marks for some unknown reason.[43] Hagin had represented Lincoln in the 1241 'Jewish Parliament',[44] and had his origins in Lincoln. He had many interests in London also. It was during his tenure of the site (1249–1275) that the *scola* was established, although there are no records of its actual foundation.

From the early 1270s Hagin was in and out of prison, almost as a hostage to other people's debts. By 1278, when his list of debts was scheduled,[45] the huge sum of £5,265 or even more in face value was documented by 37 bonds ranging in date from c.1260 to 1273, and Queen Eleanor, to whom the proceeds were assigned, had started the process of calling them in even before Hagin's death in 1280. In 1275 he had been given licence to sell his Lincoln properties to Sir Stephen de Cheynduit, and this messuage, together with the *scola*, would have been included among them.[46]

The queen probably called in the Lincoln properties at Hagin's death, as the next link in the chain of evidence is a grant by her to Cheynduit in 1286 of all the houses and rents she held which formerly belonged to Hagin. Stephen was forbidden to alienate any part of the property worth more than one mark[47]. This property was passed by inheritance to Stephen his son c.1299, when he was able to sell it all on to John of St Ives and Gilbert de Atherby.[48]

John quitclaimed his interest to Gilbert in September 1300: "...a capital messuage with the appurtenances, in the parish of St Martin, which lies between land of the Chapter on the north and land of Geoffrey de Notyngham, painter, on the south, and extends from the Great Street (*Magno Vico*) on the east to Hundegate on the west...".[49] Gilbert retained control of this site until June 1311, when he granted to Master William de Thornton "... all that tenement with five shops within it, and all appurtenances...between land of the cathedral on the north and land of Hugh le Paintour on the south...".[50] It is noticeable that the former synagogue was not referred to in either of these documents.

Thornton paid 50 marks, which went towards the debts of Stephen de Cheynduit; he had already paid four marks in 1309, suggesting that he was already in occupation at that time.[51] The mortmain licence for this and two other properties (27–28 Strait and the Jew's House) was given by the king in 1311 and Thornton received £100 from the Chapter, ostensibly from the sale of the chattels and moveable items there,[52] prior to the establishment of the Thornton and Gare Chantry in January 1312.[53] The sale price of 50 marks is measurably higher than the sums raised for the king from the sale of the other former Jewish properties in 1291/92, and may conceal other financial transactions.

A regular annual outrent of 3s per annum was paid from this property to the Black Monks outside Lincoln, the reason for which has eluded discovery. It must relate to a very early transaction or commitment which transferred to the Chapter, similar to the 6d per annum paid to the Vicars Choral from the property now called the Jew's House, and in fact listed next to it in the Thornton accounts each year. Also paid from no.262 as an outrent was a sum of 14s 8d per annum for the benefit of the Alexander Fitzmartin Chantry.[54] These three payments were still being made as late as 1450.[55]

262–265 HIGH STREET

265 High Street

POST-MEDIEVAL
DOCUMENTATION

Here there was a modest Corporation leasehold, situated on the corner of High Street and St Martin's Lane, running westward for only 34 yards; for this we have separate records only between 1542 and 1699, at which point it seems that the tenement was enfranchised and became subsumed within the territory of no.264.

In 1542 Edward Crosfeld, a member of the family which held the Cardinal's Hat for a while, was given a 40-year lease at a rent of 3s per annum; this consisted of a cottage and a small piece of ground behind it.[56] The first surviving lease, entered into the City's Lease Book, was granted on 18 February 1613[57] to Edmund Booth, tanner, who may also have held land immediately to the west for which there are few records. The occupiers at this point were Anthony Awstine and Edmund Hornsey, Notary Public. Along with the rent, the lessee had to provide one capon each year; this was later amended to 12 pigeons or 18d pa.

Simon Topliffe, cordwainer, took over the lease in 1624,[58] then came a hiatus in the records until 1656. A William Easman was probably lessee until his death in 1632, when he left his house at Dounston Lock (sic) to his son William, with the residue going to his wife Margaret.[59] Margaret became lessee in 1656.[60] William Easman and his wife Ann lived here until his death in 1664; a description of the house in his inventory includes four chambers, a high chamber next to the street, a buttery, shop and a stable to the rear. He was a barber and there was a chair and two razors in the shop;[61] the lease went to his

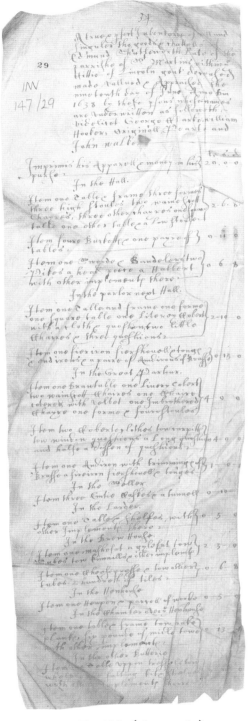

wife.[62] The description suggests a rebuilding had taken place, probably in the earlier part of the 17th century.

In 1669 Sir John Monson was lessee, although we have no actual lease and the reference is from the City's Seal Book.[63] William Bunch Darwin was in occupation, and this was a period when several of the gentry started to take up town houses for those times when they had business in Lincoln. Darwin may have died before 1676, as Anne Darwin, widow, was also occupying no.264 at that time, according to boundary information from a lease for no.263. In May 1699 the last known lessee of no.265, John Garnon, apothecary, was given his lease, for which again there is no extant text,[64] and Christopher Palmer, last named occupier of the leasehold died in 1705.[65] Thereafter no.265 lost its separate identity, although some partitioning was still evident in later records.

264 High Street

We are heavily dependent on boundary information from leases for no.263 for details of owners and occupiers of this freehold, which, from the list available, appears to have been a fairly high-status town house from the mid-17th to the late 18th centuries.

Edmund Shuttleworth, gent., a lawyer and Town Clerk of Lincoln, was the first known post-medieval owner of this house. He had other property interests in the city, including a five-acre close in the Carholme area previously belonging to the Grantham family, and an extensive farm in North Hykeham, purchased from Bartholomew Gregg. He died in 1638, leaving the Lincoln property to his wife Elizabeth for life.[66] His eldest son Leon later acquired no.264, adding it to his leasehold over the road at the Cardinal's Cap, as it was then generally called; however, he died in 1645 and the property passed to Edmund, his eldest son, who was to have use of the study, "if his calling so requires": Edmund was under 21 at the time, and does not seem to have carried on the family business.[67]

No.264 came into the hands of the Harvey family by 1649, another family with legal

Fig 108. (above right) no.265 High Street: probate inventory for Edmund Shutleworth, 1638

Fig 109. (above left) Contemporary photograph of street frontage, nos 264–265 High Street

interests. In 1676 a reference in the Chapter lease for no.263 gives the name of Anne Darwin as an occupier,[68] and Christopher Randes of the Close, associated with the Chirurgeons holding,[69] occurs in 1696. John Medley, gent. was the owner in 1710, and also held the lease of no.263. He had property in the east of the county and in the Isle of Axholme. Dying in 1726, his will, in which he left his property to his son, another John,[70] was witnessed by Francis, William and John Harvey, three members of the prominent legal family by now based at no.262. Medley was related to the Amcotts, Hall and Sibthorp families, and acted in his own legal capacity for the Sibthorps alongside the Harveys.[71]

Not so much is known of the house or its occupants in the second half of the 18th century. The Revd Mapletoft is mentioned in 1749, Mrs Nevile in 1763 and Mr Boot the surgeon, one of many of the medical profession to be based in this house, in 1791.[72] In 1805, John Flewker, Officer of Excise, was in occupation. He later took an office further down the High Street.[73] In around 1833 Thomas Charles Sympson, surgeon and descendant of Thomas Sympson the antiquarian, was based here, staying until c.1847. After him came three more surgeons, Anderson Mason, Benjamin Taplin and John Macdonald.

ARCHITECTURAL
DESCRIPTION

Both properties at the junction of High Street and St Martin's Lane are of one build and date from the late 17th–early 18th centuries. Of two stories and attics, they are brick-built throughout, with gabled wing projections to the rear (west) that contrast markedly with the elevational treatment towards High Street. The sub-division may be seen to be one that awards No.265 a smaller ground plan whose details at this level have been removed in modern alterations, leaving the upper floors and its original staircase fortunately intact. Within the stair area there is an approach to the cellar no longer in general use that has yet, to date, to be examined.

No.264 has undergone the same clearance as its neighbour so that little may be learnt from its ground-floor; hopefully the remainder of the tenement may compensate for this loss. It has recently been converted into a patisserie and restaurant. A drawing of the upper part of High Street made in 1818 by the itinerant artist William Henry Brooke is based on a view from St Martin's Lane.[74] In the foreground of the sketch he shows a projecting door frame with pediment and attached half-columns, a feature which one would reasonably accept as the principal entrance to no.264. It is not known when this was removed and early photographs of this end of the street have, to date, not emerged.

Vicars' Choral tenement in Hungate, behind no.264 High Street

As shown hitherto, documentation for the properties of the Vicars is sparse. John Tooley was their tenant from 1635 and in 1649 the Parliamentary Survey shows the occupant to be Matthew Eager. At this time the property consisted of two small rooms below and one chamber above, built of rough stone and thatched.[75] A list of leases of 1685[76] shows that William Tooley had a lease in 1666, and in an 18th-century hand the name William Hall appears. There was a John Hall, tailor, here as lessee from 1819;[77] he and his family developed an extensive tailoring business in the upper High Street over several decades. Hall's executors were lessees until 1847, the last being Benjamin Singleton, the roper; the two tenements then on the site were assigned to the Dean and Chapter to be used as part of the holding at no.263.

263 High Street

In the post-Reformation period, no.263 was assigned to the Board Rents of the Cathedral. Some late 16th-century rentals show that Edward Bowler, who held other Chapter leaseholds, was tenant here from c.1591 and had a further lease in 1615, the original of which has not survived: this was in a list written into the rental record.[78] Robert Bedam,

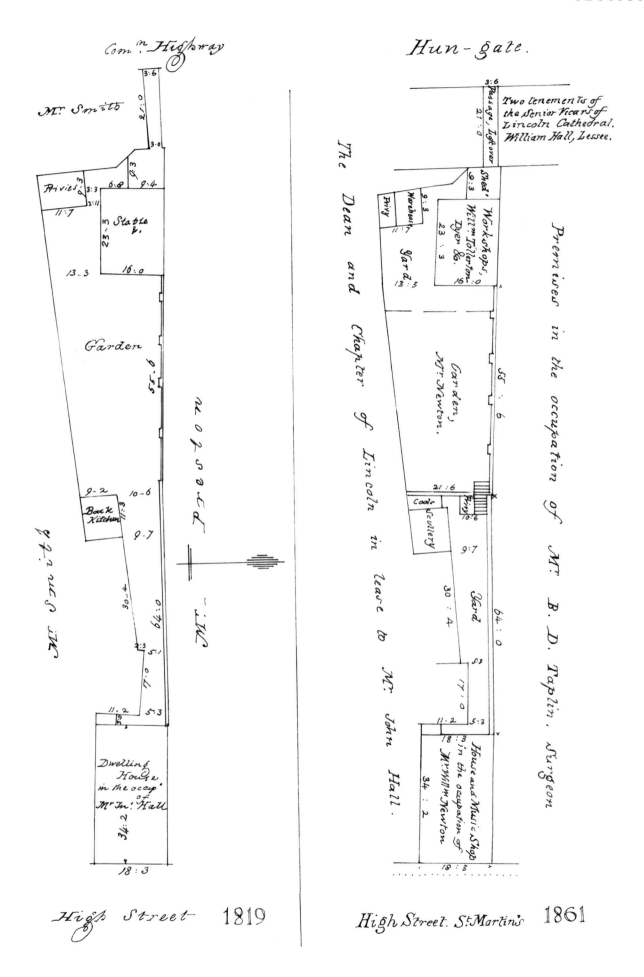

Fig 110. *Ground plans from leases, 1819 and 1861, no.263 High Street, drawn from the originals*

skinner, was here in 1633 and had a lease in 1640, for 40 years at the rent of 12s per annum.[79]

At the time of the 1649 Parliamentary Survey a Mr Storey was lessee with Stephen Gateworth as occupier. There was a hall, parlour, kitchen, buttery, three lodging chambers and a closet. At the Hungate end of the site, where a separate tenement had been situated in the early 14th century, now stood a cottage occupied by Nicholas Bishop, "anciently a barn (*sic*), built of stone and covered with thatch, consisting of one low room, two little chambers and two small gardens, one stall and hayloft, with a narrow passage leading to a back lane". The main tenement was of wood and covered with tile.[80]

Benjamin Bromhead, yeoman, was lessee from 1676, although he had been paying the rent since 1672.[81] He died in 1695, and his brother John, a Sleaford merchant, inherited the lease.[82] The probate inventory[83] lists a hall, chamber, matted chamber, chambers over the hall and kitchen, a closet, kitchen, brewhouse, corn chamber, yard, cellar, a stable with seven horses and their saddlery (valued at £30 in all), a hay chamber and a belfry.

John continued as lessee until 1704. John Medley took it over in 1707 and received leases in 1710 and 1723.[84] Although he died in 1726 his sister in law Elizabeth carried on with the rents until 1733. Under John's will she was allowed to live there rent-free, but only permitted to enjoy the part of the house in which she was living in 1726, and forbidden to "...intermeddle with the kitchen, garden, coal house and chambers above them, nor the two stalls in the back lane (i.e. Hungate), nor the coach house...".[85] The latter, previously described as a stable, was home to a very respectable and probably ostentatious equipage; we will encounter the coach house again later.

The Wood sisters, Anne and Elizabeth, lived here from c.1749. Anne dropped out before 1763, but Elizabeth stayed until c.1791, when Samuel Walker, a victualler from Horncastle, received a lease, with James Spellman as occupier. The coach house, also used as a brewhouse and stable, was assigned to John Garmston, gent., lessee of no.262. The Chapter allowed a rent reduction of 3s per annum, which was added to the rent of no.262 from 1772.[86]

In 1805 the holding was leased to Francis Mansford, the ill-fated grocer, the house then being in the occupation of Mrs Thickstone.[87] After Mansford's bankruptcy in 1815 a new lease was given in 1819 to John Hall, the tailor,[88] renewed in 1833 to John Smith, victualler and Benjamin Singleton, roper, Hall's executors.[89] Richard Hall was in occupation, replaced in 1841 by Mary Hall, tailor. The name 'Mary Hall and Sons' was to recur in street directories for another six years, until the business moved down the street to no.254.

262 High Street (latterly Garmston House)

The linkage with no.263 had by the end of the medieval period disappeared except for their common assignment to the Board Rents of the Cathedral. The rent for no.262 seems to have become standardised at 14s per annum at an early date: the Board rentals seem less erratic in that respect, compared to the Fabric rentals. In c.1461–63 the widow of John Clerk was a tenant at this rent, and in 1489 Thomas Syme.[90] Christopher Forman was listed in 1529, again paying the same rent.[91]

A boundary reference in a 1561 lease[92] for no.261 gives us the name of Ralph Skelton as lessee here; his family had several links to the Chapter over a long period of time, and they had a number of leaseholds in Lincoln. The first lease of no.262 for which we have the text[93] was given in 1586 to a bookbinder, originally from Newark, called variously Thomas Waitman or Whaitman. His father, another Thomas, had already been in occupation of the property and some of their descendants were connected to no.258 High Street.

It is probably the elder Thomas who was given the Freedom of the City in January

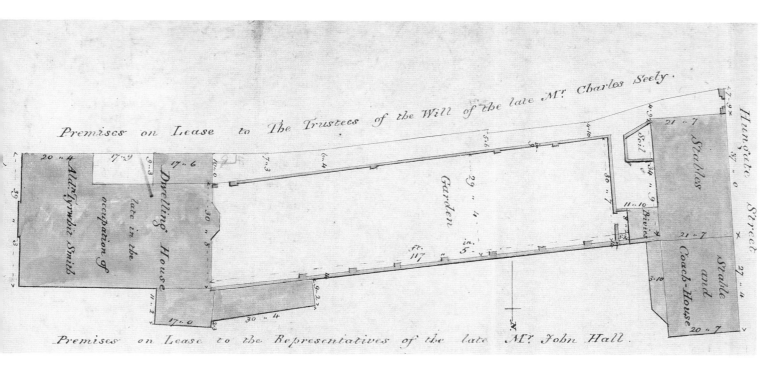

*Fig 111. Ground plan from
lease of 1831, Garmston
House, no.262 High Street*

1559, paying 10s for the privilege,[94] and taking John Hopkynson as an apprentice two years later.[95] Whaitman's widow paid rent of 13s in 1588.[96] Original [Reginald] Morris, cook, also lessee of 14 Strait,[97] took over and his wife or widow paid the rent of no.262 in 1591.[98]

To continue the unfortunate trend of rapid turnover here, by 1598 there was another tenant, Richard Knyght, according to the Board Rentals.[99] In 1601 a new lease was granted to Thomas Turbervile, gent.; this is the first to survive in the original format.[100] Thomas had left before 1614, as in that year William Darwyne died. The rooms in his inventory were: a seeled (ceiled, i.e. pannelled) parlour, a middle room, the parlour towards the street, the chamber at the stairs head, the best chamber, the black chamber, buttery, kitchen and stable. The lease of the house with the glass and ceiling etc., was valued at £80, and he had horses to the value of £18. The Black Chamber was used mostly for storage of linen and plate, appraised at £34 14s; there were 14 table cloths and 21 pairs of sheets. The buttery included a still, with more brewing equipment in the kitchen, and there was a set of hangings in the best chamber. The total value of the inventory was an impressive £293 19s.[101]

After Darwyne came John Hawdenbie (Haldenby), gent., who received a lease in 1618[102] but assigned it in the following year to Adam Glover, who, with his wife Sybil, was to reside here until 1643.[103] Sybil was given a lease in 1640 and was still in residence in 1649; at this time the Parliamentary Survey[104] showed that the kitchen was in a ruinous condition and the parlour had a boarded floor. The main tenement was of stone with a tiled roof, and the stable at the Hungate end was of rough stone and had, like other properties in the row, a thatched roof.

No.262 was one of those houses which we know were sold off by the Parliamentary Commissioners and had to be re-purchased by the Dean and Chapter in 1660. By 1655 it had come into the hands of Samuel Williams, a stationer, who with his wife Edith had arranged a mortgage loan for £70 with Robert Phillips, a Whitechapel glass founder.[105] In 1663 a new lease was given by the Chapter to John Williams of London, stationer; Edith Williams, widow of Samuel, was the occupier at this time, but she died in 1671.[106]

Her inventory was notable for two things: firstly because her name was entered as Eden, not Edith, and secondly for the informative catalogue of books and writing equipment in the little shop and the great shop. There were 99 folio volumes, 318 Quarto, 1,140

Octavo and 434 smaller Duodecimo works; three old and three new Quarto Bibles, seven Octavo Bibles and 12 gilt Duodecimo Bibles at 3s 6d each; grammars, psalters, testaments, prayer books and so on. The total book stock was worth over £105. There were sheets of parchment from Lincoln, Grantham and London in the little shop.[107]

John Williams took out a new lease in March 1678,[108] leaving the running of the Lincoln business to Samuel Williams, probably his son; there was another business in London. Samuel carried on at no.262 until 1682, when William Willerton of the Close became lessee.[109] Jane Ellis was the occupier at this time. Stephen Ludington succeeded Willerton as lessee in 1689.[110] An extra lodging chamber (to make four) had been added, and the stable had acquired a tiled roof. Ludington, however, died shortly after taking over.[111]

Francis Harvey, the lawyer, was probably responsible for the rebuilding work which ensued within the next few years; he was lessee from 1696[112] until he died 40 years later. John Harvey was then lessee, with three leases dated between 1738 and 1752.[113] He died in 1758[114] and the house and legal practice devolved to John Garmston. The house took his name over time, as did a small street near St Martin's Church. Sometime after his death another house in Newland took over the name Garmston House. His first lease was at the customary rent of 14s per annum, but by 1772 he had arranged an assignment to his leasehold of the coach house behind no.263, thus increasing his rent to 17s pa.

Garmston died in 1793, and Elizabeth, his widow, lived on here until 1798.[115] The lease was assigned to Henry Banks, another lawyer; a new kitchen had been built, together with other modifications.[116] Alderman Tyrwhit Smith acquired the lease by assignment c.1805, and remained as lessee until 1827, when Thomas Winn paid £1,860 for an assignment of this prestigious house. Winn had leases in 1831 and 1843, but sub-let the house first to George Hinde, then in 1843 to Ralph Hewitt, surgeon. The lease was assigned to John Hall, tailor and draper, in 1859.[117]

Hall remained lessee until he was able to purchase a reversionary interest from the Ecclesiastical Commissioners in 1863. It was let to Albert Wingfield Hall, grocer, in 1877, and he developed the shop, which still bore his name until 1899. In the following year it was sold to the Lincolnshire Property Board and General Finance Co. for £3,650, and some of the shop accommodation partitioned off, with a variety of tenants.

In 1911 the Lincoln Theatre Ltd took up occupation. By 1913 most of the property had been adapted for the uses of the Electric Cinema. In 1943 General Picture Theatres Ltd were still continuing with the cinema, at a rent of £500 per annum, and it later became known as the Grand Cinema.[118] During the early 1970s, after the cinema had shown its last reel, there was a threat to the whole building (and its neighbours) from a proposal to run an inner city ring road through the area. Happily for this interesting example of early 18th-century architecture, the scheme fell through.

ARCHITECTURAL DESCRIPTION

SUMMARY What proved to be the most important discovery made on site during the renovation of this building in 1990 was the remains of two conjoined and joggled arches in its north wall at ground-level. The arches had formerly topped shallow recesses and although a central section had been cut away for a later chimney flue it would appear that, at mid-span, both arches had shared a corbel or pilaster support in common. From the form of the joggling a conservative date somewhere in the later 12th century is suggested. In addition there was corroborative evidence of a similar origin in re-used masonry in the west wall of the street range. It is perhaps not unusual that party walls survived later rebuildings of the main range and none more so when of solid stone construction.[119] In 1649 the property to the north, no.263 High Street, was timber-framed and probably remained so into the 18th century. The cellar of Garmston House, noted in the Parliamentary Survey of that year, has no obvious ancient features, having been both modernised and enlarged; its former extent probably lay, in part, under the boarded parlour mentioned in the Survey.

From the late 17th and throughout the 18th and 19th centuries the house was, for considerable periods, leased as the residence of persons of substance, including town clerks, attorneys, merchants and mayors. The choice of window type, with its triple openings and usually referred to as 'Venetian' for the facade and its smaller versions facing the garden, was popular elsewhere in Lincoln – e.g. Greestone Holme, Greestone Terrace and the Archdeaconry, 2 Greestone Place – from the mid-18th century onwards. The name Garmston derives from one John Garmston, attorney, a lessee and occupier in 1758 who renewed his lease in 1772, at which date additional rooms and ground had been assigned to him from the tenement forming the north bounds, i.e. no.263. It is this expansion, together with the architectural evidence, that helps in assigning an approximate period for rebuilding and, more significantly, the persistent attachment of the improver's name to the house.

The following description is based on visits made before and during demolition work that commenced in 1990. The first site visit followed shortly after the demolition of the auditorium of the former Grand Cinema, a structure that had been built on the garden area of Garmston House c.1911. This initial clearance enabled an inspection to be carried out of newly exposed walling, and from this an assessment to be formed of what remained of this important town house after the cinema episode that had lasted up to its closure in 1962.

Prior to 1911 the street facade of the house had remained virtually unchanged since a massive refurbishment in the third quarter of the 18th century had left it with a symmetrical stone frontage in which Venetian windows played a prominent part, gracing both ground- and first-floor levels. These, together with the central pedimented entrance doorway, raised quoins and baluster panels to its parapet, marked the building out as a residence of considerable distinction and desirability. At this point in High Street at that time a number of adjoining properties were dedicated to trade, and their narrower fronts held shops. Garmston House clearly dominated the west side of the street and there is good reason to think that, as noted earlier, it originated as a substantial stone structure as early as the 12th century.

DESCRIPTION   The street front of Garmston House is generous, measuring 39ft 3in north–south, its length being remarkably close to that of the Jew's House in the Strait.[120] In 1649 the Parliamentary Survey describes the house as one of stone construction, yet so few rooms are listed for the ground-floor as to question their distribution within such an apparently ample frontage. A hall, parlour and kitchen are also listed for no.263 in the same survey but this has a more modest frontage of 18 ft 3 in, a dimension more in keeping with those individual tenements to the south of Garmston House, and where their rooms were similarly aligned from front to rear.

The Parliamentary Survey description of the house is as follows: 'Sibell Glover, all that tenement in p. St Martin consisting of a hall, a parlor (the floor being boarded), one kitchen, very ruinous, with a buttery, a cellar, 3 lodging chambers, 2 little gardens, one stable built of rough stone and thatcht, the scite and seat by estimation 1 rood, the tenement built of stone and covered with tile, abutting high street east, Mr Story on the north and upon a common lane now (sic) Beaumont Fee west. Rent 14s worth by improvement £4 13 4; lease of 1618 quoted.'[121] In a lease and counterpart of 1677/8 to one John Williams the description includes 'one shopp' after buttery in the above survey and the reference to the ruinous state of the kitchen is omitted.[122]

Of the contiguous tenements comprising nos 257–261 High Street in 1650, all were said to be of stone construction. Somewhat disquieting, however, is the evidence of an early photograph that clearly shows no.260 as a timber-framed and jettied building, albeit rendered.[123]

With the removal of the cinema's accretions, the form of the 18th-century house became clearer, showing that it had formed a 'T'-planned building. The head of the 'T' was formed by the two-storied range with attics fronting the street, and the stem by a central rear wing, similarly storied. It was presumably in this form that the house was described in 1696 as 'being newly built' when leased to Francis Harvey,[124] but the recasting may be more properly ascribed to the town clerk, Stephen Ludington, in occupation from 1689.[125] Of this later 17th-century house the part which may be claimed to have survived relatively unaltered since 'newly built' is at first-floor level where the west wall of the street range preserves two blocked window openings. These are sited, respectively, to the north and south of the junction of the rear wing with the street range and, when entire, would have contained wooden mullion and transom frames appropriate to the period. The rear wing held a central brick-built chimney stack serving its two floors and – excepting the replacement west gable end of brick construction – had stone north and south walls and was undoubtedly of the same new build. From the ragged joint that the stone walls made with the west gable end and the continuation of their wall-plates it was clear that an earlier stone gable had been deposed. Old rafters had been pressed into service as lintels for doors and windows in the north wall and these, together with irregular brick patchings and poor foundations, contributed to its instability and, inevitably, to the wing's recent partial demolition and replacement; the brick gable end to the wing was also replaced post-1990, together with its unstable stack. The brick west wall of c.1770, incorporating the rear wing's gable, had been extended, north and south, to include the lower gables of smaller attached wings or pavilions. Each lower gable preserved a Venetian window and one can be reasonably confident that this consolidation of the garden elevation was coeval with the recasting of the street range in the later 18th century.

THE ROOFS

The rear wing, conspicuously free of openings that could be credited with a medieval origin, had a span that appeared to have been dictated by the re-use of a suite of medieval roof trusses whose provenance is uncertain. From the evidence of smoke staining it would seem that they had once spanned an open hall. Each truss, of uniform scantling, had two collar beams, their overall form strongly resembling those rafter couples of the 13th-century hall roof at Deloraine Court, James St.[126] From the carpenters' marks scribed on the wing rafters it is clear that they once formed a homogeneous group combining those couples east of the chimney stack with their collar beams clasping the west face of the rafters and those to the west which had collar beams clasped or halved to the east face of the rafters. Purely in terms of numbers, and rearranged in numerical sequence, the rafter couples' total fell short of the west end of the rear wing. What in 1985, in the east bay, were confirmed as three original tie-beams, but not necessarily in situ, and in use as flooring beams for the garrets, were then available, in part, for investigation. The top of one such beam carried a central mortice which suggested that it had once held a vertical timber, possibly a crown post. The undersides or soffits of these tie-beams were mortice-free, a strong indicator that the original roof, when entire, had belonged to a stone structure rather than one of timber framing; an octagonal post, possibly either a crown post or king strut, was noted, *ex-situ*, in the east bay of the wing roof, but because of its inextricably high location regrettably it went unrecorded. In two of the rafter couples, in which both upper and lower collar beams were present, central single dowels that would have secured a collar purlin were retained on the lower beam. It was noted that the feet of rafters in the west bay, north side, were exposed and partly defaced below the level of an 18th-century plaster cornice in the first-floor room; their precise method of attachment

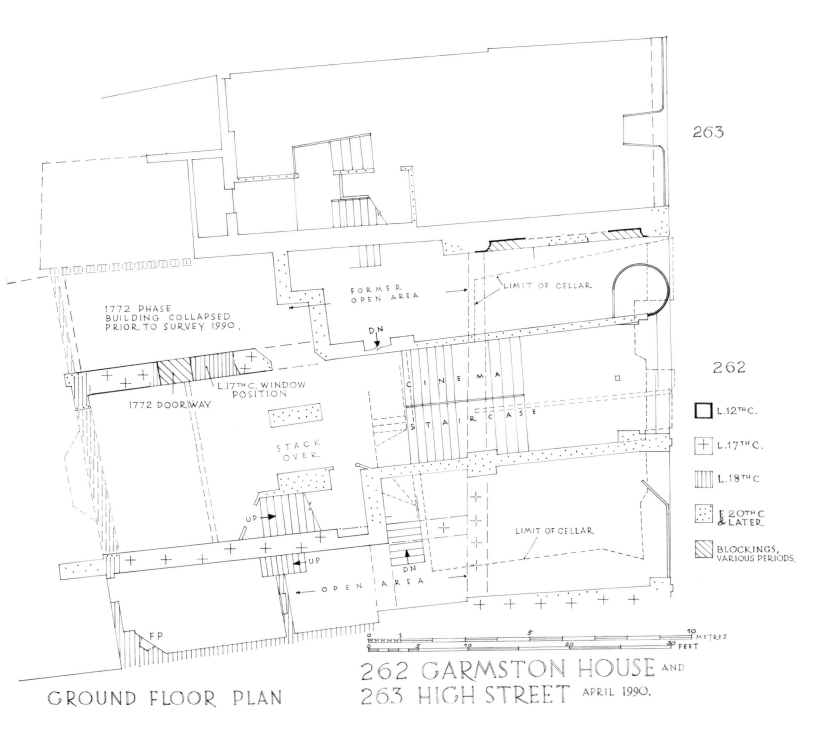

263

262

☐ L.12ᵀᴴC.

+ L.17ᵀᴴ C.

▥ L.18ᵀᴴ C

⠿ E 20ᵀᴴ C & LATER

▨ BLOCKINGS, VARIOUS PERIODS.

1772 PHASE BUILDING COLLAPSED PRIOR TO SURVEY 1990.

FORMER OPEN AREA

LIMIT OF CELLAR

L.17ᵀᴴ C. WINDOW POSITION

1772 DOORWAY

STACK OVER

DN

CINEMA STAIRCASE

LIMIT OF CELLAR

UP

UP

DN

OPEN AREA

FP

GROUND FLOOR PLAN

262 GARMSTON HOUSE AND 263 HIGH STREET APRIL 1990.

Fig 112. Ground-floor plan of Garmston House

to a buried wall-plate on this side could not be determined, as was also the case for the opposite wall.

If, as appears to be the case, the entire complement of early rafter couples is reset and centred on the chimney stack, the most likely date for this occurrence is the period late in the 17th century when the house is referred to as being newly built.[127] There is nothing to suggest a previous location for the roof members elsewhere on site.

The short roof bay, intervening as an infill between the roof of the street range and those rafter couples of the east bay in the rear wing, was marked by both a change in roof and attic floor levels to accord with those of the street range.[128] This section was a motley collection of roofing materials and carried a clasped-purlin roof.

The five-bay roof of the street range is of a form that allowed free movement at attic level. It has high collar beams and staggered purlins, a practice that suggests an 18th-

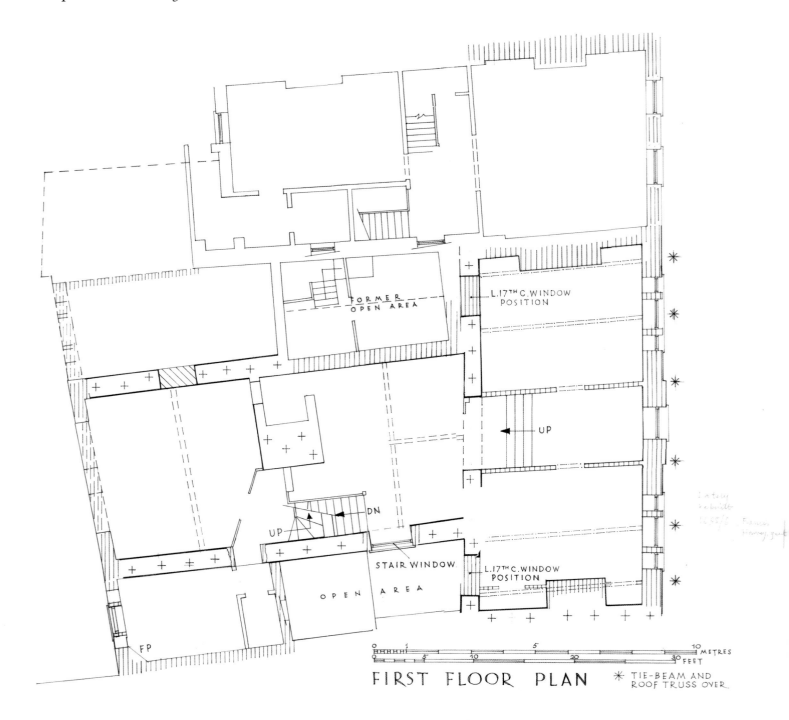

Within the plan:

FORMER OPEN AREA

L.17ᵀᴴ C. WINDOW POSITION

UP

STAIR WINDOW

L.17ᵀᴴ C. WINDOW POSITION

UP

DN

OPEN AREA

FP

FIRST FLOOR PLAN ✳ TIE-BEAM AND ROOF TRUSS OVER

0   1   5   10 METRES
0   5   10   20   30 FEET

Fig 113. First-floor plan of Garmston House

century origin and conceivably coeval with the massive re-fronting of the house towards High Street.[129]

A staircase preserved against the south side of the chimney stack in the rear wing at first-floor is of two distinct periods. The section visible at the stair foot has balusters of mid-18th-century style, whilst the upper section, approaching the attics, preserves stout turned balusters and a handrail of the later 17th century.[130] At ground-level any evidence for the stair is now removed, but for the principal staircase, introduced in the 18th-century alterations, its large round-headed sash window is retained in the south wall.[131]

The plan of the house, as transformed in the 18th century, saw the main range fronting the High Street disposed symmetrically about its central entrance hall and having on either hand a heated room of equal ornamentation and status. The principal staircase, approached via the entrance hall, was not immediately apparent from the latter, being set within the back wing, south side, and lit from an open yard. Where the kitchen was located prior to the general makeover is uncertain, other than to suppose it occupied

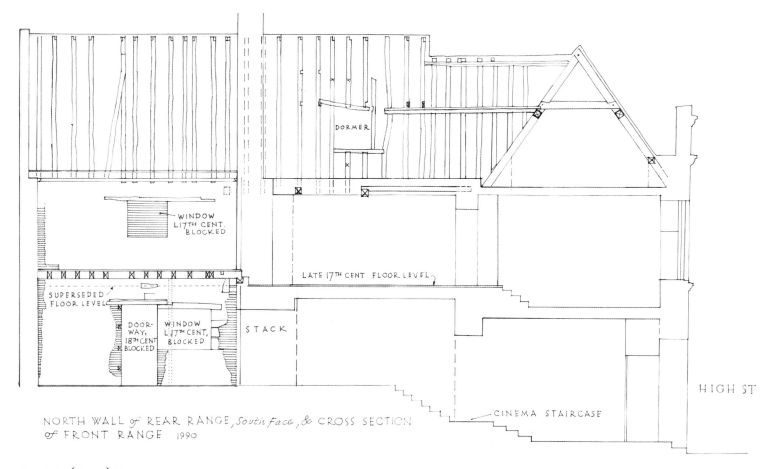

WINDOW
L.17TH CENT.
BLOCKED

DORMER

LATE 17TH CENT FLOOR LEVEL

SUPERSEDED
FLOOR LEVEL

DOOR-
WAY,
18TH CENT
BLOCKED

WINDOW
L.17TH CENT,
BLOCKED

STACK

HIGH ST

CINEMA STAIRCASE

NORTH WALL of REAR RANGE, South Face, & CROSS SECTION
of FRONT RANGE 1990

Fig 114. (above) South face of rear range and cross section of street range, Garmston House

Fig 115. Photograph of masonry in north wall, Garmston House

Fig 116. Photograph of arched recess in north wall, Garmston House

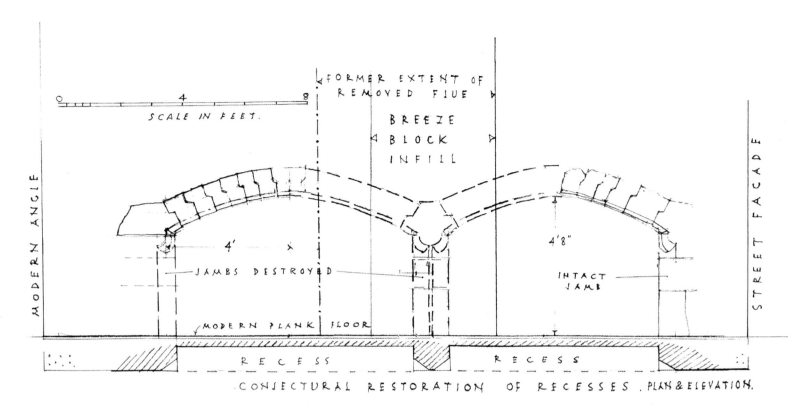

Fig 117. Conjectural restoration of arched recesses, Garmston House

Fig 118. (above) Photograph of street
frontage, Garmston House, from a slide
Fig 119. (right) Photograph of stair
window, Garmston House

Fig 120. (left) Photograph of attic staircase and balusters, Garmston House
Fig 121. (above) Garmston House: photograph of rear wing roof, east end, with reset trusses

some part of the back wing. After John Garmston's alterations it occupied that part of no.263 High St leased to him,[132] and the back wing at both levels was then dedicated to more polite uses.[133] Could the suggested change of use have necessitated a rebuilding of the wing chimney stack?

At the south end of the street frontage, and within its limits, is a doorway that gave onto a service passage, of varying widths, which ran the full length of the plot from the High Street to Hungate, the back lane.[134] It had as its south bound no.261, and for its north side, the garden wall of Garmston House. This arrangement ensured that both servants and goods could access the house and back wing without using the main entrance and, in turn, the users of the garden were guaranteed a degree of privacy. A similar arrangement has been recorded in Stamford in a house of comparable date and status but, unlike the Lincoln building, the service doorway is a better integrated feature.[135] Flanking Hungate and closing off the west end of both nos 262 and 263 were stables and a coach house, all apparently lofted over and of stone/rubble walling. It may well be that the stable to no.262 was that described in 1649 as 'thatcht'. These ancillary buildings survived into the later 20th century, post-clearance of the Grand Cinema's auditorium, having earlier served sundry uses and been independent of the main holding.

261 HIGH STREET

The name of Richard, son of James, son of the Brother, is noted as a south boundary reference on two deeds relating to no.262, 50 years apart, c.1190 and 1240.[136] Geoffrey de Notingham, painter, was living there in 1300, and Hugh le Payntor (alias Hugh Pictor) in 1311.[137] Hugh's will of 1324 stated that Catherine his wife would inherit the property,[138] and it seems to have come to the Chapter after her death. None of the references to repairs to properties in Mikelgate (for which tenants are named) have yet been identified with this building.

DOCUMENTARY
HISTORY

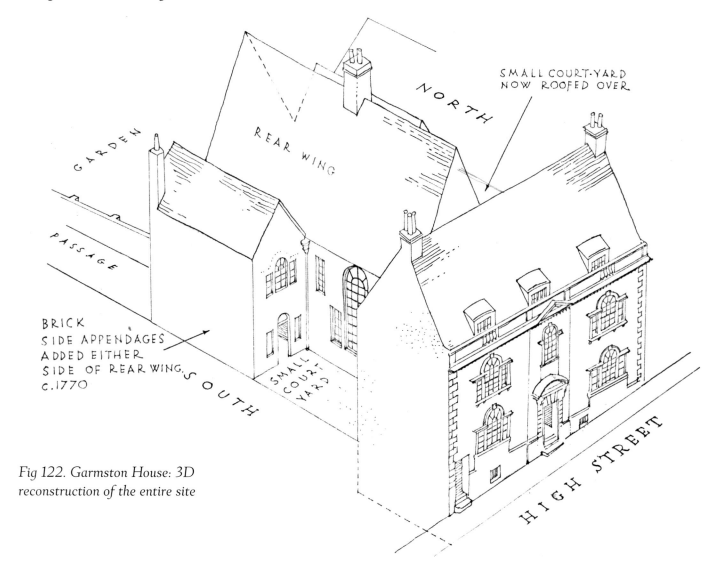

Fig 122. Garmston House: 3D reconstruction of the entire site

In comparison with some of the other Chapter properties in this area, the post-medieval history of the site is relatively uneventful, except for the lengthy period of its use as a bakery, first mentioned in 1672 and continuing for 200 years.

George Holt, mercer, was given a 60-year lease at a rent of 8s per annum in January 1562; the tenement description gives little but boundary information.[139] After Holt, the Board Rentals supply references to Jeffrey Wilson, senior, who had several property interests in Lincoln, and was lessee or tenant here in 1588 and 1598; his widow was tenant after him, in 1615.[140]

Thomas Cumberland, upholsterer, was lessee from September 1628, but after only a year he had assigned it to Adam Glover, currier.[141] Dorothy, his daughter, paid the rent in 1633, and Adam resumed in 1642, only to die during the following year.[142] Sybil Glover, his widow, is recorded as tenant in the 1649 Parliamentary Survey, by which time the building had been divided, in the occupation of Robert Fleming and Robert Wilkinson.[143] There was an error in the text: the clerk had written that this was a Fabric Fund property, whereas it was in fact accountable not even to the Board Rents but to the Common Fund.

After the Restoration John Green appears to be paying the rent,[144] but a lease was given in 1664 to George Greene of Caistor.[145] There follows a lengthy series of bakers as lessees or occupiers, including four members of the Bristow family between 1672 and 1716,[146] Nathaniel Knight and Elizabeth his wife 1719–1739,[147] Matthew Curtois 1771–93,[148] the first Charles Seely 1798–1807,[149] his widow 1816–1843,[150] and their son Charles, the politician, c.1849–57.[151] John Curtis followed Seely in 1857.[152] Herbert

Henry Woolhouse, also a local politician, was there in 1872, the last of the dozen or so bakers to have plied their trade from no.261. Rushton and Dawkins, wood turners, were using workshops at the rear of the premises in 1895 and 1897, and Halford's cycle shop was here from 1909.

260–257 HIGH STREET

This run of properties was part of the long range of Chapter properties extending from no.257 to no.263, brought together between the 12th and 15th centuries. Some charter information exists for at least one of these particular houses, but has not yet been formally linked to any of them. In April 1312 Roger de Crosholm and Elena his wife obtained a grant of property situated between land of Adam son of Martin on the south and land once of William de Neuland on the north, abutting Mikelgate and Hungate, which they were already leasing from the heirs of William Gudgeon.[153] Adam, son of John Gudgeon quitclaimed his interest in this property to Thomas de Kele and Helen his wife in 1331 before the Burwarmote Court.[154]

Moving on to 1369, what appears to be the same property was in the hands of John of Bishop Norton,[155] and in 1378 was granted to William de Carleton, cordwainer, and Alice his wife; the northern bound was by this time property of the Chapter, so must be north of no.256, and the southern bound was land of Hugh of Burton.[156] In 1421 Margaret, widow of another William de Carleton, granted it to trustees, and in 1423 it came to Nicholas Kepe, chaplain. By this time it was described as 'a tenement and two shops, with

*Fig 123.
Photograph
of jettied
front, no.260
High Street
c.1910*

Figs 124-127 Photographs of timber framing discovered during demolition, no.259 High Street, c.1961

a chamber built over and an entry',[157] so may possibly fit the later profile of nos 257–258, leased out as a single holding until the early 19th century.

Kepe granted this property to John Thetilthorpe in 1426.[158] Thetilthorpe, sometime a mayor of Lincoln, was a lay brother of the Fraternity of Lincoln Cathedral, and in January 1464 gave a tenement in St Martin, possibly this one, to the use of the Dean and Chapter, reserving to himself for life a rent of 13s 4d per annum.[159]

This group of tenements and two other premises adjoining to the south were distinguished by the encasement of substantial timber-framed structures that were three stories high in their primary stage and were retained when superseded by brickwork or render. No.260 in c.1900 preserved its rendered and jettied frontage,[160] and we are aware of it through its illustration in Laurence Elvin's *Lincoln As it Was*. One is indebted to him for photographs taken in less than favourable conditions of no.259 High Street in which its early framing was exposed behind a bland brick façade.[161]

ARCHITECTURAL DESCRIPTION

POST-MEDIEVAL DISCUSSION

260 High Street

After the Reformation no.260 was allocated to the Fabric Fund for rental purposes. The few rentals held for the period before 1572 are not consistent as to rent charged, so it has proved virtually impossible to identify any particular tenant at this stage, apart from Richard Burniston, probably a furrier, who appears as the south bound in a 1562 lease for no.261.[162] Burniston, also known as Furrier, appears in rentals until 1574, and thereafter the rent was paid by his assigns.[163]

Anne Hopkinson, spinster, received a lease for this house in September 1602. It was described in the lease book[164] as 'a messuage or tenement, tiled, with a garden adjacent, situated between property of the Works on the south and land of the Board Rents on the north'. During her 40-year term she was to pay 8s 4d per annum.

By 1617 George Farmerie, cordwainer, had taken over the tenancy,[165] and he was given a new lease in 1635, remaining as lessee and occupier until c.1660.[166] In 1649 the Parliamentary Survey provided a description of a fairly basic house cum shop: it consisted of a hall, kitchen and shop, with two chambers over the same. To the rear there was an orchard with some fruit trees, and at the Hungate boundary a thatched stable and hayloft. The main building was listed as being stone-built, but the photograph of no.260 at the turn of the 19th century, published by Elvin,[167] shows a jettied front at the upper level, typical of half-timbered construction. It could be that this frontage had been rendered over to give the impression of masonry.

Richard Farmerie, also a cordwainer, took over c.1661,[168] and for some years paid his rent regularly. There was some consideration of a new lease in 1662. Precentor Featley noted[169] that the lessee was to leave "a long lead gutter now lying on the north side of the premises", presumably in situ rather than on the ground, and to ensure repairs. Richard fell into arrears with his rent soon after, paying at intervals for the remainder of his tenancy. He did pay a renewal fine in 1681,[170] but no rent was paid until his widow paid in five years' arrears in 1686/87: the Dean and Chapter were probably surprised to get anything at all! Widow Farmerie was allowed 4d pa rebate until the lease was renewed in 1701.[171]

Jane Sibray, widow, entered into the leasehold c.1722. She had property interests on the other side of the street, so Edward Holland, plumber, was put in residence. Jane died in 1727, leaving the residue of her lease term to her niece Dailey Cater.[172] In 1735, now the wife of Thomas Greenley, a London chandler, Dailey sublet to Francis Bishop.[173] Edward Holland was lessee from 1742, followed by trustees John Garmston and Richard Barker (a schoolmaster) in 1756.[174] From 1763 to c.1777 Robert Holmes of Burgh le Marsh, grazier, held the lease with Thomas Porter, plumber, as occupier.[175] Holmes' son Robert, a butcher in Lincoln, gained a new lease in 1784. Porter, now an Alderman of the city, became lessee in 1791, setting up a candle factory in the rear premises; he renewed the lease in 1798 and 1806.[176] The Chapter threatened his successor George Varah in 1816 with a £10 per month surcharge if he continued the candle and soap business, a fire risk.[177]

John Flewker, gent., a former Excise Officer when he had an office at 264 High Street,[178] and now trustee for William Sharpe, was given a lease in 1823. The Sharpe family of plumbers and glaziers was running the family business from here from 1835 to 1870. William Lister Sharpe, a timber merchant resident in Gainsborough, was lessee from 1837.[179]

259 High Street

This was another property which was accountable to the Fabric Fund for its rent payments of 8s per annum. For some time before 1572 John Younglove was lessee and he was replaced in that year by Thomas Rawlinson, who held the lease until 1589; it may be mentioned here that Thomas Gaile is listed as making some of the rent payments during the period 1579–1584.[180]

From 1598 until his death in 1613 John Howe, skinner, was lessee.[181] He seems to have prospered in his trading activities, and was also fortunate in marrying Rose Wilson, daughter of Jeffrey Wilson, owner of several properties in the city, c.1602. John acquired leases not only from the Chapter but also from the parish of St Martin and estate owners such as Lord Burcham.[182] After Howe's death the property was apparently managed by Rose and other members of the Wilson family. A Widow Wilson was assignee in 1649, and William Farmerie, from no.260, was the occupant. The house had a hall, parlour, kitchen, three ordinary chambers with a garret over one of them and a shop fronting onto the street. At the end of the screed of ground to the west was a stable with a hayloft, built of rough stone and thatched, similar in description to other buildings on Hungate with frontages to the High Street.[183] Although the Survey entry states that the main house was built of stone, some fragments of timber framing were brought to light in 1962 during demolition work, and photographed by Laurence Elvin.[184]

In 1661 the first post-Restoration lease was granted to Thomas Hadney of the Close, a yeoman; his occupier was the suitably named Thomas Tenant.[185] Hadney died a few years later; his widow Anne took over the lease in 1672[186] and stayed resident in the Close, subletting to George Hambleton, who was still living there until 1689, when John Holland's name is found.[187]

During the 18th century there were numerous changes of both lessee (largely absentees) and occupants, including Henry Rands, who was also connected to nos 8–9 Steep Hill, and Edward Aldy, watchmaker, resident c.1760–1770.[188] Joseph Marshall, gent., held the lease between 1796 and c.1820, and was also resident in the house.[189]

Miles Hall ran an academy from no.259 c.1838–1845,[190] and Charles Akrill began his printing and bookbinding business here c.1857, remaining for about ten years. The *Lincolnshire Chronicle Co.* had its premises here from c.1877 until 1905.

257–258 High Street

These two tenements were leased as one unit until 1819, the rent of 20s per annum being allocated to the Common Chamber, although as in the case of some other properties the rent payments were registered with the Board Rentals. This has led to the discovery of three additional lessees in the early rentals: James Goodknap in 1529,[191] John Holding or Hallden, a tailor, c.1588 and his widow, who continued until c.1607.[192]

Thomas James was lessee from September 1607, with Robert Hartley, one of the sheriffs of the city, as occupier, but this fell through within a year and Hartley took it on by himself in September 1608.[193]

The Waytman family of booksellers and stationers, who had earlier been associated with no.262, appear as occupants if not lessees in the period 1617–1631. Augustine Wayteman, a very religious man,[194] was a member of this family, but there is nothing to prove his connection with the property; his daughters Ann and Alice, however, were connected to it. Ann's daughter, also Ann, married John Tompson, the bookseller, who took over the running of the shop c.1627 and acted as executrix for her mother and aunt, who both died in 1631.[195] The Tompsons were also related by marriage to the Williams family of stationers, also of no.262: Ann and Alice's niece Eden, usually known as Edith, was married to Samuel Williams.[196]

John Tompson was still lessee at the time of the Parliamentary Survey in 1649. The description is that of a modest house built of timber construction with a tiled roof, containing a 'fair shop', parlour, kitchen, wash house, two chambers and a garret, with the customary (for this area) garden, screed of ground and thatched stable with hayloft at the Hungate end.[197] He died in April or May 1650, leaving a nuncupative will, a summary of his verbal deathbed wishes. Entreated by his servant to make his will, at the instance of his daughter Margaret Rowlston, he replied, "Why need she trouble me, my hand is gone, she knows I have given her all I have [repeated]. I have nobody else to give it to but her" or words to the like effect, spoken before several witnesses, including Martin Mason, later known as a Quaker.[198]

With the leases is a deed of Bargain and Sale to Richard Wetherall, gent., who purchased this and other former leasehold sites from George Walker in 1652 during the period of the Commonwealth, when Deans and Chapters were abolished.[199] In 1660 this and the other dispersed leaseholds were recovered by the Chapter, and this property was soon leased to Henry Lambe, butcher, who renewed it in 1673[200] and held it until his death c.1687. His widow Elizabeth died in 1695 and her probate inventory catalogues two chambers over the shop, garrets above, a fore kitchen, hall, two back kitchens and brewhouse, and a boarden chamber, with three beds and other furniture worth £30. Her several leaseholds were valued at £300, amounting to a prosperous estate.[201] The Lincoln butchers were a cut above the average.

Henry Lamb, mercer, probably her son, took over her rental payments, then in 1706 was granted a lease.[202] In 1716 the property was in the occupation of John Sibray, who had property over the road.[203] A plan was included in the 1763 lease, some 50 to 60 years before they became customary. It shows a house on the High Street frontage, 18 feet/5.8 m in depth westwards, with two stables and a run of pig sties against the northern boundary, and a passage way (later called Francis Court), 4 ft/1.2 m wide on the south boundary, connecting High Street with Hungate.[204] A tenement to the rear, in the occupation of John Milward, was referred to c.1777–1790 as the Peacock Inn, a name which had been given to the hostelry at no.287 High Street in the years before 1767.[205]

By 1791 there are indications that some of the tenements, which came to be known as Francis Court, had been built on the site of the old pig sties, replacing the short-lived inn. John Francis, hairdresser, lived in the High Street premises, and Mrs Smith, mantua maker, and others inhabited the tenements. Again, a plan is attached to the lease. In 1805 a lease was given to Francis Mansford, grocer, who had been in occupation since about 1802, but he had been replaced by a plumber called Fish before 1809.[206] Mansford's financial problems, referred to elsewhere,[207] forced him and his mortgagee to assign his lease in 1810 to Joseph Ashlin, glazier. An insurance policy of 1811 shows that by now there were five tenements in Francis Court, all brick and tiled. Ashlin also had to take out a mortgage in 1813.[208]

There was a partition of the existing leasehold c.1819, forced mainly by the development of Francis Court. The house on the High Street was demolished and two separate dwellings with shops formed. No.258 was leased to and occupied by William Sharpe, plumber, at 11s pa: the lease description was "...a messuage, tenement or dwelling house with warehouses, buildings etc.", abutting south in part on the passageway and in part also on the premises of Martha Ashlin, lessee of no.257; use of the passageway was to be shared. Martha's leasehold paid 9s pa; she held a small house on the frontage, partly over the passageway, and the five tenements of Francis Court. Edward Betham inspected these tenements at some point before 1833: one was one up and one down, three were the proverbial 'two up and two down', and the other had two up, two down and a garret. William Hewson, watchmaker, living at no.257, had a cellar kitchen partly under no.258, two-rooms over the shop and the passage with a garret over it.[209]

In 1842 no.257 came into the hands of George Bainbridge, the draper, whose business across the road and also further down the High Street was booming. He bought up the freehold in 1872 for £50. Since 1859 he had been paying 9s 8d pa rent, an adjustment probably occasioned by changes to the boundary line with no.258.[210]

1   *RA viii*, no.2336; for Geoffrey, see also *SAH* iv,144 for an account of his connections to the Cathedral and the Angel Inn
2   *RA viii*, nos 2315-2320,2325
3   2 Binnall J, p. 28
4   *RA viii*, nos 2313-2334
5   *ibid.*, no.2321
6   *VC* 276
7   *ibid.*,277
8   *ibid.*,278-280
9   *RA viii*, no.2322
10 *Cant* 297-299
11 *ibid.*,300; see also C.P.C. Johnson, 'A Second Jewish *Scola*', in *LHA* 13 (1978), 35-36
12 *Cant* 301
13 *ibid.*,76
14 See pp.80-81 above
15 *Cant* 297-301 mentioned above; *RA viii*, nos 2314-2315
16 *RA viii*, no.2316
17 *ibid.*, no.2317
18 *ibid.*, no.2318
19 *ibid.*, nos 2323,2325
20 *ibid.*, nos 2320,2326-27,2328-2333
21 *RH* i,322. There is no real evidence, however, to link this property with nos 264-65
22 *RA viii*, no.2334
23 *ibid.*, no.2316
24 *ibid.*, no.2314
25 e.g. in regard to 46-47 Steep Hill, above, p.14
26 Bardney Cartulary f.50v
27 *BFees ii*,1336
28 *PRS* 38, Pipe Roll 34 Henry II (1187-88)
29 Davis *op.cit.*,190
30 *RA viii*, no.2317
31 *ibid.*,nos 2318-19,2323
32 1262: *ibid.*, no.2327
33 *SAH* iv,8
34 Bj 2.5 f.145v; Bj 5.8.9 no.43: in the latter instance it was described as being opposite Brancegate
35 *LRS* 22,22
36 *RA viii*, no.2314
37 *ibid.*, no.2315
38 See above
39 *Receipt Roll 1223, PRS* NS 52 (2007),no.1682
40 TNA DL 27/276
41 C60/32, CFR 17 *Henry III*, 3 January 1233, no.84, www. finerollshenry3.org.uk
42 e.g. TNA E372/125
43 *CChR* i (1226-1257) p. 346
44 H.P. Stokes, *Studies in Anglo-Jewish History*, (Edinburgh, 1913),33-35: the Jewish representatives were obliged to assess the tallage on their own people
45 Jewish Plea Rolls TNA E9/33, m.6; see also *CCR* (1272-79),547
46 Jewish Plea Rolls E9/20; *CPR* (1272-1279),88
47 Dij 51.1.2-2a; *Cant* 274-75
48 Dij 51.1.4-6; *Cant* 276-77
49 Dij 51.1.7; *Cant* 278
50 Dij 51.1.8; *Cant* 279
51 Dij 51.1.9; *Cant* 280
52 Dij 51.1.10-11
53 *Cant* 73
54 e.g. in 1319/20, Bj 2.5 f.15v
55 Bj 2.15 *passim*
56 L1/1/1/2 f.2v
57 L1/3/2 f.9v
58 *ibid.*,f.100
59 LCC Wills 1632/298
60 L1/1/1/6 f.57
61 Inv 162/223
62 LCC Wills 1663/584
63 Ciij 9.1/24]
64 *ibid.*,1/231
65 LCC Wills 1705/227
66 LCC Wills 1638/660
67 LCC Wills 1645-6,689
68 LL 124/2
69 See above, p.9
70 LCC Wills 1726/140
71 FL Deeds 122,205
72 LL 124/6-7; LPC 1/16/2
73 See below, p.160
74 *Fig 104*
75 CC 27/152829 3/7, p. 10
76 VC 3/2/4/1
77 VC 3/2/4/12
78 Bj 1.1.7-11 *passim*
79 LL 124/1
80 CC 27/152829 3/7, p. 7
81 LL 124/2; Bj 1.2.1
82 LCC Wills 1695&6 i,40
83 Inv 192/211
84 Bj 1.3; LL 124/4-5
85 LCC Wills 1726/140
86 LL 124/6-7; LL 125/18
87 *LPC* 1/16/2, 152738; see also p.121 above
88 2 CC 4/150762; Bij 5.9, p. 239
89 2 CC 4/150763; Bij 5.11, p. 263
90 Bj 5.13.13
91 Bj 1.1.2
92 Bij 3.16, no.4
93 Bij 3.18, no.40
94 L1/1/1/2, f.140
95 *ibid.*, f.166
96 Bj 1.1.5
97 L1/1/1/3, f.154v
98 Bj 1.1.7
99 Bj 1.1.8
100 LL 125/1
101 LCC Admons 1614/131
102 LL 125/2 ; Bj 1.1.9
103 LCC Wills 1643-4,158
104 Ciij 29.1; CC 27/152829 3/7, p. 6
105 L1/3/1 f.274
106 LL 125/3-4; LCC Wills 1671 ii,603
107 Inv 173/387; printed in the volume of Lincoln inventories edited by Dr Jim Johnston for Lincoln Record Society, *LRS* 80 (1991),33-37
108 LL 125/5-6
109 Bij 2.8, f.223v: he was also connected for a while with the Cardinal's Hat, across the road
110 LL 125/7
111 LCC Wills 1689 i,91
112 LL 125/8-13
113 *ibid.*,14-16; LCC Wills 1736/77
114 LCC Wills 1758/75
115 LCC Wills 1793/87; 1798 i,106
116 Lincolnshire County Council Deed Bundle 1393
117 LCC Deed Bundle 1393; 2 CC 4/150772-775
118 As for note 115
119 *Figs 112-114*
120 Cf. *Fig 69*
121 CC 27/152829 3/7 p. 6; see also LL 125/2
122 LL 125/5-6
123 *Fig 123*; for *no.259* see also *Figs 124-127*
124 LL 125/8
125 LL 125/7
126 *Fig 121*; cf. *SAH* iii
127 LL 125/8
128 *Figs 112-113*
129 *Fig 118*
130 *Fig 120*
131 *Fig 119*
132 *Fig 110*
133 *Fig 122*
134 *Fig 111*
135 Brasenose House, 28 St Paul's Street, Stamford: see no.383 in RCHM (England), '*The Town of Stamford – A Survey*', 1977
136 *RA viii*, nos 2314,2315; for Richard, see also the section on the Jew's House in Section 5 above
137 *Cant* 278,279
138 *BB* f.99v, no.129
139 Bij 3.16, no.4
140 Bj 1.1,5,7-9
141 LL 126/1-2
142 Bj 1.1.11-12; LCC Wills 1643-4,158
143 CC 27/152829 3/7, p. 20
144 Bj 1.2.1.1
145 LL 126/3-4
146 Bj 1.2.1; Bj 1.1.4; Bj 1.3 ; LL 126/5-7; LCC Wills 1704/21
147 LL 126/8-10; LCC Admons 1739/38
148 LL 126/15-17; LCC Wills 1793/55
149 Bij 5.6, f.74,370v; Bij 5.7, f.65,312v
150 2 CC 4/150772 2/2; Bij 5.8 p. 817; *ibid.*,9, p. 59; *ibid.*,10, p. 583; *ibid.*,12, p. 505
151 Bij 5.13, p. 457
152 2 CC 4/150776
153 Dij 75/2/18,20
154 *BB*, f.125v, no.341
155 Dij 75/2/21
156 *ibid.*,75/2/11
157 *ibid.*,75/2/14,16,17; these charters were not published in *RA viii*.
158 *ibid.*,75/2/13
159 A.2.35, f.151v
160 *Fig 123*
161 *Figs 124-127*
162 Bij 3.16, no.4
163 Bij 3.2 *passim*
164 Bij 3.19, no.137
165 Bj.1.7
166 LL 127/1
167 L. Elvin, *Lincoln as it Was* (Lincoln, 1976), vol. 2; *Fig 123*
168 Boundary reference: LL 128/1-2
169 2CC 8/152941, p. 57
170 LL 127/2; Bj.1.9
171 LL 127/3
172 LCC Wills 1727/279
173 LL 127/6
174 *ibid.*,7-9
175 *ibid.*,10-12
176 *ibid.*,13; Bij.5.6, f.75, 370v; Bij. 5.7, f.258
177 Bij.5.8, p. 817
178 See p.144 above
179 Bij.5.11, p. 778; Bij. 5.13, pp. 462,747; lease schedule for 1858 and 1865 in CC 146
180 Bij 3.2 *passim*
181 Bj 1. 7-8
182 L1/5/12, Churchwardens' Accounts; LCC Wills 1613/204
183 CC 27/152829 2/7, p. 3
184 *Figs 124-127*
185 LL 128/1-2
186 *ibid.*,3
187 LL 129/6-7
188 LL 128/11; 127/6-11
189 Bij 5.6, f.275; Bij 5.7, f.121; Bij 5.8, p. 201; Bij 5.9, p. 768ff
190 Bij 5.11, p. 945ff; Bij 5.12, p. 942
191 Bj 1.1.3
192 Bj 1.1.5,7,8
193 Bij 3.20, nos 17 and 42; LL 129/1
194 LCC Wills 1617 ii, 180
195 LL 129/2; LCC Wills 1631,240-241
196 LCC Wills 1671 ii, 603; Inv 173/387
197 CC 27/152829 3/7, p. 5
198 LCC Wills 1650/189; Hill, *TSL*,167-68
199 LL 129/3
200 *ibid.*, 4-7
201 *ibid.*,8; Inv 191/153
202 Bj 1.3, cf. LL 128/5; LL 129/9
203 *ibid.*,10; Sibray is noted at nos 276-277 High Street - see LCC Wills 1713/106
204 LL 129/16: the passageway is still *in situ*
205 Bij 5.4 f.222v; LL 157/13
206 Bij 5.6 f.88; Bij 5.7 f.121
207 See above, pp.121, 146
208 *LPC* 1/16/2
209 *LPC* 1/16/2, lease of 1819 numbered 152739 by the Ecclesiastical Commissioner; notes from the survey are endorsed on the outgoing lease
210 *ibid.*; 2 CC 9/152947w

21 WATERSIDE NORTH
THE WITCH AND WARDROBE

DOCUMENTARY
HISTORY

The extensive medieval site, of which this building now occupies only a fraction, had frontages both to the River Witham on the south and the Malt Market (*forum brasii*), now part of St Swithin's Square, on the north. It was also flanked on the west by a passageway leading to the waterside, and thus was a prime location for a mercantile residence and warehouse.

We have circumstantial evidence to indicate a strong possibility that the Le Wordi family owned this property in the late 13th/early 14th century. William le Wordi is quoted as the western boundary owner in a deed of 1270/7[1] for land in this area, and a tenement of Richard le Wordi, possibly his successor, was the subject of a rentcharge of 3s per annum conveyed to the Cathedral in 1316 by Walter of Gloucester.[2] Richard was also a tenant of Chapter property in the early 14th century.[3]

Prior to 1331 Richard gave part of his property to a son John, who then released it to William of Swineshead.[4] In this document it is noted that the main property was in the hands of William of Humberston. This is one of the few references we have for the Malt Market. William passed on his interest in this to his daughters Joan and Julia in 1349.[5] John le Wordi also made a feoffment to Alice, wife of Thomas de Yukflete, which passed to Thomas her husband by will in 1370.[6]

Fig 128. Street plan for the Witch and Wardrobe, no.21 Waterside North, from St Swithin's parish Tithe Award, 1851

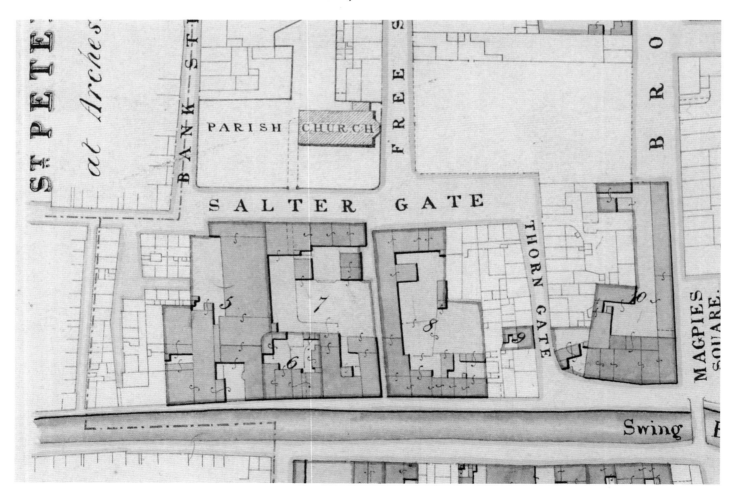

From the late 16th century to the middle of the 19th century, this area remained a major centre for the brewing of beer in Lincoln, maintaining the tradition noted here in the medieval period. It appears that the surviving late medieval building at what is now no.21 Waterside North was part of a more extensive holding which included land to the east bordering a Chapter leasehold (nos 23–24 Waterside North), which was assigned to the Board Rents of the Cathedral.[7] This connection gives us a list of occupiers for nos 21–22 and other property to the north which later became split from the original holding.

Anthony Hare is mentioned in 1580; his son Richard owned other property in the Michaelgate area.[8] The Waterside site may have been sold to a brewer named George Baines, who died in 1611;[9] his daughter Helen and son in law William Harrison sold off a part of their holding to Anthony Meres, gent., in 1617.[10] John Baines sold the remainder in 1627 to Alexander Kilne of the Bail, butcher, and Alice his wife, who passed it on in 1629 to Anthony Kent, beer brewer.[11] It was then in the hands of Thomas Thornhill and Christopher Preston. The Kent family are named in successive Chapter leases for nos 23–24 until the early 18th century, followed by Mr Lane.[12]

John Hawkshaw, gent., is mentioned as the western boundary in several 18th-century leases for nos 23–24. He died in 1732,[13] leaving the bulk of his estate to his daughter Mary Blow in trust for his grandson John Blow, neither of whom is actually referenced in connection with no.21. Thomas Mackeness, merchant, is mentioned in Chapter leases for the period 1777–1806;[14] he died in 1805, leaving his freehold properties to his six daughters.[15] The executorship phase for his estate lasted until the late 1820s, when the various premises were sold to Messrs F. & C. Winn, the brewers. In the Willson and Betham Survey of 1828, no.21, now converted to a warehouse, was rated at £35 per annum.

The Winns concentrated their brewing interests at other Lincoln sites after this, and seem to have leased no.21 to William Norton and Matthew Turton, who combined a business of ale, porter, wine and spirit merchants with a coal and corn merchant concern, as noted in the 1843 Directory. Much of the Winn estate was sold in 1857, but this property appears to have remained in the hands of Messrs Norton and Turton for another 20 years.

In 1875, no.21 and the St Swithin's Square frontage was acquired by Lincoln Liberal Club and heavily mortgaged.[16] Until 1890 the Club actually met in no.21, but after the new building was erected no.21 was relegated to storage uses. Since the mid-20th century the building has been restored and redeveloped for commercial purposes, first as a Fish Restaurant (the A1 Fish Café) and more recently as a public house, the Witch and Wardrobe.

ARCHITECTURAL DESCRIPTION

SUMMARY   The initial survey of the building was undertaken in 1975, when the property had ceased trading as the A1 Fish Cafe and was awaiting the necessary alterations for its present role as licensed premises. Photographs of the area c.1900 show the great variety of buildings that once flanked the north bank of the River Witham from the High Bridge eastwards to Thornbridge. Several of these were two-storied and of timber-framed construction, albeit stucco rendered, and interspersed with these were later substantial brick buildings mostly related to commercial uses; all in all an attractive and intriguing run of elevations, whose eventual removal was doubtless effected with little or no public regret at their despatch. It is evident from early photographic records that in size alone and treatment, the A1 Fish Cafe was in a separate category from that of its neighbours to the west.

DESCRIPTION

Having the advantage of being flanked on two sides by a public right of way, and now serving as a public house, it may be remarked that several points of interest pertaining to the building and noted in the following description are readily viewable.

In terms of its development, no.21 would appear to be the product of at least two or three main stages in the formation of its L-shaped plan, ranging in date from the 14th to the mid-16th centuries; of these the latter is dominant in the longer range with a ground story of stone topped by a timber frame containing chambers on the upper floor, and having attic accommodation. For the primary stage, the short arm of the L, aligned north–south and bordering St Swithin's Passage, retains a west wall in which, at the north end, there are two low pointed relieving arches with rubble voussoirs, which may well indicate a distant phase of building consolidation perhaps related to the canalisation of the Witham.

In the same rubble wall two features are prominent, one being a small pointed quatrefoil possibly serving as a vent and reset, the other a large square slab with a triangular piece topping it and itself topped by two short sloping slabs, the whole somewhat reminiscent of a dedicatory tablet.[17] Internally the larger feature is now exposed as a cupboard recess or aumbry, and at a level that implies it was part of the amenities of a chamber. The west wall in its southern half as part of the main range is framed and carries a run of close-set timbers at first-floor level, the studs in question being tenoned into a continuous bressummer at their base and into a wall-plate overhead. There are no window positions evident and no indications that the timber frame may have antedated the lower walling. The lower eaves level of the short west wing in its southern half is roughly original, and the higher section to the north an alteration and replacement dating from the now fully brick-built north gable end and associated east wall.[18]

The same east wall of the west wing, at its junction with the main range, preserves a principal post belonging to an internal roof truss (see below) and a now-depleted run of close-set studs; north of this section the east wall, as noted above, is a later replacement in brick. Within the roof space of the wing, stubs of sawn-off rafters remain to the east wall and one entire roof truss is *in situ* at the south end; this truss consists of a tie-beam with rafters and collar beam in a simple A form; the remainder of the wing roof northwards is modern. The step up in the west side elevation at this point marks the commencement of a higher roof of similar type to that of the short wing and there are indications that this roof continued to the south front of the main east–west range to finish in a gable.[19] Evidence for this lies in a dovetail notch on the extremity of the wing's east (and now redundant) wall-plate, a timber retained within the roof space of the main range.

THE MAIN RANGE

The south elevation of the main range facing the River Witham has a rendered upper storey, masking its timber frame; the same concealment applies internally. There is an obvious concern for symmetry in the disposition of the door and windows on this side; the mullion and transom window west of the doorway and the doorframe itself – with fanlight – are original, whilst the window to the east is modern, a close copy of its counterpart based on internal evidence of splays and lintel. Presumably the fenestration of the timber-framed upper half followed suit, including the possibility of a central oriel, perpetuated present day in the bow window of early 19th-century origin. A weathered moulded stringcourse, topping the masonry wall on which the frame rests, continues across the east end of no.21 and formerly extended to the north to the limits of the main range and beyond, as far as the westward return of the back wall. What was then exposed in 1975, namely the greater part of the east wall, is now partly masked by a modern addition. The survey drawing[20] shows its earlier state and the wall's westward return, making the case that the house had either a long and substantial lean-to against its north side with a cat-slide roof originally or a two-storied gabled projection. Here timbers forming the framed upper half of the north wall of the main range were noted as being in a near-pristine state, with no evidence of their ever having been exposed to the elements.

At the east end of the framing there is evidence of a blocked door that formerly

THE A1 FISH CAFE . 21 WATERSIDE . LINCOLN.

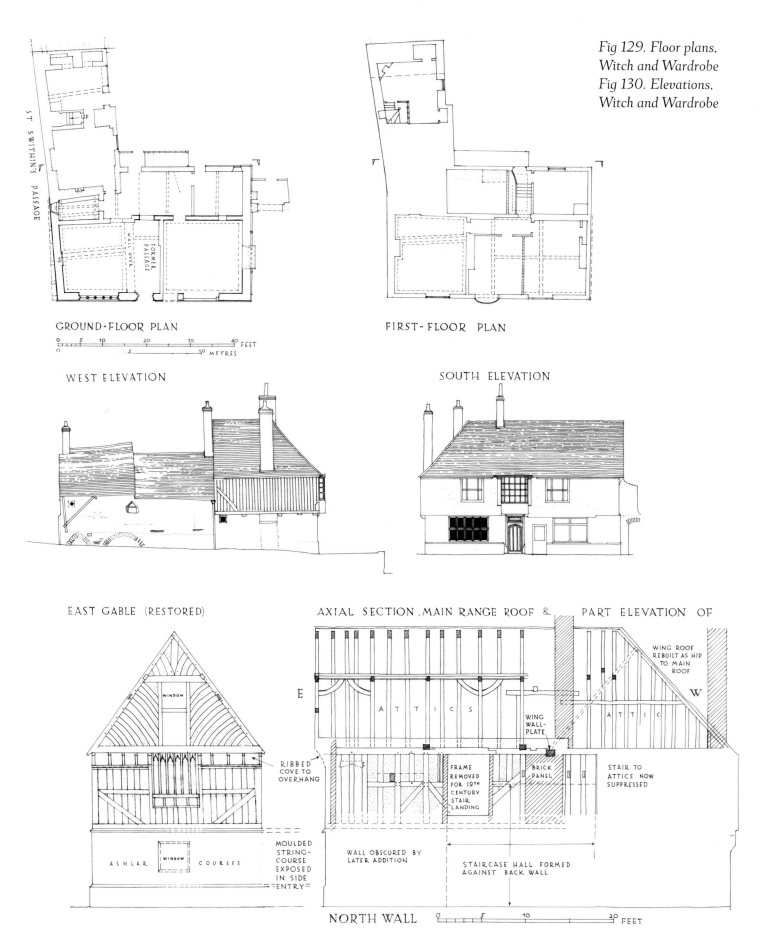

*Fig 129. Floor plans,
Witch and Wardrobe
Fig 130. Elevations,
Witch and Wardrobe*

GROUND-FLOOR PLAN

FIRST-FLOOR PLAN

ST SWITHIN'S PASSAGE

WALL OVER

FORMER PASSAGE

0 5 10 20 30 40 FEET
0 5 10 METRES

WEST ELEVATION

SOUTH ELEVATION

EAST GABLE (RESTORED)

AXIAL SECTION . MAIN RANGE ROOF &

PART ELEVATION OF

WINDOW

E

A T T I C S

WING ROOF REBUILT AS HIP TO MAIN ROOF

W

A T T I C

WING WALL-PLATE

RIBBED COVE TO OVERHANG

FRAME REMOVED FOR 19TH CENTURY STAIR LANDING

BRICK PANEL

STAIR TO ATTICS NOW SUPPRESSED

ASHLAR   WINDOW   COURSES

MOULDED STRING-COURSE EXPOSED IN SIDE ENTRY

WALL OBSCURED BY LATER ADDITION

STAIRCASE HALL FORMED AGAINST BACK WALL

NORTH WALL   0 5 10 20 FEET

Fig 131. Witch and Wardrobe: sectional drawings, gable end and coving

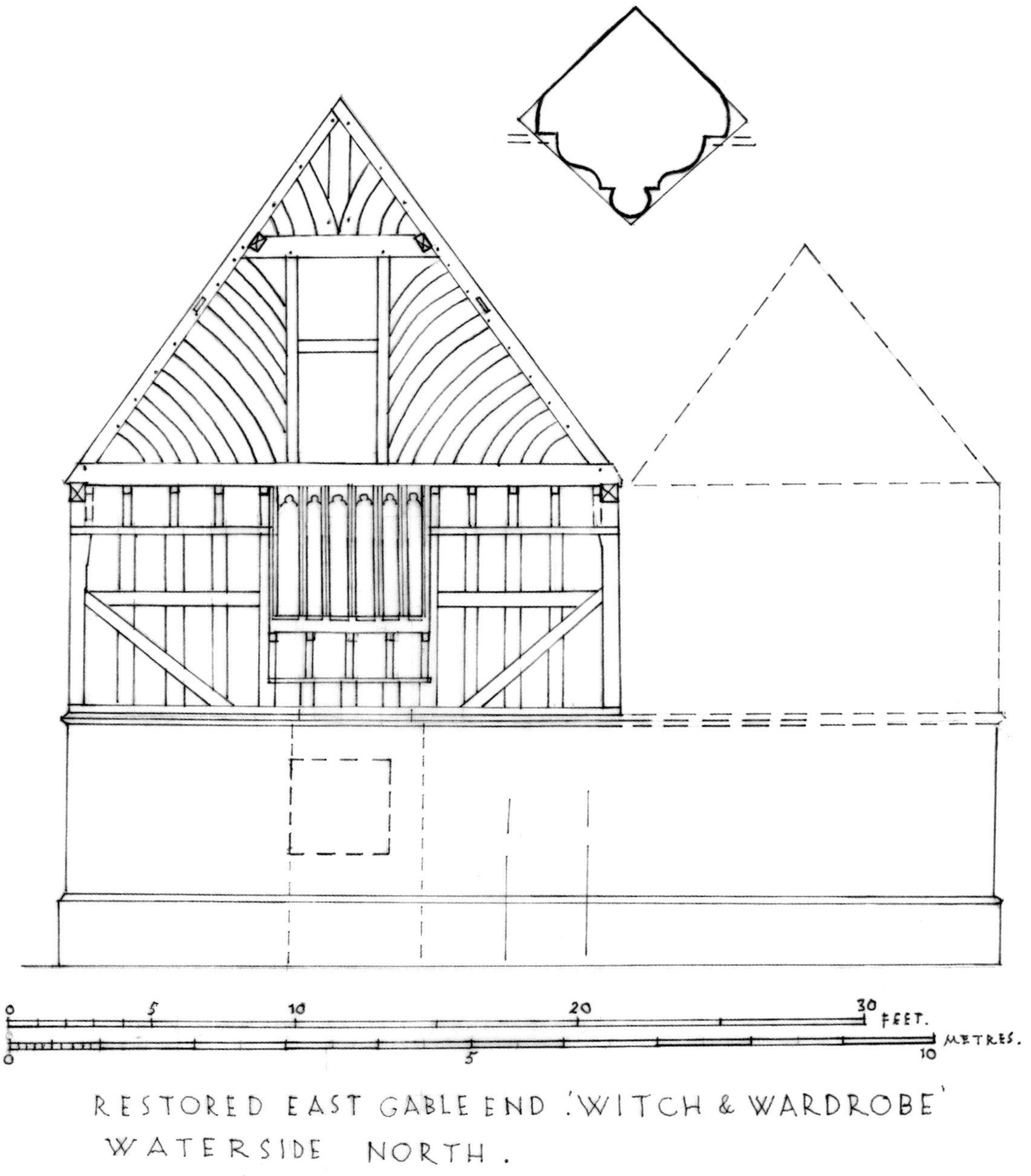

RESTORED EAST GABLE END 'WITCH & WARDROBE' WATERSIDE NORTH.

communicated with the now removed north side structure. A large gap in the north side framing, now brick-filled, may be related to an important feature missing from the Waterside house, namely a lateral chimney stack formerly serving the principal room – the hall – and its chamber overhead. None of the present chimney stacks in the house appear to be earlier than c.1800, a provision then permitting fuller use of hitherto unheated rooms or their sub-divisions. It would seem to be usual in a house of this status that the main entrance door led directly into the hall – the chief apartment – and traditionally at this date the fireplace would most probably have been sited in the north wall of the hall; the date of its removal, together with that of the integrated north side building, is uncertain, but it may well be after the building had ceased to house the Lincoln Liberal Club (1874–1890) and to trade as Clayton's A1 Fish and Oyster Saloon. The new role must account for the additional front door next to the original entrance, exclusively for the patrons of the Saloon, and implying an internal division separating shop from the domestic end of the house.[21]

What was clearly designed as a prestigious east end to the house had, in 1975, only its gable timbers exposed. With the removal of the render in the conversion to a public house, a clearer picture has emerged of the effect sought by the 16th-century carpenters; missing

Fig 132. (right)
Photograph of roof interior,
Witch and Wardrobe
Fig 133. (centre)
Contemporary photograph
of masonry wall features,
west façade of the Witch
and Wardrobe
Fig 134. (below)
Contemporary photograph
of the Witch and
Wardrobe, taken from
the south bank of the
River Witham

is a central oriel window of six lights set beneath a gable tie-beam of equal projection and flanked on either hand by a ribbed cove.[22] A moulded mullion held to have originated from this window, a fully glazed feature, had been re-used in the framework of a stair at the west end of the main roof.[23] The pattern of curved timbers in the gable, bordering the attic window, is one recorded elsewhere in Lincoln and beyond, and was clearly regarded as fashionable in the early 16th century;[24] quite how long it remained so has yet to be established. One is also uncertain about whether a coved eaves had ever completed the south wall of the house in continuation of this feature from the east gable; had it done so it would make much sense in emphasising the frontage with a show of elaborated timber framing, perhaps as a counter to the sobriety of the lower masonry wall.

The amenities of this large 16th-century residence comprised, for example, glazed windows at all levels, a heated hall and its chamber overhead, sufficient accommodation and service provision, plus, in addition, the large rear wing, or lean-to, housing the principal stair and a lesser one serving the attics in the main range. Proximity to the river and its activities on which the 16th-century occupiers of no.21 may have relied for trade may have persuaded them to rebuild the greater part of an ancient, and possibly decaying, tenement. What is not known is whether there were any ancillary buildings to the rear connected with the river trade. If one had to provide a close parallel for the choice of half stone/half timber in the new build, the former Bishop's House, 14 Eastgate, Lincoln, may be cited as an excellent local exemplar. The northern limits of the riverside plot, c.1550, appear to have extended as far as Saltergate. It may be questioned whether the potential of a riverside location saw a sub-division of the plot followed contemporaneously by the erection or development of what is now known as the Witch and Wardrobe public house.

In the conversion works, post-1975, major alterations were addressed to the east and north–east walls against which additions were made. A small stone-framed window reset as a feature in the public bar once served a bathroom at the north end of the rear building, and was recorded there, when *in situ*, by the author.

195 HIGH STREET
FORMERLY THE RED LYON INN, LATER WYATT AND HAYES, DRAPERS

DOCUMENTARY
HISTORY

In terms of identifiable documentation for this building, the sole medieval context is a boundary reference in a deed for the Walmsford Chantry property situated to the north, dated 1343, in which it is quoted as a tenement of Walter de Eboraco (of York).[25] Walter occurs as a witness on three other occasions, in two as bailiff of the city in 1316/17,[26] and the other in 1322,[27] marking him as a substantial citizen who lived in close proximity to others of his class. The Walmsford property was owned by Matilda Pinzun, widow of John Pinzun, former bailiff and mayor of Lincoln.

The latter property, described as two messuages, bounded north by Golderonstigh, one of a number of east–west lanes linking the High Street with the wharves of Brayford, took in a substantial area of land directly to the west of Walter's plot. It can reasonably be supposed, from the boundaries as shown on the Padley plan of 1842 and a most informative map drawn up in 1841 for the speculative and (thankfully) abortive London and York Railway,[28] that no.195 and its neighbours to the south, nos 193 and 194, formed a single double-fronted holding with the trademark central passageway connecting lines of outbuildings on either side of a wider rear courtyard behind the main buildings on the High Street frontage.

170

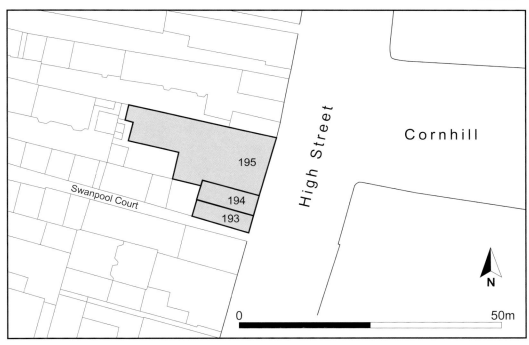

Fig 135. (left) Street plan for no.195 High Street
Figs 136-137. (above) Early 20th-century photographs showing a timber-framed building, no.194 High Street

The central passageway, depicted on the A.C. Pugin painting,[29] appears to have been lost through infilling c.1880, but a trace of it can be seen in later photographs; the roof lines adopted in the rebuilding process fortunately preserved some of the early roof timbers in no.195, but unfortunately the distinctive jettied timber-framed construction of no.194 survived only to be torn down in the 1920s.[30]

Prior to the beginning of the 18th century there was a long hiatus in the available documentation, and the only reference to be found in a Chapter lease for the Walmsford Chantry property (no.196) named a certain Roger Woode, otherwise unknown, as the

Fig 138. Lincoln High Street, A.C. Pugin, c.1818, including nos 194–195 High Street

boundary occupier.[31] Other 17th-century leases neither give names nor useful property descriptions. We are grateful for the survival of a bundle of title deeds for the period 1703 to 1875[32] to give a more complete picture of the development of this property.

One fact which does emerge is that nos 193–194, the tenements to the south of the passageway, were in separate ownership to that of no.195 for the period from before 1703, but reunited for a while under Henry Blyth, grocer, from 1827. In the first part of the 18th century no.195 was an inn called the Red Lyon, with outhouses, stables and various other appurtenances to the rear; it was heavily mortgaged. Joseph Townsend, gent., was owner and occupier until his death in 1707, leaving it to his wife Ann until their daughter Barbara became of age or married.[33] By September 1724 Barbara was married to John Reynolds of Great Barford, in Bedfordshire, and they sold the inn for £100 to John Corbett of Lincoln, a surgeon who was already in occupation. Corbett died in 1733[34] and his wife was also dead by 1738. His sister Anne Harthorpe (aka Hartrup), widow of Richard Hartrup, inherited the inn and entered into a mortgage with Clement Wood of the Castle for £40, to add to the earlier mortgage taken out by Townsend in 1703 with James Rous, which was still in force.

Wood gained outright possession of the property, no longer an inn, in 1772. After his death his executors sold it to Thomas Dawson, seedsman. In 1782 Dawson obtained a mortgage for £300 with Isaac Wood, using the capital to build a further tenement in the area behind no.195; four more tenements were added during the next eight years.

Dawson had died by 1790 and his widow Anne was living in one of the tenements. William, their son, now owed £600 to Joseph Watson of Heighington, grazier, the new lender. In 1791 William Dawson and Jane his wife conveyed the site to John Wriglesworth, senior, gent., for £1,000, £600 of which went to pay off Watson's loan. Just three years later Henry Blyth, aspiring grocer, purchased the property for £1,200.[35] No.195 was occupied by Thomas Watson and Miss Perry: to the rear there were five tenements, two nail shops and a coal yard, together with a stable, warehouse and other outbuildings.

Thomas Sawdon, inventor and builder of agricultural implements, had set up a workshop here before 1798 and later gave his name to the yard.[36]

In the same bundle of deeds are a number relating to nos 193–194, situated between the central passageway and the lane through to the Brayford which became Swanpool Court. John Hopton, blacksmith, owned this property until his death in 1766; his daughter Sarah Millington, widow, sold it for £150 to Matthias Hopton, also a blacksmith; there was one messuage, two stables and a garden, mostly in the tenancy of Joshua Drewry, barber. In 1792, after Matthias' death, William Hopton, later of Doncaster, inherited and sold it to Henry Blyth, junior for £450, his father having died in 1816. Blyth also needed finance: three mortgages were agreed between 1827 and 1831 on the security of the combined premises.

A charming and evocative depiction of this part of High Street, Pugin's painting,[37] mentioned above, may have been made c.1818, when he is known to have visited E.J. Willson. It shows the regular 18th-century brick frontage of no.195, with what may be a bow-fronted lower-floor shop window, and three sash windows above, as well as the steeply pitched roof, the remnant of which is discussed in the Architectural Description above. In contrast, nos 193–194 stand out as a survival of virtually unrestored timber framing, particularly no.194, with its tall jettied upper storey leaning precariously over the street. This was photographed at least twice during the late 19th century; one, probably datable to the 1890s, was published by Elvin.[38] The central passageway, which shows in Pugin's work that a room had been built over it, was completely infilled by the time of

Fig 139. Photograph of the High Street, 1857, including nos 194–195 High Street

this photograph: the roofline is different. The late 19th-century brick frontage seen today shows subtle evidence of the infill in the irregular vertical spacing bars in the stringcourse below the gutter.

Henry Blyth died in 1848, leaving his property to trustees, and his son, another Henry, inherited in 1860; the conveyance has an invaluable plan of the various constituent parts of the estate and lists the several occupants. Henry sold the whole site in 1875 to Hugh Wyatt, clothier and future mayor of Lincoln, who is commemorated in a fountain outside the church of St Peter at Gowts, further down the High Street. The firm of Wyatt and Hayes was still in business as recently as 1974.

ARCHITECTURAL DESCRIPTION

SUMMARY The investigation of the tenement, the former premises of Wyatt and Hayes, was carried out in advance of proposals to alter this, a Grade II Listed Building, and incorporate it into British Home Stores, a major holding in no.196. It was discovered that no.195 preserved an impressive late medieval roof set above stone walling of the same date. By analogy with other roofs in Lincoln the High Street example may be dated to the early 16th century. In this period the earlier predominant roof type of crown post and collar-purlin construction was gradually superseded. The new roof type is one that in Lincoln is associated with stone-walled structures as the following list, excepting (v), demonstrates.

> (i) The Chancery, Minster Yard: street range and chapel wing roofs of 1480–1494.
> (ii) 7. Eastgate: roof of two bays over street range c.1500
> (iii) St Mary's Guildhall, Wigford: house in courtyard, roof of early to mid-16th century
> (iv) The Ancient Deanery, Eastgate: Tower and stable range (demolished), ascribed to 1451–83. Drawing by J.C. Buckler, in Add Mss 36436, f.417 (British Library).
> (v) Bishop's House, Eastgate: roof of west wing with associated moulded joists and tie-beams ascribable on stylistic grounds to c.1500+. North, south and east walls of wing close-studded timber framing set on half-height masonry walling.

Two illustrations throw some light on the appearance of the High Street premises in the 19th century. For the early part of the century there is a watercolour drawing of High Street by Augustus Pugin (1762–1832), now in the Usher Gallery, Lincoln, which includes the frontage of no.195 and timber-framed properties south of it. A photograph taken from the same viewpoint in 1857 and reproduced in Laurence Elvin's booklet 'Lincoln As it Was' (1974)[39] substantiates the detail and accuracy of the drawing which indicates a refronting having taken place in the 18th century. When refronted again c.1900, Wyatt and Hayes incorporated a carriageway of some age that led to a back yard on the south side of their premises. The street entrance to the carriageway may be seen in Pugin's drawing, where it appears to carry a circular sign above its lintel, and at that date the ground-floor of no.195 was already given over to shops. The majority of the High Street frontages depicted date from the first half of the 18th century, including that to no.195, in which building the roof was hipped back to accompany the red-brick refronting and a general rebuilding affecting much of this and other important thoroughfares in Lincoln.

THE PRESENT ROOF The roof, five bays in length, is aligned east–west, terminating in a large hip fronting High Street and at the west end in a vertical gable where the remaining truss is embedded in modern brickwork. Including the hipped arrangement, the three eastern bays are each 12 ft in length, with two shorter bays of 8 ft, the dimensions taken from centre to centre. The average span of a typical truss, measured between the wall-plates, varies from 25 to 26 ft. With the exception of a short interval at the east end, the south wall-plate appears to be entire; the north wall-plate is inconveniently obscured and at one point a section of it has been removed for the insertion of a later chimney-stack.

There are six trusses, including that now forming the hip at the east end, at which point, when vertical, the gable presented a close-studded and window-less elevation above a stone (?) wall. In common with the embedded truss at the west end, the now hipped truss is of double collar-beam construction, but of more substantial scantling. The central trusses are identical and differ from those at the former gable ends by having single collar-beams, no infilling, and employing short principal rafters below the collar-beams. All trusses throughout have tie-beams at wall top level and two purlins on either slope. The upper purlin is clasped between the collar-beam and the common rafter in a notch cut in the former member and further retained by pegging from the back of the rafter. The lower purlin is held between the common rafter and the short principal rafter, and is similarly pegged in position. The purlins are made up in lengths that are splay-scarfed together.

The central or open trusses[40] are well finished with chamfered edges to the collar-beam and inner rafters, the chamfers terminating in neatly executed 'stops'. There is no evidence of wind-braces, but in this respect it conforms to certain characteristics of the corresponding group of Lincoln roofs noted earlier (excepting the Bishop's House in which roof the wind-braces are small, offering minimal stiffening to the roof). In no.195 the collars have central pegs, now serving no useful purpose but possibly used in erecting the present roof.

The west end truss appears to have been endowed with a pair of large in-curving braces from a point on the common rafter between the two collar beams to a more or less central position on the now removed (concealed?) tie-beam. In so doing the braces were halved across the lower collar beam. A more profuse display of curved bracing was recorded when exposed during repairs to the south gable at the Bishop's House in 1984, in which context the decorativeness reflected the general high quality of the interior fittings.[41]

THE EARLY ROOF FORM AND ITS EVIDENCES The common rafters throughout the roof of no.195 originate from an earlier roof of c.1250–1300. All rafters are of uniform scantling and carry notched lap-joints typical of the period. From their disposition it may be deduced that the 13th-century roof rested on stone walls and had a span of roughly 20 ft or more. At wall top each rafter was tenoned into a horizontal sole-piece and further rigidity was afforded the rafter by a vertical ashlar piece aligned with the inner face of the wall. At a higher point on each rafter straight struts rose inwards to a horizontal collar-beam in a simple triangulation. Two or more rafters show evidence of additional lap-joints, indicative probably of divisions within the earlier structure whatever its location. There is no evidence of smoke-blackening on the rafters and it has been suggested that the timber originated from the deposed church of St John's, Wigford (after 1549), which was sited across the High Street, on the Cornhill. Certain rafters show evidence of weathering on what would have been their outer face which is not compliant with their supposed origin.

An estimate of the length of the building that surrendered its roof may be attempted on the basis that collar rafters were set out at roughly 1 ft 8 inch centres. Allowing for those rafters divided for use in the new east hipped end, there is a total of 35 couples, suggesting a length of 52 ft, the present internal dimension of the roof from east to west. It may well be that the early roof from which the rafters are re-used was provided with

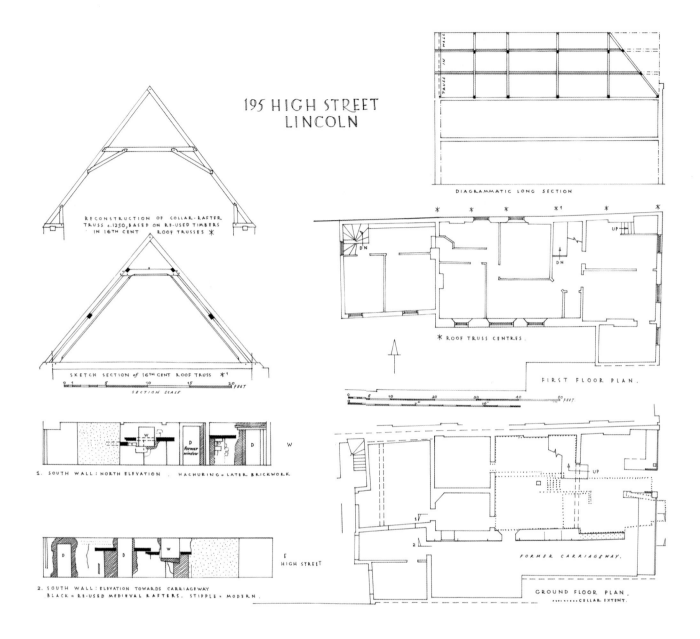

195 HIGH STREET
LINCOLN

RECONSTRUCTION OF COLLAR-RAFTER
TRUSS c.1250, BASED ON RE-USED TIMBERS
IN 16TH CENT. ROOF TRUSSES *

DIAGRAMMATIC LONG SECTION

SKETCH SECTION of 16TH CENT ROOF TRUSS *¹

SECTION SCALE

* ROOF TRUSS CENTRES.

FIRST FLOOR PLAN.

1. SOUTH WALL: NORTH ELEVATION . HACHURING = LATER BRICKWORK

2. SOUTH WALL: ELEVATION TOWARDS CARRIAGEWAY
BLACK = RE-USED MEDIEVAL RAFTERS. STIPPLE = MODERN .

E
HIGH STREET

FORMER CARRIAGEWAY.

GROUND FLOOR PLAN.
········· CELLAR EXTENT.

Fig 140. No.195 High Street: plans and long section, existing roof trusses

crown posts and a central collar-purlin, but of these members in the later roof there is no trace. The waney outline of the existing tie-beams precludes the provision of a ceiling coeval with the later roof, and additional spanning beams, six in number, plus a few that may subsequently have been reduced in length, are set out to carry the present first-floor ceiling.

OTHER FEATURES   In the south wall, ground-floor, there are a number of blockings cut through for later openings.[42] The earlier blockings appear to be those of doorways and windows, all with long timber lintels whose dimensions point to an origin as former common rafters of a deposed roof. The lintels are set well below the ceiling heights and this could imply that the latter has been reset at a higher point than its predecessor. The lintels overlap and in sequence from west to east descend in height; the third lintel, of which only a fragment remains, presumably extended a further 10 ft to the east, being sawn off when that end of the stone side wall was replaced by the present thinner wall. Much of the stone in the south wall is re-used and shows a variety of chisel toolings on the exposed north face. On the same ground-floor face and at its west end, one splayed opening has evidence of a plastered reveal and lintel, but its south face, unfortunately, is featureless. The disrupted character of both long north and south walls points to an

176

Fig 141. Photograph of roof interior,
no.195 High Street
Fig 142. Contemporary photograph
of exterior, no.195 High Street

almost total new build, and the employment of second-hand medieval timbers at both high and low levels must surely point to the building in its present form as being a structure of approximately the mid-16th century.

What, then, was the function of the building, and how was it planned? Firstly the width of the tenement is considerable and, present day, incorporates the carriageway, formerly a separated area thrown into that of the shop after 1900. On the evidence of Pugin's drawing, the refronting of no.195 in the 18th century included the carriageway, the latter being given a lower roof. The property on the north side of Wyatt & Hayes, now the site of British Home Stores, also had a narrow bay from the street to the rear. Swanpool Court, to the south of what were formerly timber-framed buildings as late as 1920 (nos 193 and 194, formerly Wingad's and Strawson's Eating House, now Timpsons and Dixons, respectively), may yet be a similar passage to the rear of a tenement at an earlier period, that in turn became a public lane. If so, then to judge from the character of the brickwork of the buildings forming the south side of Swanpool Court, the passage must have lost any High Street frontage as early as 1730 or thereabouts.

The presence of a passage against the north side of no.195 explains the blocked cellar light on that side. Its distance back from the street indicates the overlap gap of a former building on the site of the British Home Stores. Two ground-floor window openings further west in the same wall (one opening appears to coincide roughly with the blocked cellar light) also gained light from an open area to the north; both windows are now blocked and nothing may be learned of their character. The height of the blockings suggests, however, that the openings are perhaps no older than 18th century, to which period the first-floor windows in the south wall belong. The upper half of the south wall was plastered internally and not available in the survey. There were no surviving chimney stacks of any age and no firm evidence for the whereabouts of one that may have been added or rebuilt when the roof was constructed in the 16th century.

No transverse partition walls have survived from the earliest phase and it may be supposed that these were of stud and plaster or wattle and daub and consequently easily removed. In the continuation of the range westwards, the north side wall has at some time prior to 1900 carried a roof lower than the present one and considerably below that of the main range. The spring of the former roof is marked by a pronounced off-set in the wall at first-floor level, above which the wall has been heightened to carry a modern roof of softwood construction.

352–355 HIGH STREET
SIBTHORP HOUSE

DOCUMENTARY
EVIDENCE

This was an extensive site, covering more than five acres, and one of the largest in this area of Wigford, but little is known of its owners in the medieval period. The occupier c.1200 was William de Kelstou,[43] noted as a boundary reference in a grant made by Nocton Priory to Hamo the Smith, son of Lambert. Peter de Meldeburn was named c.1321.[44]

There was industrial activity in the form of milling carried on in the area. The Vicars Choral property to the south was, in the mid to late 13th century, occupied by William the miller and the site of Sibthorp House itself was in the hands of Richard the miller c.1235–40.[45] The property to the north of this house was at one time in the ownership of the Black Monks[46] and after the Reformation was acquired by the city, becoming Maltby's Mill House.

These references aside, there are insufficient clues to prove any indication of a

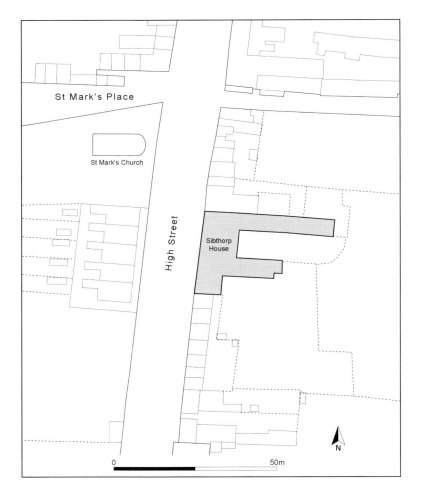

Fig 143, Street plan for Sibthorp House, nos 352–355 High Street, based on Padley plan of 1842

particularly important residence on the site of Sibthorp House in the medieval period, apart from the existence of a capital messuage here c.1527. The discovery in the 1950s, during the demolition of the north range, of what may have been some substantial late 14th-century roof trusses[47] seems, on reflection and given the comments made by E.J. Willson in his notes on the building in 1816, to point to a re-use of trusses from elsewhere.

Among the Towneley MSS held at Lancashire Record Office is a 1526/27 rental[48] of property in Lincoln belonging to Christopher Wymbyssh, which previously formed part of the estate of Sir Thomas Knight of Ingleby, d.1503.[49] According to the rental Wymbyssh reserved for his own use a capital messuage in the parish of St Mark, together with a close and a barn and stable in the occupation of Thomas Edmondson, and a series of three cottages, later called 'The Rentes'. These were next to the north wing of the main house. Wymbissh also owned eight cottages in 'le Beydhouse Lane' in the same parish, possibly near the church on the other side of the High Street. The occupiers of the Rentes were Robert Milner, Edmund Atkynson and Elizabeth Bellow; an Edmund Atkynson was in 1550 a citizen and Alderman of Lincoln.[50]

Nothing further is known of this house during the 16th century. It was not listed among properties belonging to the Towneley family in 1604, although the Rentes were included. The Yarburgh family seem to have purchased the estate surrounding the Rentes in the late 16th century, as "the Lincoln house" is mentioned in the 1595 will of Francis Yarburgh of Northorpe.[51] The most likely purchaser was Edmund Yarburgh Esq, who was married to Margaret, a member of the Grantham family, prominent in Lincoln. His grandson Robert (1582–1619) was the owner of this site in 1615, when the Rentes were conveyed by Thomas Johnson, tanner, to William Knyght, gent., and Elizabeth his wife.[52] These were later acquired by the Savile family. Robert Yarburgh, who also owned land in St Martin's parish, died in 1619, leaving an only daughter Mary, who married Thomas Savile of Newton by Folkingham.

Thomas died leaving no sons but three daughters, Alice, Ann and Mary.[53] Mary married William Burnell, who became one of the Savile trustees, together with Anne Middlemore, whose son Richard became agent for Sir John Brownlow,[54] and Alice Savile, spinster. In April 1688 the Savile trustees were doing business with Gervase Sibthorp, and this led to him purchasing the messuage in St Mark's parish, now reunited with the three cottages (the Rentes).[55] At this time Robert Snowden Esq was living in the old house, obviously still habitable, and Henry Bell, Widow Putterill and Widow Eblethwaite in the cottages.

A biography of the Sibthorp family, who were copyholders of the archbishop of York at Laneham in Nottinghamshire in the early 17th century, is given by Maddison.[56] Gervase was the husband of Judith Marshall, widow of Benjamin Marshall, a Lincoln mercer who had died in 1664.[57] They married c.1666 and probably set up home in the Marshall home in St Peter at Gowts parish. Joan Varley, in her notes on Sibthorp House,[58] suggests that they moved into the old house in St Mark's in 1688, as Judith their daughter was buried in St Mark's Churchyard. Gervase was churchwarden there in 1693/94 and died in 1704,[59] just two years after his wife Judith.

Nothing is clear in the records about when the house was rebuilt; it would have been either in the period 1691–1702, if by Gervase himself, or c.1704–10 if built by his son John. The house was not devised by Gervase's will, so would have been the subject of a family settlement which has not survived. It may have been John who added the south wing in any case, as it appears later in style and is shorter than the north range.

John Sibthorp died in 1718, and the house descended in the family, but eventually with the development of Canwick Hall it became of less importance. In May 1790 Dr Humphrey Sibthorp conveyed the 'capital mansion house', with the stables, coach house and other outbuildings, and the close of five acres to the east of it, to Robert Lowrie,

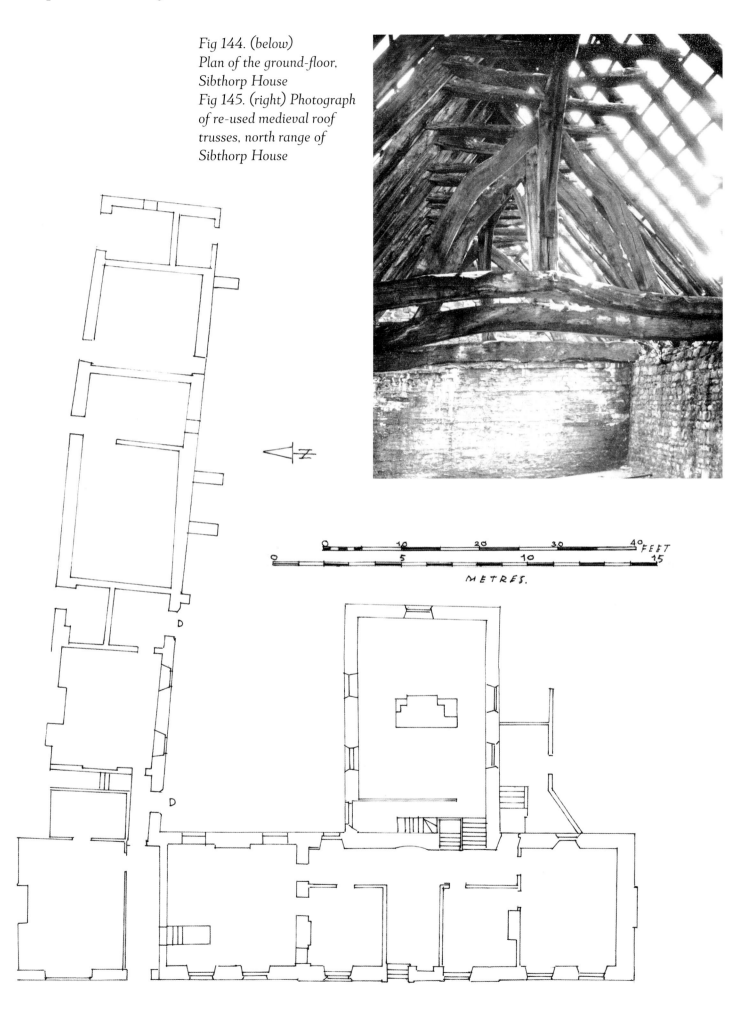

Fig 144. (below)
Plan of the ground-floor,
Sibthorp House
Fig 145. (right) Photograph
of re-used medieval roof
trusses, north range of
Sibthorp House

Fig 146. (above, left)
Photograph of street
frontage, Sibthorp
House c.1955, prior
to demolition

Fig 147. (left) Photograph
of courtyard and north
range, Sibthorp House

Fig 148. (above)
Photograph showing
the south range,
Sibthorp House

mercer and draper of Lincoln, for the sum of £1,100. Robert made some alterations, pulling down the coach house and some other buildings, and erected two new tenements, possibly on the site of the present-day nos 350–350a High Street. He died, however, in May 1810.[60] Robert, his eldest son, born in 1776, died at Vitoria, Spain in 1813; another son, Charles, was a captain in the 69th Foot, later promoted to major. He inherited the house and set up a family trust for his four daughters.[61]

In July 1848 Charles and two of the daughters (the others having previously released their shares) conveyed 3,727 square yards of the five-acre close for the formation of the new Manchester Sheffield and Lincolnshire Railway for more than £2,200, and the following June a further 1.25 acres was sold to the Revd Francis Swan, who was buying up land for a proposed road scheme and speculative housing. A further tranche of land to the south of the house was sold in 1852.[62]

Major Lowrie died suddenly, at St Mark's Railway Station in 1855,[63] leaving his daughters Mary and Harriet as co-owners. A half share in the house and the remainder of the land was offered for auction in 1868, and two further plots were conveyed to the Railway Company in 1868 and 1875/6. The former paddock was now busy with railway lines and lineside equipment, leaving just the house and a small area of land remaining.

The old mansion house was last recorded in the Lowrie family's occupation in 1857, when Harriet was still in residence. George Fountain came in as keeper or caretaker from c.1863 to 1881, followed by Henry Hare and others, all presumably railway employees. The Inland Revenue and Stamp Office held sway there from 1867, and a number of coal merchants took office space in the house. By 1956, when a plan of the premises was drawn for British Railways, there were three cellars, a scullery and a pantry area in the basement, and a hall and four offices on the ground-floor. Demolition and a decidedly 'carbuncular' replacement shop and office block swiftly followed; a handful of photographs remind us of what has been lost with the old Sibthorp House.[64]

It may be claimed unreservedly that Sibthorp House was a unique building in Lincoln in several respects. Firstly as a town house whose pavement length of 60 feet plus and a single-storied frontage executed in limestone ashlar is such that one might have anticipated a fully two-storied facade; there is neither parallel nor close exemplar for comparison. The plans of the house,[65] the last executed in the demolition year, enable one to comment on aspects of planning and attempt to allot uses for the main range and its ancillary buildings. It is clear that the owner/builder was intent on occupying the full length of his plot bounds with the High Street and part of this extent was to include an adjoining tenement at the north end of two full stories in order to provide a through passage from the street to the rear courtyard. The passage also connects directly with the north range, and it is suggested, given the alignment of the latter, south of east, that it was more formally integrated with the north end street tenement; this much may be inferred from the accompanying plan produced in 1956. It is acknowledged that the plan incorporates alterations effected over three centuries, yet does not indulge in archaeological analysis; it is sufficient to have to hand a carefully measured survey.

We are fortunate in having photographs of the house taken by Laurence Elvin prior to demolition to supplement the plans.[66] From these it may be seen that the street frontage had an elevation of seven bays divided into two bays north and south with the central three bays containing a modest entrance doorway. A single large sash window is the major feature in each bay, with a lower basement window at podium level and matching its square shape overhead at parapet level is a series of blank panels. Dormer windows on the street range's west roof slope point to use made of the roof void to accommodate domestics and others connected with the household. What appears to be a fully two-storied wing is to be seen as a major eastward extension attached to the rear of the street range at a central point. It was a well-appointed addition with a large central chimney heating rooms on two levels. The photographic evidence shows the first-floor of the back wing employing windows with wooden high cross frames fully glazed with small glass panes. The window type is one in use in the later 17th and early 18th centuries.

On plan we are shown that at the wing's junction with the street range there are three staircases in close conjunction; the southern stair apparently giving direct access to the first-floor of the wing and its neighbour also in an upward direction, serving the attic levels in both wing and street range; the third stair, at a guess, may have accessed the basement. From these observations we may conclude that the back wing was an essential and coeval unit in the working of the principal building. Its location at a mid-point with central stack recalls the once substantial wing at Garmston House, no.262 High Street, that on documentary evidence was rebuilt c.1670.[67] What limited finish was allotted to the street range of the Wigford house did not extend to anything similar to the rear elevation – we do not know whether the stables and associated buildings that were demolished in the 19th century were of comparable age or quality.

Perhaps by far the most intriguing aspect of Sibthorp House is that of re-used medieval material in the north range. In the matter of the precise location of three crown post and collar-purlin roof trusses known to have been reset, the photograph offers little help. Two arched doorways that are shown in a view of the back of the street range can be identified on plan as being located at the west end of the north wing. In appearance both are similar and presumably from the same superseded building which could, conceivably, have been part of an earlier establishment on site. But why their new placements and when and who can have conceived their re-use? Two framed windows in the wall interval between the doorways have segmental arched heads and could be considered as part of a small scale conversion of the western end of the north wing, perhaps to a habitable unit. It is likely that the doorways marched with the medieval roof trusses. It can be shown that the roof trusses were part and parcel of a stone-walled structure and not survivals from a timber-framed phase.

The symmetry of the main range is such that to the north and south of the small entrance hall on plan there is an equal disposition of rooms that could imply the accommodation was shared. It is when one looks closely at the two southern bays that one is aware that they are not as extensive as their northern counterpart. Another difference may be seen in wall thicknesses within the southern half of the main range – here one is at the mercy of the surveyor draughtsman – yet it makes sense perhaps to see the change as part of a two- or three-phased building operation.

It is unlikely that we will obtain additional information that throws light on how the interior was decorated; given the simplicity of the street elevation this may have been reflected internally in the ceiling and wall treatment of Sibthorp House.

12–14 BROADGATE
THE SCHOOLMASTER'S HOUSE

DOCUMENTARY
EVIDENCE

The indications from the early Padley plans are that this property was originally part of a more extensive holding based on the Wheatsheaf Inn, with lengthy frontages both to Broadgate and to St Rumbold's Lane. Relevant documentation, however, is lacking for the period before 1792, although it is possible that one of the Winn family branches may have owned it at an earlier period. They did hold the inn in 1828,[68] together with a major

Fig 149. Street plan for nos 12–14 Broadgate

Fig 150. Plan of the ground-floor, nos 12–14 Broadgate

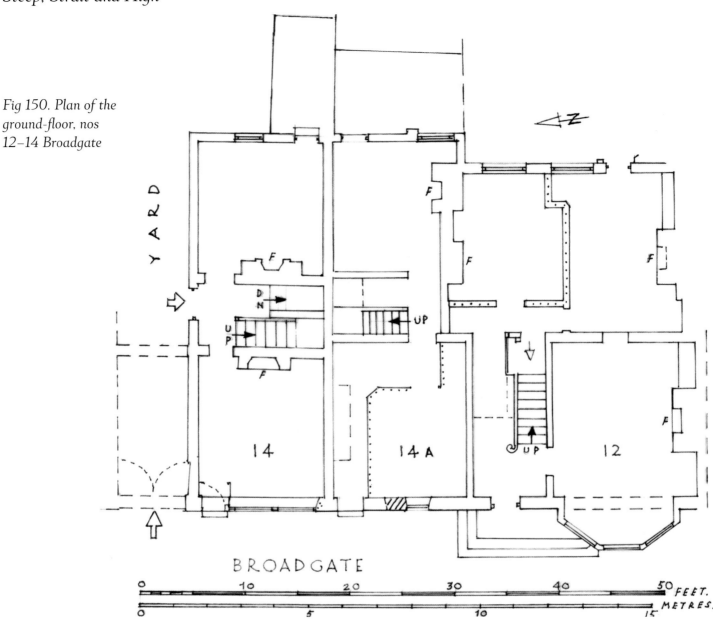

brewery complex to the south of St Rumbold's Lane.[69] Other neighbouring properties in Broadgate were mostly freehold, thus reducing the likelihood of informative boundary details being found.

What evidence we do have suggests that this range was sold off by the owners of the Wheatsheaf sometime in the mid-18th century, and was then developed from a single-storey wing of the inn. No.12 did share the same building line as the Wheatsheaf. A set of photographs, fortunately taken by the RCHM for the National Monuments Record in 1972 or 1973 prior to demolition, shows a panelled room and an 18th-century staircase which could be the twin of those in nos 21 and 23 Minster Yard, and is certainly similar to that to be found at no.3 Pottergate.[70]

By 1792 this house was in the tenure of local trustees, Henry Swan, surgeon, Revd Francis Swan and a Mr Milnes, possibly Henry; they were acting for unidentified vendors. The Governors of Lincoln Grammar School, then situated across Broadgate in the Greyfriars building, were searching for a convenient residence for the schoolmaster and sufficient boarding accommodation for some of the pupils. Negotiations for the purchase, involving as it did the Corporation (as landlords) were protracted, but in March 1793 the purchase price of £600 was agreed.[71]

The master, a friend of E.J. Willson, the Revd John Carter, moved in with about 10 boarders, and was granted immunity from local taxes by the Corporation, later commuted

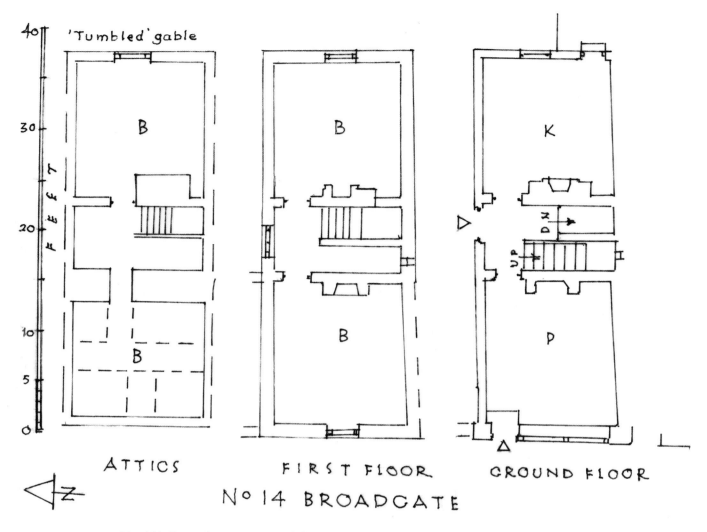

'Tumbled' gable

40

30

20
F
E
E
T

10

5

0

B

B

ATTICS

B

B

FIRST FLOOR

K

UP

DN

P

GROUND FLOOR

N° 14 BROADGATE

Fig 151. Room layouts, ground-floor, first-floor and attic, 12-14 Broadgate

Fig 152. Nos 12–14 Broadgate: photograph of street frontage 1972, prior to demolition

185

*Fig 153. (Right)
Photograph of principal
staircase, no.12 Broadgate
Fig 154. (opposite, top)
Photograph of main room,
first-floor, no.12 Broadgate
Fig 155. (opposite, below)
Photograph of the rear of
no. 14 Broadgate, from the
north-east*

to a fixed £9 per annum grant. In 1821 Carter retired, and in 1828 the Revd James Adcock was appointed: his 22-year 'reign' eventually became a disaster for the school. Both school and house were closed for some months before 1851, when the Revd George Foster Simpson introduced several reforms.[72]

By this time the Broadgate premises were quite dilapidated and woefully short of modern facilities. Simpson was able to arrange some short-term improvements, but it was felt by the city authorities that the master and boarders should have new quarters on a site near the school. This inhibited further investment in the Broadgate buildings, and a debate, heated at times, rumbled on until 1861, when a new headmaster, the Revd John Fowler, was appointed.[73]

The plan to move the residence across Broadgate to a site near the school had fallen through for various reasons, but a new site for the house was found in Upper Lindum Street;[74] this left Broadgate vacant, and in 1862 the council sold it to John Would Lee, whose family already owned land to the north of the master's residence. In the meantime, it was let to Francis Keeling, proprietor of a private boarding and day school: he had found an alternative site in Danesgate by 1867.[75]

Lee found more suitable tenants. Renovations were put in hand by Josiah Elsey, a partner in the Lincoln building firm of Otter and Elsey. Internal alterations and improvements were carried out in 1869.[76] The 1872 Directory shows that the Broadgate properties were renumbered at this time to take account of recent developments. Elsey lived at no.12 and his partner John Otter at no.13. Elsey and his wife were both dead by c.1890, and Matthew Otter was shown as occupant of no.12 until c.1911, followed by William Otter.[77]

Fig 156. Photograph of ground-floor shop, no.14 Broadgate

These three properties, brick-built and two-storied with attics, were constructed in the second quarter of the 18th century. There were no indications of an earlier phase and from the high quality of the fixtures and fittings throughout no.12 for example, the residence was very much that of minor gentry status. No.14A, as the plan hopefully makes clear, appears to have been divided off from no.12 and given its own front door to the street; in connexion with this, internally, an inconvenient chimney breast appears to have been removed to create a through passage. That there might be another acceptable explanation is demonstrated by the plan form of no.14, in which the house entrance, as opposed to that via the shop, is sited roughly midway in the north side wall; this side door led into a small lobby which housed the main stair and a lesser one leading to the cellar. Off the lobby the room to the west, serving as a shop prior to demolition, had a fine suite of 18th-century fielded panelling; its subsequent shop role may have been falsely reinforced by its receiving a large framed window to Broadgate in the later 19th century. It will be seen that the stair form in no.14A is similarly located, and as poorly lit, the difference being that in no.14 the stair well is backed by chimney stacks serving both east and west rooms at ground and first-floor levels. In no.14A the corresponding rooms have hearths sited in opposed side walls. No.14 has a small single-storied scullery off its east wall, a possible pointer to the larger room it adjoins as having once functioned as a kitchen.

A photographic record by the Royal Commission on Historical Monuments (England) was undertaken, after notification, of the above properties, and well before their demolition date. Given the high quality of the interior fittings it is extraordinary that, present day, the group should not have been listed.

Fig 157. Photograph of front room, first-floor, no.14 Broadgate

1   *RA viii*, no 2241
2   *Cant* 187
3   Bj 2.5 *passim*: arrears lists
4   *BB*, f.165v, no.531
5   *ibid.*, f.206v, no.704: the main tenement was described as extending from the Witham to the Malt Market
6   *ibid.*, f.271v, no.963,
7   See LL 104,147
8   L1/3/1 f.167v
9   Inv 111/321
10   L1/3/1 f.221
11   *ibid.*, f.251v
12   LL 104/1-3; LL 147/2
13   LCC Wills 1732/102
14   LL 147/9-10; 2 CC 21/151643; L3/774/151562
15   LCC Wills Misc. P/40
16   *ARMH* 2007/081 deposit: proposal for new Club building 1889
17   *Fig 133*
18   *Fig 130*
19   *Fig 132*
20   *Fig 130*
21   *Fig 129*
22   *Fig 130*
23   *Fig 129*
24   *Fig 130*
25   *Cant* 1152
26   Dij 77/1/13-14; *BB* f.77v

27   *RA viii*, no.2362
28   Lind Dep Plans 2/28
29   'Lincoln High Street', early 19th century, Usher Gallery, *LCNUG* 1927/152; a photographic copy of this is at *LCL* 3091
30   L Elvin, '*Lincoln As It Was*', 2 (Lincoln 1976)
31   LL 166/1
32   *TSJ* 3/Bundle 4756 (Wyatt)
33   LCC Wills 1706/152
34   LCC Admon 1733/24
35   *TSJ loc.cit.*
36   C. Page, 'Thomas Sawdon, machine maker, and Sawdon's Yard', in A. Walker (ed.), *Brayford Pool: Lincoln's Waterfront through Time* (Survey of Lincoln 2012), 19-23
37   *Fig 138*
38   *Figs 136, 137*
39   *Fig 139*
40   *Figs 140, 141*
41   *SAH iii*, 120-126
42   *Fig 140*
43   *RA x*, no.2970
44   *VC* 337
45   *ibid.*,340
46   LC Charters 6/54
47   Photograph taken by

Laurence Elvin and copied to Sir Francis Hill: Hill, Historical Photographs, no.40
48   Copy at LAO, *MCD* 161, m.2
49   Some wills and a deed of arbitration concerning this estate are in the O'Hagan MSS at Lancs RO, ref. K/22/18,20
50   FL St Mark's Deeds 3/1
51   *BNLW* 1/1/39/1
52   L1/3/1, f.212
53   Holywell 91/1
54   *BNLW* 1/7 *passim*
55   FL Deeds 78,159
56   AR Maddison, *An Account of the Sibthorp Family*, (Lincoln, 1896)
57   LCC Wills 1665/22 and 33; LCC Admon 1667/131
58   Survey of Lincoln Project working files
59   *LRS* 80; LCC Wills 1701-04,146
60   *BS* 29/46/270
61   Lincolnshire County Council Deed Packet 3426
62   *BS* 29/46/270; R.C. Wheeler,'Housing Development between Sincil Dyke and Canwick Road', in A. Walker (ed.), *South-East*

Lincoln: Canwick Road, South Common, St Catherine's and Bracebridge (Survey of Lincoln, 2011),18-20
63   2 Binnall Gg, p. 71
64   *Misc Don* 1268/6-7; *Figs 144-148*
65   *Fig 144*
66   *Figs 145-148*
67   *Figs 114, 121*
68   Willson and Betham Survey
69   *LCL* 5208ff
70   *Figs 153-157*; see also *SAH i*,99; iv,107
71   L 1/1/1/7 pp. 793,795; Charles Garton, Lincoln Grammar School 1792–1850 (unpublished typescript), 1631–1635 *passim*
72   Garton, *op.cit.*,1767-1801 *passim*
73   L 1/1/1/10, pp. 512-538 *passim*
74   *ibid.*, pp. 638-39
75   Street Directory
76   LC Planning Applications 144
77   Street Directories

APPENDIX

THE SURVEY OF ANCIENT HOUSES IN LINCOLN 1970–1996

During this period the Survey Working Party, as the group was termed, produced four *Fascicules* in A4 format, under the auspices of the Lincoln Civic Trust. Below you will find a digest of the contents of each of these volumes, none of which has an integral index. A combined index of the *Fascicules* is under consideration. Stock for each of the volumes is kept by Lincoln Civic Trust.

I: PRIORYGATE TO POTTERGATE

Stanley Jones, Kathleen Major and Joan Varley, with a contribution by Christopher Johnson
1984

II: HOUSES TO THE SOUTH AND WEST OF THE MINSTER

Stanley Jones, Kathleen Major and Joan Varley
1987

WORKING PARTY MEMBERSHIP

This list includes some guests and visiting speakers, and is listed roughly in chronological order of first appearance, commencing in 1971. Several other people, notably at the City Planning Office, the Archives Office and the Archaeological Unit, also gave welcome assistance to the work of the *Survey* at various times.

1971
Tom Baker
Chris Bedford (*Secretary 1971–74*)
Glyn Coppack
Judith Cripps
Mary Finch
Stanley Jones
Prof. Kathleen Major (*Chairman*)
David Smith
Joan Varley
Catherine Wilson
Michael Lloyd

1972
Mr C.F. Martin
Len Woodford
Christina Colyer
Ray Crownshaw
Nick Moore
John Marjoram
Richard Olney
Paul Everson
Sir Francis Hill
Flora Murray
Chris Page
Mr A. Whitehead

1973
Mick Jones
Canon Peter Binnall
Mr T. Marshall
Chris Johnson (*Secretary 1974–96*)

1974
Carol George
Bob Jones
Richard Lucas
Miss J. Oyler
Mr E. Swabey
Dick Whinney
Tony Gunstone
Richard Higginbottom

1975
John Anderson
Andrew White

1976
Nick Lincoln
Bob Pilling
Gerald Parker

1977
John Manterfield
David Vale
Maggie Darling
Timothy Ambrose

1978
Keith Briscoe
Guenever Moyes
Alan Dobby
Prof. Maurice Barley

1979
Brian Gilmour
Lauren Adams

1980
Carol Bennett
Arthur Ward

1981
Elizabeth Melrose
David Stocker

1982
John Magilton

1983
Peter Hill

1984
A.M. Snell
R. Bradley
Susan Noble

1985
Gershom Knight
Margaret Graham
Elizabeth Nurser

1987
Chris Guy
Mary Short
Amanda Goode

1988
Eleanor Nannestad
Kate Steane
Pam Marshall
Alan Vince
Peter Washbourn
Dr J.W. Baily

1989
George Kurucz

1990
Anne Coltman
Alastair Harton

1991
Lisa Donel
Stephanie Gilluly
Martin Maw

1992
Roland Harris

1993
Miss P. Graves
Adrian Wilkinson

1994
Jeremy Ashbee

GENERAL INDEX